# THE RISE OF DEMOCRACY

# THE RISE OF DEMOCRACY

## Revolution, War and Transformations in International Politics since 1776

Christopher Hobson

EDINBURGH
University Press

Edinburgh University Press Ltd
13 Infirmary Street, Edinburgh, EH1 1LT
www.euppublishing.com

First published in hardback by Edinburgh University Press 2015

Typeset in 11/13pt Monotype Baskerville by
Servis Filmsetting Ltd, Stockport, Cheshire

A CIP record for this book is available from the British Library

ISBN 978 0 7486 9281 1 (hardback)
ISBN 978 1 3995 7075 6 (paperback)
ISBN 978 0 7486 9282 8 (webready PDF)
ISBN 978 0 7486 9283 5 (epub)

# CONTENTS

# PREFACE

Layers upon layers. Much like the concept I have been studying, this work is marked by different periods, experiences and places. It represents my first substantive attempt to come to grips with democracy: a beguiling, ambiguous and slippery idea and reality that I expect to be grappling with for a long time to come. While commencing from international relations (IR), this book is not much concerned with disciplinary questions, except in so far as the artificial line we have drawn between the domestic and international realms has limited our ability to fully understand democracy. Most IR scholars have either ignored democracy or employed a shallow conception of it, devoid of most that marks it as worthy of study. Meanwhile, political theory has – until recently – largely failed to deal with the wider international context, a crucial condition of possibility for state-based democracy. This book seeks to chart a course between these problematic tendencies and in doing so, tends to blur between international relations, political theory and history. In this regard, perhaps I have accidentally been overly influenced by the approach of early English school thinkers, especially Hedley Bull and Martin Wight. Yet the book departs from these scholars in ultimately having a more critical intent. In this regard, the purpose of this study is not to explain or theorise, but to contrast, disrupt and denaturalise. For instance, how can we so easily talk of the Arab Spring – referencing the earlier European experience – but still be dismayed that the outcome of these political transitions remains unclear only a few years later? It took Europe more than a century to arrive at something approaching stable democratic government; why should it be expected that other countries can reach a similar destination in a fraction of the time? This reflects an overwhelming tendency to view democracy as something freestanding, almost devoid of a past.

Strangely enough, in such a situation simply providing a historical contrast becomes a valuable and necessary corrective. This is what the book's cover is meant to convey. The image is hardly how we might depict democracy today; even contemporary critics would portray their scepticism in different terms. Yet we tend to forget that it is the current situation which is the historical anomaly, and not the other way around. In reminding us of this, my aim is not to bolster the lazy scepticism towards democracy that is too often evidenced by those of us lucky enough to have the freedoms that allow us to be so blasé. The book very consciously avoids *that* quote by Winston Churchill, which tends to become a cheap crutch for doubters who have yet to abandon democracy but find little left to love in it. Even if we have legitimate grounds for being frustrated with the many failings of democracy, outright cynicism is not the solution. Democracy has its flaws, but one of its greatest virtues is precisely that it provides space to complain, identify problems and hopefully induce change. To this end, here I provide the foundations and the first cut of a normative defence of democracy. The chief technique employed is to ask us to look at democracy through the foreign eyes that history provides. There are perhaps no remarkable discoveries here; much like democracy, its contribution is modest and straightforward, but hopefully still of value.

This book has been completed in iterations over the past decade across three countries, three democracies: Australia, the United Kingdom and Japan. This work bears the marks and influences of these different periods. Unfortunately one consequence of my globe-trotting is that I have been stripped of my right to vote in Australia, and I remain a denizen in my current home of Japan. As I can no longer vote, teaching and writing is perhaps where my voice can be best heard. In this sense, this book is partly meant to be a democratic act.

Scholarly endeavours like this are for the most part thoroughly solitary, but are punctuated by – and ultimately reliant upon – the input and support of others. This book has been made possible through decisive and valuable interventions from those around me, while the flaws and limitations found within are ones I am solely responsible for. My sincere thanks to loved ones, friends, mentors and colleagues who have supported me, to varying degrees and in different ways, during the slow process of seeing this project to completion. I am also very appreciative of the considerable patience and assistance shown to me by the staff at Edinburgh University Press. The book is dedicated to my parents, Paul and Vivien. I am deeply grateful for the opportunities and love they have given me.

'When *I* use a word,' Humpty Dumpty said in rather a scornful tone, 'it means just what I choose it to mean – neither more nor less.'

'The question is,' said Alice, 'whether you *can* make words mean so many different things.'

'The question is,' said Humpty Dumpty, 'which is to be master – that's all.'

Lewis Carroll, *Through the Looking-glass, and What Alice Found There* (1871)

*Chapter 1*

# INTRODUCTION:
# BEYOND THE 'END OF HISTORY'

We have suffered in the past from making democracy into a
dogma, in the sense of thinking of it as something magical,
exempt from the ordinary laws which govern human nature.

(Lindsay 1951: 7)

The exponents of liberal democracy make the mistake of ignoring
the all-important fact that democracy is not something given once
and for all, something as unvarying as a mathematical formula.

(Hogan 1938: 10)

## INTRODUCTION

Little over 200 years ago, a quarter of a century of war fundamentally
reshaped the European international order. That conflict was triggered
by the advent of popular doctrines in revolutionary France, and fears
that it might seek to export 'all the wretchedness and horrors of a wild
democracy', as the British ambassador Lord Auckland described it at
the time (quoted in MacLeod 1999: 44). In stark contrast, today 'rogue
regimes' are defined by the fact that they are *not* democratic. In the
intervening period a remarkable series of revisions took place in the
way democracy was understood and valued in international society.
In a relatively short space of time, popular sovereignty went from
being a revolutionary and radical doctrine to becoming the foundation
on which almost all states are based, while democratic government,
long dismissed as archaic, unstable and completely inappropriate for
modern times, came to be seen as a legitimate and desirable method
of rule. This book examines these changes in the concept of democracy, and considers how these processes have interacted with the
structure and functioning of international society. Put differently, this

study is structured around the historical contrast between, on the one hand, the high degree of acceptance and legitimacy that democracy now holds, and on the other, the strongly negative perceptions that defined democracy when it reappeared in the late eighteenth century, which should have seemingly limited the possibilities of it becoming understood so positively.

The book seeks to throw new light on a central feature of the current international order, in which – according to Nobel Laureate Amartya Sen – democracy has become a 'universal value', having 'achieved the status of being taken to be generally right' (Sen 1999: 5). It explores the remarkable reversal that took place, accounting for democracy's rise from obscurity to its position as a central component of state legitimacy. In contrast to the influential accounts of liberals, who too easily universalise democracy's current meaning and suggest its 'triumph' was somehow inevitable, this book illustrates the opposite: just how unlikely this outcome was. Indeed, the success of these changes is reflected in the extent to which they go unquestioned today. This is hardly a new phenomenon, however. As the opening quotes from Hogan and Lindsay attest, there has been a longstanding tendency to reify, if not deify, democracy. Consequently, we often forget that its recent ascendance is not a natural or inevitable condition, but the result of political and sociological processes that have led to a certain set of ideas and institutions prevailing. In this regard, the book uses history as a resource for better understanding the contemporary challenges democracy faces, and in doing so, it develops a normative defence of democracy based on its uneven and contingent past. It reminds us that a world in which democracy is the dominant form of government is not the norm, but a historical anomaly, which in turn should promote a sense of humility.


## DEMOCRACY VICTORIOUS?

When considering the standing of democracy in contemporary politics, a logical starting point is the end of the Cold War. With the collapse of the Berlin Wall, democracy was left alone and ascendant, having seen off the great twentieth-century challenges of fascism and communism. Francis Fukuyama famously heralded this as signalling the 'end of history', in so far as liberal democracy presented itself as the ideational endpoint for societies to move towards (Fukuyama 1989; Fukuyama

1992). While his thesis has been widely criticised for its excessive tri-umphalism, Fukuyama did verbalise a significant transition that was unfolding. As democratisation scholar Juan Linz noted at the time, 'ideologically developed alternatives have discredited themselves and are exhausted leaving the field free for the democrats' (Linz 1997: 404). In the early 1990s it certainly appeared that a new democratic era was dawning. As Thomas Carothers and Saskia Brechenmacher recall, 'the decade was marked by a strong sense of liberal democracy as a univer-sally valid normative ideal. The remaining authoritarian regimes were in a phase of relative weakness as the tide of history appeared to be running against them' (Carothers and Brechenmacher 2014: 22). The 'third wave' of democratisation was reaching its peak: having traversed much of the globe from southern Europe across to Latin America and Asia, it was then spreading through eastern Europe and Africa. This represented a truly unprecedented expansion of democracy, reflecting that it had become an aspiration for people across the world and an important marker of state legitimacy.

A quarter of a century later and much of the initial bravado has since disappeared, but democracy – even if bruised and battered – remains ideationally in the ascent. Larry Diamond, a leading democratisa-tion scholar, still regards it as being without peer: 'no other broadly legitimate form of government exists today, and authoritarian regimes face profound challenges and contradictions that they cannot resolve without ultimately moving toward democracy' (Diamond 2014: 8). This is reflected in the fact that few, if any, states openly repudiate the label, while most authoritarian governments tend to either claim to be demo-cratic or suggest that they are progressing towards it (McFaul 2010: 37–41). Even China, widely seen to embody the most serious challenge to liberal democracy, does not directly deny the ideal, although it cer-tainly does so in practice (Economist 2014a). In the speeches of world leaders, democracy is taken as a 'natural' state of affairs compared with the 'distortions' of dictatorship and other forms of authoritarian rule. Reflecting on the current state of affairs, Fukuyama's position is now much more nuanced, but he maintains that 'in the realm of ideas … liberal democracy still doesn't have any real competitors. Vladimir Putin's Russia and the ayatollahs' Iran pay homage to democratic ideals even as they trample them in practice' (Fukuyama 2014a).

The present ideational supremacy of democracy reflects both its institutional successes and the failures of its historic competitors. The spread of democracy across the world since the end of the Second World War is a remarkable achievement that is unlikely to suddenly disappear (Levitsky and Way 2015; Ulfelder 2015). Following the 'third wave' of democratisation from the 1970s through to the 1990s, and the subsequent Colour Revolutions and Arab Spring, different forms of democracies can now be found across all regions of the world. According to the most recent Freedom House report, 89 out of 195 states are considered 'free', collectively making up nearly 2.9 billion people or 40 percent of the world's population (Freedom House 2015: 7). The vast majority of the world's most stable and prosperous countries are democratic, suggesting that 'there is a broad correlation among economic growth, social change, and the hegemony of liberal democratic ideology in the world today' (Fukuyama 2012: 58). Democracy is seen to be uniquely capable of providing a wide range of domestic and international goods, from better protecting human rights and preventing famine, to behaving peacefully and following international law. These beliefs have helped inform the liberal ordering strategy the United States has pursued since 1945 in which the advancement of democracy has played a central role (T. Smith 1994; Ikenberry 2000).

The breadth of acceptance of democracy is further reflected in the increasingly prominent place it occupies in the programme of the United Nations (UN). While the UN may now closely align itself with democracy, this represents a marked change from the original charter, which is noticeably free of any references to it. This was updated by the 2005 World Summit outcome document, which included an explicit statement that 'democracy is a universal value' (United Nations General Assembly 2005: 30). It was followed by the UN secretary general's guidance note on democracy, which proposed that

> democracy, based on the rule of law, is ultimately a means to achieve international peace and security, economic and social progress and development, and respect for human rights – the three pillars of the United Nations mission as set forth in the Charter of the UN. (Ban 2009: 2)

Further examples can be found in the establishment of the UN Democracy Fund in 2005, which reflects the pivotal position that democracy now plays in post-conflict reconciliation and peacebuilding efforts, what has been dubbed the 'New York consensus' (Hassan and

Hammond 2011: 534). These developments have been partly motivated by arguments from academics and think tanks that propose that the spread of democracy will help foster a more peaceful and prosperous international order (Parmar 2013; T. Smith 2007). Not only is democracy presented as a universal value, it is seen as having instrumental value in that it is seen to offer the best route to peace and prosperity. As such, democracy is supported and advanced for both ethical and practical reasons.

Performance legitimacy, a lack of peer competitors, and the nominal backing of the global hegemon have certainly provided strong foundations for the ideational dominance of democracy. Yet initial hopes that the end of the Cold War would mark the dawn of a new, and fundamentally better, era of international relations – defined by the spread of democracy – have failed to come to full fruition. Instead, the 1990s now appear as something of a liberal interregnum. This change of affairs has led Azar Gat to suggest that we have reached 'the end of the end of history' (Gat 2007). Democracy is increasingly questioned, as doubts about its normative value and institutional strength proliferate. These growing concerns have been reflected in a spate of recent books on the health of democracy and whether it is now in crisis (Coggan 2013; Dunn 2013; Kurlantzick 2013; Ringen 2013; Runciman 2013). Certainly the challenges democracy faces are manifest and they are real. A number of significant trends are pulling at the threads of democracy, threatening to slowly unravel it. The continued rise of non-democratic China, the resurgence of an increasingly authoritarian Russia, a United States weakened by political dysfunction at home and costly adventurism abroad, growing dissatisfaction and disengagement in many established democracies, the failed attempts to democratise Afghanistan and Iraq, the 'third wave' leading to a proliferation of 'hybrid regimes' rather than functioning democracies, and a growing backlash against democracy promotion efforts, are among the most obvious negative trends that are leading some to question democracy's future.

It may seem strange to be publishing a book entitled *The Rise of Democracy* at a time when people are increasingly wondering if it is decline. Few can doubt that democracy's standing has weakened since the early 1990s. This is hardly a surprise given the excessive optimism and confidence of that moment. Nonetheless, it is here that Fukuyama's kernel of truth remains relevant: democracy still does not face a clearly defined ideological competitor in the way it previously did with fascism and communism. To date, increasing dissatisfaction with the way democracy works has manifested itself more in discontent and calls for better-functioning democracy. It has not yet led to widespread support for alternative political systems, although there is no reason to believe this cannot change. On the whole, Sheldon Wolin's summary of the situation in 2004 remains largely accurate:

> One of the most striking facts about the political world of the third millennium is the near-universal acclaim accorded democracy. It is invoked as the principal measure of legitimacy, as the standard for any new states wishing to gain entry into the comity of nations, as the justification for a pre-emptive war, and as the natural aspiration of peoples struggling anywhere for liberation from oppressive systems. Democracy has thus been given the status of a transhistorical and universal value. (Wolin 2004: 585)

This is not to deny the limitations and weaknesses of contemporary democracy, or the considerable challenges to it that presently exist, but to appreciate that there has been a remarkable consensus over its normative and political desirability in the post-Cold War world, and that the historical trend has been broadly in the direction of democracy, albeit not in any simplistic, unidirectional manner. Jørgen Møller and Svend-Erik Skaaning are ultimately justified in concluding that 'the democratic *zeitgeist*, though less ebullient than . . . it was just after the Cold War ended, still reigns' (Møller and Skaaning 2013: 106). In this context, what this book illustrates is that democracy is simultaneously more secure and more vulnerable than is commonly appreciated.

## TOWARDS AN INTERNATIONAL HISTORY OF DEMOCRACY

> Since we are all democrats (or so one may hope!), we tend to see democracy as the fulfilment of our political destiny and as the political system that will remain with us for the rest of human history. For what alternative is there to democracy?
>
> (Ankersmit 2002: 10–11)

Is democracy's time in the sun coming to an end? Or are the reports of its demise greatly exaggerated? It is here that returning to democracy's past becomes such a productive and necessary exercise. On the one hand, doing so guards against a misplaced faith that democracy's recent ascendency reflects some deeper Truth or answer to History. On the other hand, it also warns against excessive pessimism, given democracy's remarkable resilience and its ability to provide comparatively convincing answers to some of humanity's most challenging political questions. By returning to a time where democracy had yet to be endowed with the positive connotations that now shape it, this study seeks to counter the tendency to be 'bewitched' by this normatively powerful concept (Skinner 2002: 6). In this sense, it is a 'history of the present', which examines democracy's past as a way of better understanding its current role in international politics and what its future may hold. Adopting such a perspective foregrounds the limitations and fragility of democracy, and cautions against the excessive confidence that has too often defined the dominant liberal account.

The book undertakes a macro-historical study of democracy's conceptual development in modern international politics, considering how it emerged in relation to changing understandings of legitimacy and sovereignty. These principles are what help identify democracy as an international issue, as legitimacy and sovereignty are closely related phenomena that extend across and shape both the domestic and the international realms (Bukovansky 2002; Wight 1972). In considering these historically shifting and complex conceptual relationships, the study simultaneously provides a series of snapshots of the way democracy has been interpreted at different moments in time. Through examining the conceptual history of democracy, it will be seen that it has developed in close relation with the functioning of international politics (Fukuyama 2014b: 534–7). As a study by UNESCO reveals, the changing and contested nature of democracy is linked to the most basic issue that dominates the discipline of international relations (IR): 'it is not only a problem of philosophy … it is a problem of war and peace' (UNESCO 1951: 514).

The focus is primarily on moments of revolutionary upheaval and war, as these are times when the meanings of basic concepts undergo great change, and principles of legitimacy are challenged and revised. As Raymond Aron explains, 'the phases of major wars – wars of religion, wars of revolution and of empire, wars of the twentieth century – have coincided with the challenging of the principle of legitimacy and of the organization of states' (Aron 1966: 101). The study commences with the American Revolution. While clear precursors to the doctrine of popular sovereignty can be found, most notably in Britain (Morgan

1988), it was with the founding of the United States that it was explicitly introduced into, and interacted with, international politics. The majority of the study focuses on the period between the American Revolution and the end of the First World War, by which time popular sovereignty was embedded in international society, and democratic government had come to be recognised as a legitimate form of constitution. What would follow was a contest that raged until 1989, which Philip Bobbitt terms 'the long war', between different forms of domestic constitutions – democracy, communism and fascism – ultimately leading to the widespread acceptance of democracy as the most legitimate form of government (Bobbitt 2002). Underpinning these observations, and the book as a whole, is a conception of international society, as questions about legitimate forms of statehood and domestic governance, which frame much of this investigation, only make sense within some kind of interpretative community where shared assumptions, norms and beliefs exist. These theoretical assumptions are outlined in more detail in the next chapter.

In considering democracy's conceptual development, it can be seen that historically democracy has meant two things: a form of state, what is commonly referred to as popular sovereignty, and a form of government, a set of domestic governing institutions, how democracy is now generally understood. Employing Kant's distinction between *forma imperii* (state form) and *forma regiminis* (government form), it is argued that to properly appreciate democracy's conceptual development and emergence in international society both meanings must be tracked. In ancient Greece, where the origins of modern democracy lie, *dēmokratia* was a direct form of rule where the people both constituted the polity and exercised power. Popular sovereignty and democratic rule existed together. When democracy reappeared in modern politics, these two dimensions were disaggregated. Popular sovereignty was separate from democratic institutions, and preceded it. The former was able to receive far greater and quicker acceptance in international society because it was more limited: the location of sovereignty was challenged, but its nature was left untouched. Furthermore, popular sovereignty did not necessarily entail a certain set of domestic institutions: it may point towards democracy, but it need not. One need only recall Hobbes's theory or the fascist regimes of the twentieth century for important examples of where consent-based notions of sovereignty did not entail popular rule. As a form of government, democracy struggled against a diachronic structure that strongly advised against it. Nonetheless, through a series of conceptual revisions, ridding it of the negative connotations that had plagued it for so long, democracy came to be regarded as a legitimate form of domestic constitution. Once this occurred, the nature of the contestation shifted, with much of the twentieth century being defined by a battle between different domestic regime types. With communism following fascism into the dustbin of history, democracy was left standing alone at the end of the twentieth century, but most of the conceptual innovations that laid the foundations for this outcome had finished being laid almost a century earlier.

The account provided is one that emphasises the historical contingency of democracy, detailing how its meaning and significance changed as a result of political contestation and conflict. During the founding of the United States, the classical interpretation of democracy dominated the revolutionaries' imaginary, meaning that they constituted their new country on the basis of popular sovereignty, while actively denying the concept of democracy. The peripheral location of the United States, and the conformist aspirations of the founders, served to blunt the impact of this new republic being constructed on legitimacy principles that contradicted those that prevailed in Europe. With revolution in France, however, democracy powerfully emerged as a political force at the heart of international society. In comparison to America, there were two conceptions of popular sovereignty at play – representative and direct – which strongly shaped the impact of the revolution on France and the rest of the society of states. The *ancien régime*, built on custom and precedent, was violently challenged and undermined in a way that it would be impossible to recover from. Despite attempts by the statesmen at the Congress of Vienna to turn back the clock, it was not long before democracy would reappear. In America one finds a particularly early re-evaluation of the concept. While democracy retained radical connotations during the revolutions of 1848, in the United States it was widely supported and conceived of positively. In the second half of the nineteenth century, the rise of democracy was increasingly seen as something almost inevitable, and monarchical principles of legitimacy were further eroded through the institution of constitutionalism. It was the First World War, though, that would prove determinative in shaping democracy's fortunes. Through America's entry into the war, which resulted in the reframing of the conflict in terms of democracy, followed by the subsequent defeat of the Central Powers, democracy emerged fully as a legitimate form in international society. The war led to popular sovereignty supplanting monarchical sovereignty in relation to principles of international legitimacy, and through the ideological innovations of Woodrow Wilson the positive evaluation of democracy as a form of government was transposed from the American domestic context to the international realm. What would follow until 1989 was primarily a contest around the legitimacy of the constituted power: the people as the constitutive power had become a foundational premise on which international society still rests.[1]

## DEMOCRACY AND INTERNATIONAL RELATIONS

Democracy has the rather odd distinction of being central to the history and contemporary functioning of international politics, but occupying a marginal place in IR as an academic discipline. If one looks at the most significant conflicts and upheavals over the last few centuries, democracy and popular sovereignty have regularly played an important part. The American and French revolutions, the 'springtime of the peoples' of 1848, both world wars, the Cold War and the War on Terror: democracy has figured in all of these. Yet if one turns to the field of IR there has been remarkably little interest in the nature of democracy and its role in international affairs. Writing just over a decade ago, Hazel Smith posed the right question: 'why is there no international democratic theory?' (H. Smith 2000). Neither her account, nor much of the scholarship since, has offered a compelling answer, however. For the most part, IR scholars have tended to view democracy as a topic best left for political theorists and comparativists. 'IR theory's neglect of democracy lingers on in certain core assumptions,' Ian Clark observes, which has fostered a perception that the discipline is 'entitled to pay scant regard to democracy except inasmuch as, as an attribute of some actors, it has an effect on international outcomes: it is not, by itself, the stuff of the subject' (Clark 1999: 146). Meanwhile, political theorists have regularly failed to account for the wider international context within which democracy has appeared and operated.[2] On both sides of the disciplinary divide, reflecting the domestic/international dichotomy, there has been a common inability to appreciate democracy's emergence in more holistic terms. In contrast, this book denies too strict a division between the state and international levels, instead regarding the two realms as ontologically related. It follows Robert Jackson's observation that 'international theory and political theory diverge at certain points but they are branches of one overall theory of the modern state and states system' (R. Jackson 2005: 39).

Some may counter this argument by pointing to the sizeable literature by liberal scholars centred on the empirical claim that a zone of peace exists between stable, liberal democracies (Geis and Wagner 2011; Hayes 2012; Hegre 2014). In one sense, this certainly represents a significant corrective to the lack of interest that has previously prevailed in IR. Yet on closer inspection, this shift is much less dramatic than what it may first seem. These scholars, relying heavily on quantitative large-$N$ studies, reduce democracy to a variable, of use in so far as it helps explain state behaviour and international outcomes. Yet understanding democracy in such a fashion, detached of its historical and normative roots, takes away the very features that make it such a politically significant concept in the first place. As Mikkel Vedby Rasmussen observes, 'democratic peace theorists need not relate to the desirability of democratic peace or the consequences of establishing it. They are in the business of describing, not prescribing' (Rasmussen 2003: 9). This means that the argument for democracy ultimately becomes rather functional: its value lies in its contribution to interstate peace. Thus, the democratic peace claim – and the wider democratic distinctiveness literature – ends up looking like an exhibition at Madame Tussauds: the likeness may be extremely close, but it is missing something vital that distinguishes the real thing from the replica. To understand democracy, to come to terms with its complicated reality and the equally complex concept that signifies it, one must grapple directly with its normativity. And to do this, it is necessary to reconnect democracy with history and political theory. Democracy is much more than a variable in a data set.

A central claim of this book is that an appreciation of the contested and contingent nature of democracy's past can provide foundations for a strong normative defence of democracy, one rooted in its fallible, incomplete and exploratory nature. The value of adopting such an approach is expressed by Pierre Rosanvallon: 'democracy takes on meaning and form only as a *construction in history*' (Rosanvallon 2006: 205; original emphasis). He further explains that 'the object of such a history ... is to follow the thread of trial and error, of conflict and controversy, through which the polity sought to achieve legitimate form' (Rosanvallon 2006: 38). This effectively blurs the lines between history and political theory, as genealogy becomes the foundation of a normative argument for democracy. It is inspired by Reinhold Niebuhr's assertion that 'democracy has a more compelling justification and requires a more realistic vindication than is given it by the liberal culture with which it has been associated in modern history'(Niebuhr 2011: xxxi). In this regard, there is no pretence that this study has been completed by an objective bystander assessing democracy from afar. It has been undertaken and completed in democracies, and has been unavoidably shaped by that context. This is hardly a revolutionary claim, but it is worth making precisely because so much scholarship on democracy commences from an unstated preference for this regime type. Indeed, as Patrick Deneen notes, 'contemporary research in the social sciences and humanities is now almost universally undertaken with the assumption that democracy is the sole legitimate form of political governance' (Deneen 2009: 42). This is particularly evident in the case of democratic peace research. As John Owen observes, 'of all the statistical correlations with war that *could* be uncovered and *could* spark a large literature, it is no accident that several US researchers discovered *this* one and found it worth pursuing' (Owen 2011: 162; original emphasis). Yet the vast majority of that work lacks the theoretical resources to defend the researchers' unstated normative preference. In contrast, this study demonstrates how work on democratic peace, and democracy in IR more generally, can be strengthened through actively engaging with normative arguments, rather than trying to banish them.

Seriously engaging with the history of democracy leads neither to unabashed confidence nor to corrosive scepticism, but instead to a cautious recognition of both its achievements and its limitations. The misplaced and excessive optimism that has defined much of liberal thought following the fall of the Berlin Wall reflects its presentism and a shallow, linear understanding of democracy's past. Democracy is not the ultimate harbinger of freedom or equality or any other value, though it may provide some of these to a greater degree than many of its historical competitors. Instead, it represents a form of rule that remains open and adaptable in a way that reflects individual and collective desires for liberty, and provides a framework for peacefully reconciling the differences and disputes that unavoidably shape politics. The rise of democracy does not mean the dawn of a new, more peaceful and prosperous age. It certainly does not mark the endpoint of humanity's ideational evolution, even if liberal democracy remains the most widely accepted and legitimate form of polity in contemporary politics. Ultimately, what democracy offers is something much less grand, but still very significant. As Niebuhr memorably puts it, 'democracy is a method of finding proximate solutions for insoluble problems' (Niebuhr 2011: 118).

## CHAPTER OUTLINE

Chapter 2 commences with a deeper consideration of existing scholarship on democracy in IR, focusing primarily on the democratic peace research programme, arguably the most influential version of liberal internationalism at present. It is argued that this scholarship reproduces a limited, incomplete understanding of democracy, stripped of historical context and normative meaning. While these shortcomings are noted, it is also suggested that critical democratic peace research needs to move from critique to further substantiating an alternate way of studying the complex and ambiguous relationships between democracy, peace and war. This is a core aim of this book, which is fulfilled by demonstrating how insights can be generated through examining the historically contested nature of democracy in an international context. The remainder of the chapter provides the theoretical and conceptual framework for the historical study to follow. It identifies how conceptions of democracy have developed in relation to principles of sovereignty and legitimacy in international society. It is proposed that an effective methodology for studying these issues is the conceptual history approach, which is outlined by drawing on the work of Quentin Skinner and Reinhart Koselleck.

Chapter 3 focuses on the United States, which since its birth has been democracy's most important international champion. Yet the role played by democracy in America's founding is much less straightforward than is often presumed. The revolutionaries held a highly sceptical view on democracy as a form of government, while at the same time strongly supporting popular sovereignty. Their thinking was heavily shaped by classical interpretations of the concept, which is illustrated through a pre-history that identifies how democracy's meaning remained structured by the negative legacies of ancient Athens. The result was what may now seem like a rather odd arrangement: the attempt to base the United States on popular sovereignty and establish a government that was answerable to the people, while steadfastly refusing to label it a democracy. The chapter explores how the founders sought to reconcile these contradictory aims through instituting a representative form of rule based on the will of the people. While the founding of the United States did not significantly alter conceptions of democracy as a governmental form, popular sovereignty was asserted in a very powerful manner and in so doing, the Americans helped introduce a new, and revolutionary, conception of sovereignty into international society.

Chapter 4 considers the monumental French Revolution. This period is pivotal in terms of the narrative of the book, as it represents the intersection of fundamental changes in the nature of international politics with the modern appearance of democracy as a political force. The chapter examines in depth the way the concept of democracy was used and contested during the revolution, and how two conceptions of popular sovereignty emerged. These developments directly challenged an international society composed of monarchs, and ultimately manifested themselves in the revolutionary wars. A strong holistic narrative is developed locating the changes within the international context of *ancien régime* Europe, arguing that France became both 'behaviourally' and 'ontologically' dangerous to the existing order.[3] What makes the period so crucial to this study is that monumental shifts in the nature of international relations took place in unison with and in response to the democratic principles emerging from revolutionary France.

The fifth chapter explores the way the popular doctrines that emerged from the American and French revolutions developed across the nineteenth century. The chapter opens by considering the negative standing of democracy at the end of the revolutionary and Napoleonic wars. At the Congress of Vienna the new international order was constructed against the popular doctrines that had emerged from revolutionary France. The international order constructed at Vienna was able to endure for a century, but conservative attempts to re-establish monarchy based on principles of legitimacy were ultimately unsuccessful. Like the proverbial genie in the bottle, once released the principle of popular sovereignty could not be fully contained. While the peace was held between the great powers, ongoing nationalist struggles and domestic unrest peaked in the revolutions of 1848, marked by an outburst of discussion over democracy. The old international order survived, although it was hollowed out from within. There was a growing perception in Europe that democracy – in one form or another – was somehow inevitable. The chapter concludes with the end of the nineteenth century, being a transitional moment for popular sovereignty and democracy: emergent, but still on the defensive.

Chapter 6 examines the First World War, which would decisively shape democracy's rise in international politics. When the war commenced, it was fought for old-fashioned reasons, with little concern for democracy. This changed drastically in 1917, due to revolution in Russia and America's entry into the war, two events that are considered in depth. The reframing of the conflict as one of democracy versus autocracy was facilitated by events in Russia, but it was Woodrow Wilson's intervention that was crucial in thrusting democracy onto the international agenda. With the defeat of the Central Powers, popular sovereignty supplanted monarchy as the dominant form of state legitimacy. This also confirmed democracy's remarkable ideational transformation into a normatively acceptable, and for many desirable, method of government. The final section of the chapter considers the attempts to build a new international order at Versailles and the role that democracy played in these plans.

The seventh chapter focuses on the 'long war' that was waged between competing ideologies for most of the twentieth century, which ultimately resulted in democracy left alone without peer. With popular sovereignty confirmed at Versailles, the conceptual battles surrounding democracy in the twentieth century were no longer with the *ancien régime*, but the modern doctrines of fascism and communism. Immediately after Versailles, democracy was in the ascent, but only decades later its very existence was in question. The Allied countries would fight in democracy's name, but ultimately it was a war for survival against the vicious imperialism of the Axis powers. The grand alliance between the democratic powers and the Soviet Union was able to defeat fascism, but this was due in large part to force of numbers and the self-destructiveness of the Nazis. Now contestation would continue between the two remaining ideologies of democracy and communism. The ideological tensions between the East and West meant that the international society founded after the Second World War would be strongly pluralist, with an emphasis on sovereign independence and equality. In 1989 the 'long war' finally came to an end, with the fall of the Berlin Wall and the ensuing collapse of the Soviet Union. The ideological contestation that had defined so much of the twentieth century had stopped, replaced by a remarkable consensus around liberal democracy. The chapter concludes by reflecting on the

liberal *zeitgeist* of the post-Cold War era, considering the many ambiguities, contradictions and tensions underlying the supposed 'triumph'
of democracy.

The conclusion returns to the somewhat contradictory position
democracy finds itself in early in the twenty-first century, in which it
remains without peer but its future is being increasingly questioned.
Building on the preceding study, it is proposed that history can provide
the foundations for a normative defence of democracy. It is argued that
a deeper recognition of the way democracy has historically developed
– one that appreciates not only its strengths, but also its ambiguities
and weaknesses – is necessary for dealing with the challenges it now
faces. Returning to democracy's past is a way of demystifying it, ridding
ourselves of simplistic platitudes about its virtues or shallow scepticism
bred by its shortcomings. And by being more attuned to democracy's
uneven, contested and fraught trajectory, there is cultivated a sense of
humility and cautious appreciation of its strengths.


## LIMITS AND CAVEATS

> On all great subjects much remains to be said.
>                           John Stuart Mill (quoted in Bagehot 2001: 3)


The only way a study of this magnitude can be managed is through a
strict demarcation of the nature and scope of the enquiry, which unavoidably limits the work in certain ways. The macro-historical approach
utilised sacrifices a degree of depth for breadth. It is simply not possible to trace the development of the concept of democracy in international politics without forgoing the level of detailed analysis found in
case-specific studies. When considering major and complex historical
events, the focus is limited specifically to the way these were connected
to popular sovereignty and democracy. Unlike some other macro-
histories in IR, this work is not trying to understand systemic change
at the international level. Neither does this study attempt to provide a
'theory' of democracy in international politics, *per se*. Rather, it seeks to
understand and account for the development of democracy in relation
to shared principles of international legitimacy and sovereignty. This
is also the reason that the focus is primarily on changes in Europe and
the United States. Practices and understandings of democracy have
certainly existed elsewhere, but the conception now dominant is one

that emerged from the West. As John Dunn observes, 'the main bat-tleground on which the struggle for democracy's mantle was initially fought out was the continent of Europe' (Dunn 2005: 153). Moreover, international society as it presently stands is one that has grown out from Europe, even if this interaction has not been in the form of a unidirectional expansion (Keene 2002; Suzuki 2009). Finally, the study does not deal with democracy between or above states, nor with the amount of democratisation in international politics. What it does illus-trate, however, is that democracy is much more closely intertwined with the state form and the anarchical international environment than cosmopolitan democrats may wish to admit.

### Notes

1 This distinction between 'constitutive power' and 'constituted power' is taken from Sieyès, and is considered in more detail in Chapter 4.
2 Recent scholarship on transnational and cosmopolitan democracy has begun to correct the tendency for political theorists to ignore the larger international context, yet it tends to do so through a contemporary lens, while empirical political scientists have been slow in incorporating inter-national factors into their considerations on processes of democratisation, although this has been rectified to a large degree.
3 These categories are taken from Donnelly (2006).

*Chapter 2*

# THUCYDIDEAN THEMES:
# DEMOCRACY IN INTERNATIONAL RELATIONS

## INTRODUCTION

The discipline of International Relations (IR) has often mirrored major real-world trends, and this has certainly been the case with democracy. There was a considerable growth in work on democracy after the end of the Cold War, as part of a more general resurgence of liberal ideas, policies and scholarship (Jahn 2013: 1–12). A further surge in interest followed the central role accorded to democracy and its promotion during America's 'Global War on Terror'. For Tony Smith, these trends have been closely linked: the development of liberal internationalism between 1989 and 2001 would defend the position 'empirically, theoretically, and philosophically that the promotion of democracy was not only feasible, but that it would serve American security concerns' (T. Smith 2007: 49). This expansion in scholarship on democracy appears to be a significant change from the longstanding practice of regarding it as the preserve of political scientists and comparativists. As Ian Clark observes, 'in general, IR theory has not been much exercised by concerns with democracy' (Clark 1999: 146). This situation has only been partially rectified: a majority of the studies undertaken have been by liberal scholars, with other traditions continuing to display limited interest.

Despite this notable increase in the volume of work on democracy in IR, it has not resulted in a comparable development in our understanding of the way democracy is influenced by, and interacts with, the international realm. The nature, shape and possibilities of democracy have long been regarded as determined exclusively within the confines of the state (Walker 1993: 141–58). Alexander Wendt expresses this point well:

> The Westphalian approach to sovereignty allowed democratic and
> IR theorists to ignore each other. The former were concerned with
> making state power democratically accountable, which Westphalia
> constituted as strictly territorial and thus outside the domain of IR
> theory; the latter were concerned with interstate relations, which
> were anarchic and thus outside the domain of political theory.
> (Wendt 1996: 61)

The most influential example of this tendency is structural realism's separation of systemic and unit level phenomena, whereby democracy is consigned to the unit level, and thus beyond the purview of IR (Waltz 1979). Against Waltz, democratic peace scholars have argued that the internal (democratic) nature of states does have a consequential impact on their international behaviour. This appears as an important corrective, but on closer inspection the shift is much less dramatic than it may first seem. Rather, both approaches commence from similar ontological and epistemological positions, with the crucial point of difference being that liberal scholars disagree in arguing that unit level characteristics are relevant. This reflects a pervasive way of thinking about democracy in IR, which is based on the strict separation between the domestic and the international spheres.

Given that liberal international theory has dominated discussions on democracy in IR, it is this literature that this study is primarily responding to. In particular, the focus is on democratic peace research, the most prominent body of IR scholarship that deals with democracy, and arguably the most influential version of liberal internationalism at present. In this regard, limitations and omissions present in this research are significant precisely because its findings have extended well beyond academia (Bueno de Mesquita 2002; C. Hobson *et al.* 2011; Ish-Shalom 2013; Parmar 2013; T. Smith 2007). Conclusions from this literature have underwritten claims about democracies being more legitimate than other states, and have also provided a strong rationale for the expansion of democracy promotion practices (McFaul 2010; Rawls 2001; T. Smith 2007). While the politicised version of the democratic peace finding differs from the more cautious, probabilistic claims of scholars, there is a link between the way it has been studied and how it has been adopted by policymakers. The proposition that democracies do not fight each other, and that they are generally more peaceful, has come to occupy a central place in the foreign policy and rhetoric of the

United States. Notably, the theory was adopted by neo-conservatives and occupied an important place in the Bush administration's attempts to legitimate the 2003 Iraq war (Ish-Shalom 2007; T. Smith 2007). The influence of democratic peace research in theory and practice generates a need to reflect on it critically.

## THE DEMOCRATIC PEACE RESEARCH PROGRAMME

In the last three decades a flourishing research programme has swiftly emerged around the core finding that modern democracies have rarely, if ever, fought one another (M. Brown *et al.* 1996; Chan 1997; Geis and Wagner 2011; Hayes 2012; Hegre 2014).[1] The inspiration for most of this work remains Immanuel Kant's 1795 essay, *Perpetual Peace: A Philosophical Sketch* (Kant 1970). Building on pivotal early contributions by Dean Babst and R. J. Rummel in the 1970s that first highlighted an apparent correlation between democracies and peaceful behaviour, Michael Doyle's promotion of the modern relevance of Kant's ideas was crucial in igniting contemporary scholarship (Babst 1972; Doyle 1983a; Doyle 1983b; Rummel 1979; Rummel 1981). Discussion continued to increase through the 1980s, and in Bruce Russett's influential 1993 book, *Grasping the Democratic Peace*, he was able to confidently talk of 'the fact of democratic peace', by which he meant that democracies have rarely, if ever, fought one another (Russett 1993: 4, 10). Notably, the empirical correlation of a dyadic democratic peace has been widely accepted, even by critics (Rosato 2003: 585). The success of this original, limited, claim laid the foundation for a wider range of studies on the 'unique' behaviour of democracies in international politics, giving rise to what Anna Geis and Wolfgang Wagner usefully label the 'democratic distinctiveness' research programme (Geis and Wagner 2011). This body of work suggests that democracy is a powerful variable in explaining different dimensions of state behaviour, such as making and keeping alliances and international agreements, joining international organisations, protecting human rights, resolving disputes amicably and following international law.

In highlighting the relevance of democracy for explaining international outcomes, quantitative large-$N$ studies have become a trademark of democratic peace research (Chan 1997; Hayes 2012). Committed to a neo-positivist epistemology, researchers define the basic terms enabling analysis at the outset, allowing them to focus on constructing and studying data.[2] These studies continue to rely on a number of standard definitions and data sets, while rarely questioning the implications of these foundational decisions. Rather, the widespread agreement over how to understand democracy, peace and war is regarded as a sign of scientific progress (Chernoff 2004: 57–65; Van Belle 2006: 292–94). The definition of democracy generally used is the one dominant in American political science, taken from the influential contributions of Joseph Schumpeter and Robert Dahl (Schumpeter 1943; Dahl 1971).[3] Employing standard definitions may allow for certain empirical relationships to be identified and greater commensurability between studies, but it comes at a price. Georg Cavallar makes this point in strong fashion: 'We decide upon the outcome of our research and reasoning the moment we define democracy' (Cavallar 2001: 238). Political concepts – such as democracy, war and peace – are deeply infused with historical and normative contestation, which problematise attempts at straightforward interpretations. Moreover, there is a widespread tendency to understand democracy in terms of American values, institutions and experiences, which then shape the way democratic peace is interpreted (Oren 1995; Tanji and Lawson 1997). This reflects the fact that definitional processes cannot be neutral, and the accounts to emerge from studies framed by these terms can never simply reflect empirical realities.

Most versions of democratic peace theory are explicitly ahistorical, attempting to identify a correlative relationship and causal pattern between democracy and peace that holds across time and space. In so doing, democracy is interpreted in terms of contemporary values, institutions and experiences. Taking an ahistorical definition, however, prevents an appreciation of the way democracy's meaning has altered over time (Barkawi and Laffey 1999; Duvall and Weldes 2001; C. Hobson 2009; C. Hobson 2011; Shaw 2001). The Correlates of War data beginning in 1816 is regularly employed, but the definition of democracy used is not adjusted to different periods. The problem is that what democracy meant in 1816 is noticeably different from what it meant in 1919 or 1989, as this book will explore. Related to this point, implicit in the theory is that for peace to hold between democracies, states must recognise each other as being democratic (Risse-Kappen 1995; Williams 2001). Yet the United States did not identify itself as a democracy until almost the middle of the nineteenth century, and it would take another half a century for other states to begin to follow suit. If peace between democracies is underpinned by a mutual recognition of each party's democratic identity, it is most unlikely this will happen if the states in question do not adopt the democratic label in the first place. Furthermore, whether democracy is understood as warlike (as in ancient Athens), anarchic and violent (as in the French Revolution) or stable and peaceful (as at present) will have important consequences for threat perception, the chances of democratic zones of peace to exist, and more fundamentally, what being a democracy means. This study will show how democracy's past reveals a story far more varied and complex than most democratic peace scholarship allows for.

An impressive body of work has certainly developed out of the core dyadic finding. This has undoubtedly been aided by the vast majority of scholars sharing a commitment to neo-positivism, with many having a strong preference for quantitative analysis. Reflecting this, a majority of challenges to their claims revolve around issues of coding, correlation and causation. Proponents and sceptics may disagree over the nature and significance of the findings, but they largely agree on how these issues should be studied. David Lake highlights the importance of this common ground when identifying the democratic peace research programme as an exemplar of theoretical progress in IR, noting that such theories advance 'only through sets of shared assumptions and common epistemologies and ontologies that allowed theory to be extended to new topics, additional hypotheses to be deduced, and propositions confronted with evidence according to agreed-upon standards' (Lake 2013: 579–80). There are negative consequences that also come with these choices, however. Against the platitudes about this body of work being an exemplar of scholarly conduct, it is necessary to recognise the almost complete failure of the neo-positivist mainstream to engage with non-positivist democratic peace research. Questions over correlation, causation, modelling and coding are responded to in a detailed and thorough manner, whereas challenges to their underlying assumptions are comfortably ignored. In this regard, Ido Oren's seminal 1995 *International Security* article is perhaps the only outside critique that mainstream democratic peace scholars have readily acknowledged, even if they are yet to provide a convincing rebuttal (Oren 1995). Meanwhile, the work that has built on Oren's intervention has received scant attention. To take one example, Tarak Barkawi and Mark Laffey's 1999 *European Journal of International Relations* article represents another important early contribution to critical democratic peace scholarship, yet has been largely ignored by mainstream researchers (Barkawi and Laffey 1999; Barkawi and Laffey 2001).[4]

Mainstream democratic peace scholars have also been remarkably quiet in relation to major recent real-world events and trends, especially the 2003 Iraq war, which was partly justified using democratic peace arguments (Ish-Shalom 2006; C. Hobson *et al.* 2011). In a literature review on democracy and armed conflict published in the *Journal of Peace Research* in 2014, Håvard Hegre devotes all of half a sentence to the 2003 Iraq war and notably does not cite any of the critical democratic peace literature on this topic (Hegre 2014). Likewise, in a forum in *International Studies Quarterly* in 2013, the discussion predictably revolves around causation, data and modelling, with little concern for real-world changes and how these may impact on the participants' research (Dafoe *et al.* 2013; Gartzke and Weisiger 2013; Mousseau 2013; Ray 2013). In concluding their contribution, Allan Dafoe, John Oneal and Bruce Russett reflect on the way the democratic peace research programme has developed, reaffirming the value of the literature's core contribution: 'in a subject of study where reliable insights are rare, the robust finding that democracies are more peaceful toward each other remains an important empirical regularity for future scholarship to build upon' (Dafoe *et al.* 2013: 213). Strictly speaking, Dafoe, Oneal and Russett may be justified in making this statement: despite the array of problems and challenges that democracies now face, none directly undermines the core dyadic claim. Yet if one looks at the course of international politics over the last twenty-five years, an increasingly prominent phenomenon – which became most apparent following the September 11, 2001 terrorist attacks – is the belligerence of some of the world's oldest democracies, notably the United States, the United Kingdom and Australia. While this seriously undermines the monadic argument, it does not directly contradict the probabilistic, dyadic claim that lies at the heart of the democratic peace research programme. Yet if this is indeed 'the most important research program in the study of international politics', as Michael Mousseau suggests (Mousseau 2013: 186), then its increasingly limited and detached account of international relations is much more problematic. The lack of focus on democratic belligerence is all the more troubling because it does fit with dyadic claims, which readily acknowledge that democracies are just as warlike as other regimes when dealing with non-democracies (Geis *et al.* 2013). Furthermore, it represents a refusal to engage with scholarship that does examine the darker side of democratic peace. In this regard, Tony Smith's forthright claims in *A Pact with the Devil* about the role of democratic peace research programme in helping to fashion the intellectual framework for the 2003 Iraq war have been met with deafening silence (T. Smith 2007). Brent Steele has powerfully argued that the failure by mainstream democratic peace scholars to acknowledge and respond to outside critique like Smith's can have powerful disciplining effects (Steele 2010). In this sense, while one appreciates Lake's understandable preference for 'progress *within* paradigms rather than war *between* paradigms' (Lake 2013: 580; original emphasis), this can quickly become an apologia for not engaging with – or worse, marginalising – other approaches, which has been the dominant tendency when it comes to the democratic peace literature.

There is certainly a need for mainstream scholars to be more open to dialogue with alternative approaches, but the onus is not just on them: critical democratic peace scholarship must also further develop its research programme. Initially this body of work arguably suffered from being overly conceptual and from not being fully substantiated. Ido Oren's article was significant, yet his book-length study had a wider focus on American political science (Oren 2002), and he has yet to publish further on democratic peace. Likewise, Barkawi and Laffey made important interventions (Barkawi and Laffey 1999; Barkawi and Laffey 2001), but have not published again on the topic. There were a number of other valuable forays, often in the context of related issues such as US foreign policy and liberal internationalism, which were also not further substantiated (Desch 2007; Steele 2007). One scholar that did expand his research, however, was Michael Mann, who completed a book-length study on democracy's dark past with genocide and ethnic cleansing (Mann 2005). Despite being authored by a leading sociologist, and providing an important rejoinder to the work of monadic theorists, Mann's contribution was something of an outlier and has not received much attention from democratic peace scholars, mainstream or critical. The collective result was that early critical scholarship on democratic peace raised important questions and outlined some significant critiques, but it had trouble crystallising into a more sustained research programme.

The major exception to this trend was the 'Antinomies of Democratic Peace' project, an initiative undertaken by the Peace Research Institute

Frankfurt (PRIF) and led by Harald Müller.[5] This represents the most sustained contribution to the development of a critical research programme through exploring the tensions, contradictions and 'dark sides' of the democratic peace. The PRIF project has resulted in a series of publications, including two important edited books: *Democratic Wars: Looking at the Dark Side of Democratic Peace* (Geis *et al.* 2006) and *The Militant Face of Democracy: Liberal Forces for Good* (Geis *et al.* 2013), which explore the relationship between democracy and war 'as the flipside of democratic peace'. Piki Ish-Shalom has explored a related set of issues, focusing on the ways the academic findings of democratic peace theory have been translated and used in the political sphere through a series of articles (Ish-Shalom 2006; Ish-Shalom 2007; Ish-Shalom 2008a; Ish-Shalom 2008b; Ish-Shalom 2009), ultimately culminating in a book-length study, *Democratic Peace: A Political Biography* (Ish-Shalom 2013). Collectively these contributions represent a maturation of critical democratic peace scholarship, demonstrating theoretically and empirically that mainstream research has missed important dimensions of this phenomenon.

*The Rise of Democracy* is a conscious attempt to further advance this body of critical scholarship, and does so in a way that seeks to join some dots between previous works. It lies at the intersection between the historical sociology of Mann, the more discourse-orientated approach of Ish-Shalom, and the theoretical explorations of Müller, Geis and other members of the PRIF project. In this regard, Christian Reus-Smit has argued that an important aspect in the rise and acceptance of constructivism in IR is that it demonstrated its value by moving beyond theoretical debate and engaging in sustained empirical research (Reus-Smit 2005a). Elsewhere I have argued that critical democratic peace scholarship could benefit from this example, utilising critique as a starting point for further developing a non-positivist research programme focused on the complex and ambiguous relationships between democracy, peace and war (C. Hobson *et al.* 2011). This is a core goal of this book, an aim which is fulfilled by demonstrating how insights can be generated through examining the conceptual and historical dimensions of democracy. One of the most significant and telling lines of critique developed by Oren, and Barkawi and Laffey, has centred on the contested nature of key concepts, such as democracy, and the problems this creates for neo-positivist scholarship. The full consequences of this argument have yet to be worked through, however. It is here that this study intervenes by examining the historically contested nature of democracy in detail and identifying its relevance for international relations.

Rather than taking democracy's meaning as constant, as neo-positivist democratic peace work does, this book demonstrates how important insights can be derived through examining the shifting nature of such concepts. It seeks to explore what most scholarship takes for granted, namely, how the current relationship between democracy and peace was first able to come into being. This entails engaging in the broader historical trajectory of democracy, which is deeply intertwined with the development of the modern international system. The study shows how contemporary conceptions of the relationship between democracy and peace are not natural or inevitable, but historical arte-facts. Through appreciating how the concept of democracy has had varied meanings and usages at different moments in time, insight is also gained into how the realities it operated within changed, as con-cepts play a key role in shaping social practices and structures. There is certainly a strong material dimension to this story: the outcomes of wars, from civil to worldwide, helped to create the conditions within which a more limited democratic peace could subsequently exist. Yet these processes have had an equally important ideational component: the way 'democracy' has changed over time, and how it has been related to ideas such as 'war' and 'peace', has in turn shaped what 'democratic peace' means. This reflects that a 'democratic peace' does not exist 'out there' in the world; it becomes real and tangible only through being labelled and described as such. It could never be a 'brute fact' in John Searle's terminology; it is partly constituted through being identified and explained by the researchers that 'observe' it (Patrick Jackson 2008).

Reflecting on Kant's role as the figurehead of the democratic peace research programme is a useful way of contrasting the approach adopted here with that which presently dominates. Considering the centrality of *Perpetual Peace* to this scholarship, it might be surpris-ing to recall that in this text Kant explicitly dismissed democracy. He was certain that his desired end point could not come about between democracies, but only through republics. Kant clearly differentiated between these two types of rule: 'the Republican Constitution is not to be confounded with the *Democratic* Constitution', as the latter is 'necessarily *a despotism*' (Kant 1970: 99–102; original emphasis). Most contemporary theorists using Kant equate his republican regimes with modern democracy, in so far as they are both based on constitutional, representative systems. While this move can be justified as analytically convenient given the similarities between the two, it betrays a distinct lack of curiosity with democracy's complex history. Democracy's past is lost both in the desire to claim Kant's legacy and by employing a stable definition of the concept. This study takes inspiration from Kant in a different way, in as much as he is an important reference point for critical theorists (C. Hobson 2011). It instead illustrates how a non-positivist approach can generate a different set of insights about democracy, peace and war in international relations through focusing on conceptual contestation and change.

## SOVEREIGNTY AND LEGITIMACY IN INTERNATIONAL RELATIONS

Most work in IR that considers democracy, including the vast majority of democratic peace research, commences from the assumption that the domestic and international are two wholly distinct realms, with democracy exclusively being a property of the former. In contrast, this study argues against such a stark rendering. Rather, as Ian Clark explains, 'the fate of the democratic state is attached to the international order, not in the sense that the latter can now rectify the problems of the former, but because the former is already and indistinguishably a part of the latter' (Clark 1999: 161). He makes this point in the context of discussing globalisation, echoing the observation made by proponents of cosmopolitan democracy (Archibugi and Held 2011; Archibugi *et al.* 2011). Certainly globalisation has altered – and arguably further blurred – the distinction between the domestic and the international, but democracy's fate has long been intertwined with the international; this is not a new phenomenon. In this regard, democracy's relationship with the international realm has been primarily determined by two fundamental and closely related principles: sovereignty and legitimacy. These need to be outlined in more detail, as does the larger structure of an international society that links these elements together.

Sovereignty has been historically central to democracy's development in so far as it has both defined the international realm as anarchic and provided the possibility for separate polities to be self-governing. Sovereignty is a defining feature of modernity, a principle that demarcates the present epoch from the Middle Ages and Latin Christendom (R. Jackson 2007).[6] There are clear conceptions of sovereignty in the work of Bodin and Hobbes, but these theorists and their rulers were more concerned with its domestic consequences (Osiander 2001: 281–2; Shinoda 2000: 35). Only in the post-Christendom era did a conception of sovereignty emerge that incorporated both internal supremacy and external independence, thereby spatially and temporally demarcating states from each other (Walker 1993). It was Rousseau and Vattel that first highlighted this duality: the concomitant principle of self-determination within the state was independence and anarchy between them. Here one finds the foundation for both modern democracy and the modern states system.

Sovereignty is not determined by material forces, it is 'inherently social' (Biersteker and Weber 1996: 1–2). This observation reflects that the constitution and boundaries of any state cannot be fully resolved internally, as they are constructed through recognition between states. As such, sovereignty is not strictly an attribute of the state, but 'is produced and reproduced by the collectivity of state rulers; it is the outcome of ongoing interactions between states in which the practically derived norms of sovereignty emerge' (Thomson 1994: 5). In this structurationist reading, the state becomes fully constituted and sovereign only through its relations with other like entities. Thus, the international realm provides the possibility of existence for individual states. Anthony Giddens explains that '"international relations" are not connections set up between pre-established states, which could maintain their sovereign power without them: they are the basis upon which the nation-state exists at all' (Giddens 1985: 263–4). The international and the state are co-constitutive, neither existing independently. 'Sovereignty simultaneously provides an ordering principle for what is "internal" to states and what is "external" to them' (Giddens 1985: 281), and thus becomes the condition of possibility for both spheres.

The corollary of sovereignty being a social construct is that the international realm as a whole has a social dimension to it. As C. A. W. Manning explains, 'what it means to be a sovereign state is understandable only incidentally to an understanding of the nature of international society' (Manning 1962: 103). Processes of recognition that enact and regulate sovereign statehood operate in relation to shared values and identities that exist between states. These practices help to construct an international society, which is 'a reflexively monitored set of relations between states' (Giddens 1985: 263–4). Following the work of the English school, international society is understood here as the normative and ideational structure within which states are embedded and operate.[7] The society of states is a composite of norms, rules and institutions that helps to shape the identities of its members and define the kind of behaviour that is acceptable. Tim Dunne explains:

> International society exists as a social fact. Like all social structures it is unobservable but its effects are real. The structure embodies rules for identifying who gets to count as a member, what conduct is appropriate, and what (if any) consequences follow from acts of deviancy. (Dunne 2001: 89)

As English school scholars have demonstrated, societal relations may not exist in such a thick and developed sense as that found within the state, but there is a sufficiently shared purpose and set of understandings between states to talk of a society existing at the international level without the term being stretched too far (Alderson and Hurrell 2000: ch. I).

Underpinning this society of states is a constitution: a complex of rules, norms and principles that define legitimate membership and practice (Philpott 2001; Reus-Smit 1999). As Martin Wight notes, 'international society exists and survives by virtue of some core of common standards and common custom' (Wight 1966: 103). The way this constitution is historically constructed, understood and reproduced is necessarily mediated through language, in which concepts play a pivotal role. It is in this sense that international society has been the interpretative community within which democracy's conceptual development has occurred. What exactly these shared norms are, as well as their breadth and depth, will be determined by the kind of international society that exists. English school theorists normally distinguish between 'pluralist' and 'solidarist' forms of international society. The former corresponds approximately to a 'practical association' and the latter a 'purposive association' in Terry Nardin's influential analysis.[8] Yet this separation is overly stark. Following Barry Buzan, it is more helpful to think of pluralism and solidarism as existing at different ends of a spectrum marking how 'thick' or developed the international society is.[9] In conceiving of pluralism and solidarism in this way, it is worth emphasising that international society has never been a purely 'practical association'; it has always included a 'purposive' element (Bukovansky 2002: 21–22; Reus-Smit 1999: 36–39).

Even within a more pluralist international society, shared values still exist, which are most clearly evidenced in the way sovereignty is collectively understood. For a state to be fully sovereign, its claims must be acknowledged and reciprocated by other states. As a social process, this act of recognition is based on shared conceptions about what a state should be. For a state to be acknowledged and accepted as sovereign by others, it needs to conform to certain shared expectations. These may be more or less extensive, but there will nonetheless be a basic set of criteria or beliefs for recognising states as sovereign members of international society. This reinforces Reus-Smit's argument that 'sovereignty has never been an independent, self-referential value. It has always been encased within larger complexes of metavalues, encoded within broader constitutive frameworks' (Reus-Smit 1999: 6). Sovereignty's substance is effectively filled out by some shared standard of legitimacy within and between states. As Mlada Bukovansky observes, 'legitimacy is the meaningful, cultural substance of sovereignty, just as territory or population is its material substance. Sovereignty is conditioned by the terms of legitimacy' (Bukovansky 2002: 23). What this means is that democracy has been relevant not only in more solidarist international societies, but also in more pluralist ones.

Principles of legitimacy, through shaping practices of state recognition and sovereignty, structure international society by determining its composition. And as Thomas Franck observes, 'it is because states constitute a community that legitimacy has the power to influence their conduct' (Franck 1990). It is in this sense that Manning likens the society of states to a club: 'as membership of a club depends on acceptance as a member by the other members, so does membership in international society, the club, the "international", that is, of sovereign states' (Manning 1962: 103). This analogy is helpful, as it points to the primary role played by international legitimacy, which is to determine membership and codes of behaviour in the 'club' of states. This is reflected in the classic definition of international legitimacy provided by Wight, who describes it as 'the collective judgment of international society about rightful membership of the family of nations' (Wight 1977: 153). As such, principles of legitimacy are a constant element not only of domestic politics, but also of international relations, as Ian Hurd has convincingly argued (Hurd 1999). This is where the domestic makeup of states, of which democracy represents one configuration, becomes of concern to international society at large. International legitimacy has been the primary framework through which democracy's relationship with international society has been mediated, as it has been closely tied to questions about legitimate forms of statehood and domestic governance. It is in this sense that Wight observes that 'principles of legitimacy mark the region of approximation between international and domestic politics' (Wight 1977: 153).

## DEMOCRACY AND SOVEREIGNTY

When considering democracy's relationship with sovereignty, it is necessary to recognise that historically it has been understood both as a form of state and as a form of government. Kant provides a useful description of these two dimensions of democracy, one which will be employed throughout this study:

> The first classification goes by the form of sovereignty (*forma imperii*), while the second classification depends on the form of government (*forma regiminis*), and relates to the way in which the state, setting out from its constitution … makes use of its plenary power. (Kant 1970: 100–1)

Democracy as a state form (*forma imperii*) corresponds to the people acting as the constitutive power, otherwise known as popular sovereignty. Democracy as a form of government (*forma regiminis*) represents the constituted power of the people, which in contemporary terms manifests itself in the form of representative democratic government. Carl Schmitt explains this relationship:

> Democracy is a state form … The people are the bearer of the constitution-making power and, as such, grant themselves their constitution. At the same time, the concept of democracy can provide a method for the exercise of certain state activities. It also designates a form of government or legislative form. (Schmitt 2008: 255)

Today democracy is understood largely in reference to the latter meaning, but historically both dimensions have been central to its reception.

In ancient Greece, the distinction between *forma imperii* and *forma regiminis* was not made; it was not necessary. *Dēmokratia* was a direct form of rule where the people both constituted the polity and exercised power. When democracy reappeared in modern politics these two dimensions were disaggregated. The form of sovereignty, *forma imperii*, was separated from the form of rule, *forma regiminis*. In this regard, a central claim that shapes this work is that it is necessary to investigate both the shift to popular sovereignty (*forma imperii*) and the revival of democracy as a form of domestic rule (*forma regiminis*). Looking at democracy only as a form of government ignores the extent to which it has historically been understood as a form of state. Meanwhile, the tendency to study popular sovereignty by itself can result in overemphasising its relationship with nationalism. As such, what this study does is chart the emergence of democracy as a form of government which was preceded by, and to a certain extent predicated on, the rise of popular sovereignty. These are separate, albeit heavily interrelated, phenomena and need to be considered together. It is only in the twentieth century, when popular sovereignty became widely accepted and the dominant state form, that this historically strong connection between *forma imperii* and *forma regiminis* faded into the background. Instead, contestation for most of the twentieth century would be centred on *forma regiminis*, between the rival systems of democracy, communism and fascism.

Popular sovereignty was able to receive far greater and quicker acceptance partly because it was more limited in its consequences, as it left much of the basic structure of international society intact. It entails a situation where the people, not a god or a monarch, are the basis of the polity. This understanding grows out of the tradition of *lex regia* as it was reinterpreted in the late Middle Ages, with a stronger notion of consent-based sovereignty emerging in the contract theories of Hobbes, Locke and Rousseau, which was later activated in the great revolutions of the late eighteenth century (Canovan 2005: 10–39). As the constitutive power, the collective body formed – the people – are the ultimate holders of sovereignty, and they, in turn, determine the nature of the polity. Istvan Hont usefully describes this as 'indirect sovereignty', in so far as the people are sovereign, but apart from exceptional circumstances they do not actually exercise sovereignty, as it is mediated through the power it has constituted (Hont 1994). Historically the transition from the sovereignty of kings to the sovereignty of peoples did not fundamentally affect the nature of sovereignty: its locus altered, its character did not. This contributed to it being more easily accepted into international society, as what changed was the cast rather than the script. As James Mayall observes, 'it is still a society of states but the states now belong to the people' (Mayall 1990: 148).

Popular sovereignty does not necessarily demand a specific set of domestic institutions: it might logically point towards democratic government, but it is still compatible with other constitutional forms. This meant that the principle of popular sovereignty was capable of emerging and existing in more pluralist forms of international society. There is a long history of consent-based notions of sovereignty underpinning monarchies and other non-democratic constitutional forms. One only need look to Hobbes's *Leviathan* for the classic theoretical exposition of this position, and to the fascist regimes of the last century for important real-world examples. The opposite arrangement, where democratic government exists but the prevailing philosophy of sovereignty is not popular, is much less plausible logically and historically. Even if popular sovereignty does not automatically entail democracy, historically it has created the most space for this possibility. As Ingeborg Maus notes, 'the internal sovereignty of the democratic nation-state has from the beginning been … nothing other than popular sovereignty' (Maus 2006: 465). It is unlikely to be a historical coincidence that reconsideration of democracy as a form of rule corresponded with and followed the emergence of contract theories. What this suggests is a fundamental, but complex and historically variable, relationship between democracy as *forma imperii* and as *forma regiminis*. The exact link between the two, and also where they diverge, will be extrapolated over the course of this book. In order to properly examine the historically shifting nature of democracy and its connections to sovereignty and legitimacy, this study will employ a conceptual history methodology.

## CONCEPTUAL HISTORY

> Only that which has no history is definable.
> Friedrich Nietzsche (1989: 80)

Democracy is a concept famous for its contested nature and multiple meanings. For this reason, W. B. Gallie identified it as an ideal typical example of what he termed 'essentially contested concepts' (Gallie 1964: ch. 8). These concepts are distinguished by the fact that contestation over their meaning is fundamental to their character. The approach taken by most democratic peace research, as noted, is the exact opposite, instead providing a fixed definition on which to base empirical investigation. Neither is satisfactory: one exaggerates the level of contestation by regarding it as an essential part of the concept's character; the other effectively denies it completely. What is needed is a historically sensitive way of recognising the conflict and change that has undeniably shaped the concept of democracy, without falling into the trap of ignoring the continuities and shared understandings that have helped determine its trajectory. An approach which does this is conceptual history. When viewing democracy from the vantage point of conceptual history, its historically contingent and contested nature is not a problem to be overcome or avoided, but a source of insight into the concept and the social world it interacts with.

Two major strands of conceptual history are the 'Cambridge school' and the German approach, *Begriffsgeschichte*. The framework utilised here builds on scholarship that regards these as compatible (Palonen 2001; Palonen 2003; Richter 2003), and draws primarily on the leading exponents of these two respective schools of thought: Quentin Skinner and Reinhart Koselleck. *Begriffsgeschichte* provides a useful overarching structure for analysis, identifying a two-stage process in charting the history of a concept (Koselleck 1985: ch. 5; Koselleck 1996: 63). First, a diachronic account explores how a concept is structured by previous historical usages and interpretations. This shapes the kind of conceptual change possible. As Koselleck explains,

> every concept ... has a diachronic thrust against which anyone seeking to add a new meaning must work. Yet what is new can be understood for the first time only because of some recurring feature, some reference to a previously unquestioned, accepted meaning. (Koselleck 1996: 63–6)

Concepts thus have a kind of weak path dependency that influences, but does not determine, their trajectory. Second, a synchronic analysis considers the way concepts are understood, challenged and sometimes revised or overturned at pivotal moments. Emphasis here is placed not on continuity, but rupture. As concepts are ultimately human constructs, there is still considerable room for agency in determining their meaning. It is in this sense that Skinner suggests 'we are all Marxists' (Skinner 1969: 53), recalling one of Marx's less deterministic moments, where he observed how historical structures may shape but not forestall the possibility for agent-driven change: 'Men make their own history, but they do not make it as they please' (Marx 1995). Through combining these two modes of analysis a strong framework is constructed: the synchronic analysis explores the way the concept is understood and utilised in a specific historical context, while the diachronic analysis orders meanings and usages from different moments into a larger history.

Of primary interest are 'basic concepts' (*Grundbegriffe*), which are 'an inescapable, irreplaceable part of the political and social vocabulary' (Koselleck 1996: 64–5). These act as 'pivots' around which argumentation occurs and political contestation takes place, a characteristic that separates them from other ideas and parts of the vocabulary. The pivotal role of basic concepts ensures that they play a fundamental part in the constitution and reconstitution of the social world. In so far as these concepts shape the perceptions and actions of agents, conceptual shifts do not merely reflect material changes, they actively inform such transformations by constituting actors, shaping behaviour and helping to remake material structures. Recognising the causal role concepts play highlights the close dynamic that exists between conceptual and political change. According to Kari Palonen, 'there cannot be any politically crucial action that would not have a linguistic dimension' (Palonen 2003: 58). To put it in strong terms, fundamental changes in the political world are unlikely, if not impossible, without corresponding conceptual shifts.

The highly political nature of basic concepts means that they do not develop in some predetermined manner or through a gradual unfolding of reason, but in a somewhat haphazard fashion in response to the outcomes of previous political battles. This is emphasised by Skinner, who, in a Weberian vein, sees the political sphere as a realm of conflict and contestation for power, and it is through this lens that he views the role of language (Palonen 2003: 48). Drawing on the insights of Wittgenstein, Austin and Searle, Skinner focuses on linguistic acts: 'We need … to grasp not merely what people are saying but also what they are *doing in* saying it' (Skinner 2002: 82; original emphasis). He is particularly concerned with the illocutionary force of key concepts in terms of how they are used and the impact they have. From this perspective, concepts can play a limiting or enabling role in shaping the range of actions possible in a situation. Actors need to legitimate their behaviour, which places certain constraints on what they are able to do and say. Skinner puts this proposition forcefully: 'Any course of action will be inhibited to the degree that it cannot be legitimised' (Skinner 2002: 156). And it is precisely this need to legitimate behaviour that can drive conceptual change.

Skinner identifies 'innovating ideologists' as actors that attempt to alter a concept in a manner which enables them to legitimise behaviour that has not previously been accepted (Skinner 2002: ch. 8). Susceptible to this kind of manipulation are 'evaluative-descriptive terms', which are distinguished by the dual speech acts they perform: 'Whenever they are used to describe actions … they have the effect of evaluating them at the same time' (Skinner 1973: 298–301; Skinner 2002: 148). When the term is employed to describe something it also passes judgement on it, and vice-versa. This leaves two options available to innovating ideologists. On the one hand, they can attempt to alter the descriptive component by extending its range in such a manner that their behaviour is now included within the concept. On the other hand, they can try to shift the evaluative dimension by revising its normative content. This can be done through neutralising a term previously considered negatively, turning a neutral term into a positive one, or the more radical move of reframing a negative term in a positive light. Clearly these revisions do not take place in a vacuum, as they need to be accepted by the target audience. In order for this to happen, innovators must carefully adjust both their project and their language so that they can be related to existing understandings. For their attempts at conceptual revision to be successful, innovators' actions must remain compatible both with the previous diachronic structure of the concept and with the fashion in which they have redrawn it.

Conceptual revision is made more difficult by the fact that at moments of crisis and upheaval, when attempts at innovation will be most likely, competing actors are acutely aware of how language can be used as a power resource, and of the potentially major repercussions of conceptual redefinition or reaffirmation.[10] In this regard, Skinner identifies an actor that operates in a parallel but opposed manner to that of the innovating ideologist: the 'apologist' for the existing order (Skinner 1973: 301–3; Palonen 2003: 55–6). Apologists aim to limit or cause conceptual change in such a manner that the status quo is preserved. To do so, 'any apologist will need to be able to show that these unfavourable characterizations [of the status quo] can in some way be *defeated* or at least *overridden*' (Skinner 1973: 302; original emphasis). As such, when conceptual change occurs it is likely to proceed in a dialectical fashion, driven in part by contestation between ideologists and apologists. The outcome of these conceptual battles subsequently shapes the diachronic trajectory of the concept. It is with this sense in mind that Terence Ball observes, 'The language we now speak is the result of the most long-lived and successful of those earlier attempts at conceptual revision' (Ball 1988). Throughout this study emphasis will be placed on identifying innovators and apologists and how they sought to alter or reaffirm the way democracy was understood.

Just as concepts seldom appear *de novo*, they also rarely appear in isolation. Rather, concepts operate within a larger discourse, ideology or semantic field. Reflecting this, an important component of conceptual change is the way concepts are related to each other, which means that 'charting the boundaries separating related concepts is an indispensable part of conceptual history' (Richter 1995: 42). It is therefore necessary to consider subtle relationships where similar or related concepts may converge or diverge at certain moments. Basic concepts are shaped not only by closely related concepts, but also by those that are diametrically opposed. 'Counter-concepts' operate in a co-constitutive fashion: in reflecting each other, they help to define themselves. Key examples are the civilised–barbarian pairing, and with respect to this study, the monarchy–democracy and democracy–autocracy pairings. The relationship between the elements of a counter-concept pairing is generally not equal but asymmetric, in which one is identified as inferior (Koselleck 1985: ch. 10). In this regard, João Feres explains that asymmetrical counter-concepts are 'used by a given human group to confer a universal character to its own identity while denying others a claim to self-assertion' (Feres 2003: 14). Thus, opposed concepts can play a central role in defining others, as well as influencing the possibilities of political agency. These larger semantic fields have to be considered as part of doing conceptual history.

To summarise: at the heart of this discussion is a straightforward observation: basic concepts, such as democracy, are deeply political. They are sources and/or sites of contestation between political actors attempting to realise their own ends through the strategic use of language. It is through the rhetorical actions of agents operating in specific historical contexts, responding to different questions and dilemmas, that basic concepts are altered or reaffirmed over time, as the strategies of actors are reconciled with the diachronic structures of the concepts they are employing. Clearly these processes take place in a reality that is not simply linguistic, as material forces influence the context within which conceptual contestation and change occurs. Nonetheless, ideational factors give meaning to the material world. On this point, Tzvetan Todorov explains that 'ideas do not make history on their own: social and economic forces also intervene; but ideas are not purely a passive effect, either. They make acts possible, in the first instance; and then they make it possible for these acts to be accepted' (Todorov 1993: xiii). To the extent that concepts help constitute the reality inhabited by these actors, such conceptual shifts can fundamentally alter the nature of the political realm within which they operate. The consequence, as James Farr notes, is that 'the study of political concepts now becomes an essential not an incidental task of the study of politics' (Farr 1989: 29).

## THUCYDIDEAN THEMES

As a way of concluding the chapter and linking it to the history that follows, it is valuable to consider Thucydides' *History of the Peloponnesian War*, as it illuminates many themes and arguments central to this book. In so doing, this study builds on recent scholarship that has challenged the longstanding habit of reading Thucydides out of context (Bagby 1994; Bedford and Workman 2001; Lebow 2003; Welch 2003). Realists are not the only ones guilty of this: one of the most prominent democratic peace theorists, Bruce Russett, has tried to enlist Thucydides in a rather tortured attempt to extend contemporary democratic peace arguments back to ancient Greece (Russett and Antholis 1992). This can be taken as a prototypical example of the kind of understanding of democracy being argued against here. Despite numerous examples in Thucydides of war between different *dēmokratiai*,[11] most notably between Athens and Syracuse, Russett and William Antholis still manage to force the conclusion that 'to some degree the norms that "democracies should not fight each other" were just being born' (Russett and Antholis 1992: 430). This claim is emblematic of the pervasive tendency to adopt a Whig interpretation of democracy's history, whereby the observer reads back into the past what is valued in the present (Butterfield 1950).

One of the most notable features in the diachronic structure of democracy is the central role played by the classical Greek experience in shaping how the concept came to be understood. This will be considered further in the next chapter, but for now it suffices to note that the *History of the Peloponnesian War* significantly contributed to a longstanding negative interpretation of democracy that lasted into the eighteenth and nineteenth centuries. Following the disappearance of democracy in ancient Greece, there was little direct experience with it until modern times, which meant classics such as Thucydides were central to how it was received across the centuries. In this regard, democracy's bad reputation was one of venerable origins, with the major texts to reflect on it also representing the beginnings of written history (Herodotus and Thucydides) and political thought (Plato and Aristotle). The first written examples of the Greek word *dēmokratia* can be found in the *Athenian Constitution* by the 'Old Oligarch' and in the *Histories* of Herodotus, neither which employed it in a positive sense (Rhodes 2003: 19). When combined with the writings of Thucydides, Plato and Aristotle, Western political thought commenced with a 'profoundly anti-democratic bias' (McClelland 1989: 2). This situation was reinforced by the oral culture of Athenian democracy, whereby those who supported it did so through actively participating in democratic practice and rhetoric (Ober 1998: 32). As a result, when the democratic experiment of Athens came to an end, left were not the practices or values that may have vindicated it, but texts written by its enemies that told of its follies and flaws. Even if Thucydides' reflections on democracy were more ambiguous than received wisdom suggests (J. Roberts 1994), his work was widely interpreted as a thorough indictment that illustrated how the fickle and wilful rule of the Athenian *dēmos* ultimately brought about the ruin of the once great city. And there was plenty in the text to support such a reading. In *History of the Peloponnesian War* it was the voice of Alcibiades that spoke loudest, describing Athenian democracy as an 'acknowledged folly', with Hobbes stating in the introduction to his translation that 'for his [Thucydides'] opinion touching the government of the state ... it is manifest that he least of all liked the democracy' (Hobbes 1975: VI.89, 13–14). When explaining his appreciation of Thucydides, Hobbes would later write: 'He teaches me how foolish democracy is, and how much more than an assembly one man knows' (quoted in Evrigenis 2006: 303). Not only did Thucydides directly influence the way democracy was historically received, his work also exemplifies the strong diachronic structure of the concept. As explored in the ensuing chapters, for democracy to emerge as a legitimate form of rule it had to negotiate and overcome this damaging Athenian legacy.

Despite being read as a strong critique of democracy, Thucydides' actual account is more complex. Indeed, it is possible to find two opposing images of democracy present in his work. One is emblematic of how democracy was negatively conceived of throughout much of history; the other is the positive and laudatory image that now prevails. These two faces of democracy are represented in the contrast between two central protagonists in the Athenian polity: Pericles and Cleon. Pericles is best known for his Funeral Oration, often taken as one of the definitive statements on democracy. Emblematic of this judgement is Karl Popper, who suggested that this speech presented 'the democratic creed ... in a manner which has never been surpassed' (Popper 1966: 42).[12] Pericles proudly announced:

> Let me say that our system of government does not copy the institutions of our neighbours. It is more the case of our being a model to others, than of our imitating anyone else. Our constitution is called democracy because power is in the hands not of a minority but the whole people. (Thucydides 1954: II.37, 145)

Throughout the speech Pericles extolled the virtues of the Athenians – such as their courage, public-spiritedness, love of knowledge and tolerance – and identified these as characteristics stemming from its democracy. In this oration, the rule of the people is presented as the best and most legitimate form of polity.

In stark contrast, Cleon was the great danger of democracy personified: the archetypal demagogue. In Thucydides' words, he was 'remarkable among the Athenians for the violence of his character, and at this time he exercised far the greatest influence over the people' (Thucydides 1954: III.36, 212). Cleon represents the image of democracy that prevailed for centuries after the demise of the Athenian experiment: a form of rule that was immoderate, rash, passionate, selfish, wilful and violent. Those weaknesses were most clearly witnessed in the Mytilenian debate, in which Cleon manipulated the anger of the Athenians to such a degree that in the 'fury of the moment' it was determined that the whole adult male population would be put to death, and slaves would be made of the women and children (Thucydides 1954: III.36, 212). The next day the decision was reversed, as Diodotus's words prevailed over those of Cleon. In addition to exemplifying the susceptibility of democracy to demagogues, this scene further highlighted the erratic and wilful nature of the *dēmos*, liable to change their mood from one day to the next.

Drastically different images of democracy can thus be found in these two central characters in *History of the Peloponnesian War*. There is the dangerous, unstable and violent form of rule identified with the demagogue Cleon: an interpretation of democracy that would long shape its meaning and warn against it. The other image of democracy is the one that now prevails: a politically legitimate and normatively desirable form of rule in which popular power is identified as virtuous and valuable. This book traces the conceptual shift between these two visions of democracy: from that represented by Cleon to the one embodied in Pericles' funeral oration.

In Thucydides one also finds insight about conceptual change, the core focus of this study. Concepts are especially susceptible to contestation and alteration during moments of political instability, most often manifest in times of revolution and war. Flux and change in the political and social order is reflected, and informed by, corresponding shifts in language. As Richard Ned Lebow notes, 'Thucydides' understanding of the story is not linear. Economic and political developments also had ideational roots ... ideas and language are the medium through which any kind of change takes place' (Lebow 2003: 373) A particularly powerful example of this is a passage in *History of the Peloponnesian War* where Thucydides observed that 'to fit in with the change of events, words, too, had to change their usual meanings' (Thucydides 1954: III.82, 242). In identifying this state of affairs, Thucydides pointed to the constitutive role played by language in shaping the social realm, in which concepts form a crucial component. From this vantage, his history charts the breakdown of Athenian civilisation through the collapse of shared understandings and conventions (Lebow 2003: 117, 147, 161–2). In this regard, Thucydides' awareness of the way conceptual change operates in relation to the political and social realm reflects one of the key assumptions informing this work.

## CONCLUSION

The present shape of international politics, one where popular sovereignty is a doctrine accepted by all states (plus many more who seek
entry), and where democracy is widely acclaimed as a form of government, only became possible as a result of transformations in the way
the concept of democracy had been understood and used. The more
one thinks about it, the more remarkable it is. For the greater part of
two millennia there was a very high level of consensus over democracy,
and this was wholly negative: it was considered a dangerous, unstable,
violent and antiquated form of rule. It was only in the last two centuries that the descriptive and evaluative dimensions of democracy were
contested, challenged and changed, so that democracy has emerged
as the most legitimate form of polity in international society. In this
sense, much of this book is about democracy *becoming* a basic concept
in international relations. And through appreciating how the meaning
and value attached to democracy has altered over time, insight is also
gained into how the international order within which it has operated
has changed. This study is thus engaging in a form of constitutive analysis: examining the question of how democracy's meaning and value
have been constructed over time in international politics and in so
doing, 'tracing the processes of *how it mattered*' (Price and Reus-Smit
1998: 276, 282; original emphasis). The book charts how this occurred,
with one eye towards the past, and the other towards the future. It is
a story that begins in the second half of the eighteenth century in the
United States, the subject of the next chapter.

### Notes

1  The literature on this topic is already enormous and continues to expand (if
   not go round in circles). R. J. Rummel has compiled a comprehensive bibliography of work on democratic peace theory, available at https://www.
   hawaii.edu/powerkills/BIBLIO.HTML (up until 2000) and http://www.
   hawaii.edu/powerkills/DP.BIBLIO.2009.HTML (2000–9) (both accessed
   16 February 2015).
2  In operationalising democracy, scholars largely rely on the Polity and
   Freedom House data sets, while the Correlates of War project (CoW) is the
   primary source for determining war and peace in the international system.
   A comprehensive list of different regime type data sets is provided by Paul
   Hensel at http://www.paulhensel.org/datapol.html (accessed 16 February

2015). For the CoW project, see http://www.correlatesofwar.org (accessed 16 February 2015).

3  Representative is the definition provided by Russett: 'For modern states, democracy (or polyarchy, following Dahl 1971) is usually identified with a voting franchise for a substantial fraction of citizens, a government brought to power in contested elections, and an executive either popularly elected or responsible to an elected legislature, often also with requirements for civil liberties such as free speech' (Russett 1993: 14).

4  According to Google Scholar, Barkawi and Laffey's 1999 article has been cited 147 times as at 14 January 2015. Of these, Nils Petter Gleditsch and Steve Chan are the only mainstream democratic peace scholars that have referenced it. It is also not listed in R. J. Rummel's seemingly comprehensive bibliography on the democratic peace.

5  For more information about the programme, see http://www.hsfk.de/Antinomies-of-Democratic-Peace-2000-2009.819.0.html?&L=1 (accessed 16 February 2015).

6  The history and theory of the concept of sovereignty have been considered in detail elsewhere (Bartelson 1995; Biersteker and Weber 1996; Hinsley 1966; R. Jackson 2007; N. G. Onuf 1991; Philpott 2001; Shinoda 2000; Thomson 1994).

7  The classic definition is provided by Hedley Bull: 'A society of states (or international society) exists when a group of states, conscious of certain common interests and common values, form a society in the sense that they conceive of themselves to be bound by a common set of rules in their relations with one another, and share in the working of common institutions' (Bull 2002: 13).

8  'Purposive association is a relationship among those who cooperate for the purpose of securing certain shared beliefs, values, and interests, who adopt certain practices as a means to that end, and who regard such practices as worthy of respect only to the extent that they are useful instruments of the common purpose. Practical association, in contrast, unites those engaged in the pursuit of different and sometimes incompatible ends through their recognition of the worth of those ways of life constituted by the authoritative practices that apply to them as moral agents or as members of a political community' (Nardin 1983: 14).

9  There has been considerable debate among English school scholars about the relative merits of pluralism and solidarism. While providing certain insights, at times it has been confused by these categories being used in both empirical and normative senses. This study largely sidesteps that discussion, and here pluralism and solidarism are understood empirically (Buzan 2004: 159–60).

10  This suggests that while the meaning of concepts may remain in flux at

certain moments, the difficulties of actively bringing about conceptual revision lead to more continuity in concepts than the earlier emphasis on contingency would seem to imply (Ball 1988; Richter 2000).

11  In a critique of attempts at applying democratic peace theory to ancient Greece, Eric Robinson observes in relation to the quantitative data Russett and Antholis compile from Thucydides that 'the results are striking: the government with the highest incidence of war against its own type is, by a hair, democracy!' (Robinson 2001: 599).

12  What is regarded as the other great speech announcing democracy's essence – Lincoln's Gettysburg address – has been interpreted by scholars as being strongly influenced by and modelled on that of Pericles (Stow 2007).

*Chapter 3*

# FEAR AND FAITH:
# THE FOUNDING OF THE UNITED STATES

A great revolution has happened – a revolution made, not by
chopping and changing of power in any of the existing states, but
by the appearance of a new state, of a new species, in a new part
of the globe. It has made as great a change in all the relations, and
balances, and gravitation of power, as the appearance of a new
planet would in the system of the solar world.

> Edmund Burke (1782) (quoted in Armitage 2007: 87)

The People are the King.

> Gouverneur Morris (quoted in Madison 1787)

## INTRODUCTION

The founding of the United States may seem a somewhat paradoxical
place to begin this history. On the one hand, it certainly appears as an
obvious starting point, considering the central role the country played
in the subsequent rise of democracy in international politics, what
Azar Gat terms the 'United States factor' (Gat 2009: 6–8). Scholars
such as Daniel Deudney, Michael McFaul and Tony Smith have strong
grounds to suggest that no country has played a more significant part
in the defence and spread of democracy (Cox *et al.* 2000; Deudney
2007; Kagan 2015; McFaul 2004; T. Smith 1994). The close relationship between the United States and democracy thus encourages one
to revisit its founding. On the other hand, if one does return to this
point in time, an awkward fact soon appears: the American Revolution
was not primarily about democracy, at least understood as a form of
government. Democracy was little thought about or discussed during
colonial times, and this never changed sufficiently for it to become

central to political discourse during the revolution (Kenyon 1962: 158; Lokken 1959: 570–1).

That the United States, a country which now associates itself and its legacy so strongly with democracy, actively denied this label just over 200 years ago offers a stark reminder of how recently the concept has come to signify something positive. Through an examination of the way democracy was understood in the founding period, the historical layers of meaning which shaped the concept can be identified, as can its stubbornly classical nature. While the revolutionaries steadfastly maintained a sceptical view of democracy as a form of government, popular sovereignty was widely extolled. Indeed, one finds what may now seem like a rather odd arrangement: the attempt to found a polity on popular sovereignty and institute a government that was answerable to the people, but at the same time, consistently refusing to identify it as a democracy. Rather, the revolutionaries saw themselves as constructing a republic. In this regard, democracy may not have been a pivotal concept in revolutionary discourse, but republicanism certainly was (Bailyn 1967; Pocock 1975; Wood 1969). During the founding of the United States the relationship between these concepts was complex, for they were used by some as synonyms and by others as antonyms. What linked democracy and republicanism was the overarching notion of popular sovereignty. For the founding fathers what separated the two, and created the possibility for a state based on the people without it being a democracy, was the principle of representation. Representation offered a way of mediating between the people as the constitutive power (popular sovereignty) and the people as the constituted power in the form of the executive and legislature (democratic government). The consequences of these developments would ultimately reach well beyond the United States, with the advancement of popular sovereignty during the revolution representing the beginning of the shift from international legitimacy being exclusively monarchical (Bukovansky 2002).

## A PRE-HISTORY OF DEMOCRACY IN
## REVOLUTIONARY AMERICA

The American Revolution did not commence with the aim of independence: it initially started as a protest against colonial misrule, with taxation being the main source of discontent. American complaints stemmed from a belief that the British constitution had been corrupted by the king and his ministers. At the time, discourse was structured more in terms of the distinction between free and arbitrary government, than the specific principles it should follow or the kind of institutions it should have (Stourzh 1970: 40–2). Democracy was not considered extensively. 'There was no controversy over the meaning of the term "democracy" in colonial America,' as Roy Lokken explains, 'the colonists gave little thought to it, and the word seldom appeared in their political writings, speeches, sermons, public papers, and private correspondence' (Lokken 1959: 570).

This widespread lack of interest in democracy stemmed from a number of factors. First, the mixed constitution was still held in high esteem. The problem was identified as the corruption that had come to define British rule, rather than the form of constitution *per se*. In contrast, democracy was generally understood as an unmixed form, something that had been strongly warned against by theory and history. Second, the limited amount of serious discussion about the possibility of independence ruled out extensive considerations of any form of government, democracy or otherwise. Third, democracy remained a somewhat antiquarian term, with its meaning strongly shaped by the classics. Each generation of thinkers had largely accepted the received wisdom handed down from the ancients that democracy was a dangerous and unstable form of rule.[1]

Given the strong influence of classical interpretations in shaping democracy's meaning during and after the revolution, it is necessary to reflect on them in more detail. As James Farr notes, the pre-history of any concept is an essential component for constructing a larger conceptual history (Farr 1989: 38). Democracy's origins were seen as lying in Athens and the other city-states of ancient Greece. Well into the nineteenth century Athens remained 'the immediate antecedent and model of modern democracy' (Canfora 2006: 47). Of primary significance were not the actual democratic practices of ancient Greece, but how they had been recounted and interpreted historically, something that had been done mostly by democracy's enemies (J. Roberts 1994; Keane 2009). Democracy was a direct form of rule, as indicated in the etymology of *dēmokratia*: the people (*dēmos*) ruled, they held and exercised power (*kratos*). That the people were both the source and direct executors of power endowed democracy with connotations of anarchy, instability and mobbishness, which were at the heart of how the concept was understood in revolutionary America.

The direct nature of democracy in Athens – the *dēmos* exercising *kratos* – was fundamental to how the concept was historically interpreted. While Athenian democracy may have included some forms of representation, it was neither theorised nor interpreted as a defining characteristic, and it is an essentially modern trait (Manin 1996; Pitkin 1967). Representation became relevant only once the size of the polity grew, and democracy was disaggregated into a form of state and a form of government. The directness of the Athenian system meant that for the people to be able to assemble and deliberate the *polis* had to be small. Moreover, a certain level of equality among its members was needed. The implications of these perceived requirements were significant. Regardless of whether or not democracy was considered desirable, these practical requirements seemed to render it impossible for modern states far greater in territory and population.

The direct nature of democracy generally precluded such practical questions, however, as putting power in the hands of the people was seen as particularly ill advised in the first place. There were two primary concerns. First, from an eighteenth-century perspective, there was no separation of powers. The executive, legislative and judicial powers were all held by the same people. This was seen as a recipe for tyranny, if not complete disaster. The directness of democracy meant it was susceptible to the whims of the erratic *dēmos*, and liable to fall under the sway of ruthless and power-hungry demagogues, such as Cleon in Athens. This was connected to a greater problem, whereby power was invested in those least capable of exercising it properly. Instead of the philosopher-kings Plato hoped for, or the enlightened leadership Pericles represented for Thucydides, it was the unstable, passionate, self-interested *dēmos* that ruled in a democracy. These concerns crystallised around the fear of mob rule, which was central to the way democracy was historically interpreted. The conclusion handed down from ancient Greece was that the direct exercise of power by the *dēmos* was necessarily mistaken. Reflecting this perception, James Madison proposed that, 'had every Athenian citizen been a Socrates, every Athenian assembly would still have been a mob' (Madison 2001: 288).

The concern over democracy's perceived tendency to degenerate into mob rule stemmed, in part, from it being understood as a social form of rule. In this understanding, the *dēmos* were not the whole political community but one specific grouping: the poor multitude. In the influential works of Plato and Aristotle democracy was identified as a form of government where the poor many rule over the privileged few. Plato's Socrates stated that 'democracy comes into being after the poor have conquered their opponents, slaughtering some and banishing some, while to the remainder they give an equal share of freedom and power' (Plato 1901: 267). Aristotle was less dramatic but formulated a similar understanding: 'A democracy is a state where the freemen and the poor, being in the majority, are invested with the power of the state' (Aristotle 2006: 87). The equality that democracy was seen to require furnished it with a dangerous levelling instinct, making it a threat to landed and propertied interests. This further challenged its relevance for modern states, especially in the incipiently liberal America.

Contemporary understandings of democracy were also shaped by the highly influential 'numerical' approach of Aristotle, which identified six forms of governance for the *polis*: three virtuous and three corrupted, each triad comprising rule by one individual, rule by the few and rule by the many.[2] What separated the virtuous forms of rule from the corrupted was whose interests the rulers ruled in: those of the *polis* or their own. Democracy was identified as a perverted form of rule because it ruled in the interests of one class, the poor. This 'numerical' approach was later replicated and renovated by a host of classical and medieval thinkers. It is here that one can identify the roots of a second meaning of democracy prevalent during the American Revolution, in which it was understood as part of a mixed regime. Underpinning the logic of the mixed constitution was the notion that each form of rule was susceptible to a certain kind of corruption. Unmixed regimes were seen as trapped in a cyclical process in which each virtuous form eventually mutated into its unvirtuous alter-ego, before in turn being replaced by the next virtuous form of rule. This interpretation was particularly prominent in the histories of Polybius, which were widely read and cited during this period. Polybius proposed that the solution to this revolutionary cycle could be found in Rome, which he suggested had a mixed constitution composed of the one, the few and the many, thereby balancing the dangers posed by each in their simple forms. In this system, democracy was a necessary part of the mix, but it had a very limited role. The idea of a mixed constitution would later famously be found at the heart of Montesquieu's *Spirit of the Laws*, which was highly influential in late eighteenth-century America, especially during the creation and ratification of the constitution (Carpenter 1928). In this tradition, the unmixed form of democracy was seen as complete folly, but when carefully balanced and given a limited role, it took on a more positive meaning.

Democracy was thus understood in two main ways during the colonial and early revolutionary periods. First, there was the simple, unmixed variant most commonly associated with Athens, which was dismissed as an antiquated form of rule inapplicable to and unadvisable for the modern world. The second conception of democracy also had classical roots, but was more immediately connected with the famed British mixed constitution. Democracy was regarded in social terms, in which it represented one social order, which was then combined with aristocratic and monarchic branches of government to create a mixed constitution, thereby protecting against the forms of corruption each branch suffered by itself. In its unmixed form, democracy was almost uniformly condemned, but when forming part of a mixed constitution it was seen as having a more positive role, on the proviso that it was carefully checked and limited. As America moved towards independence, questions related to sovereignty and forms of rule became more prominent.


## FROM REVOLT TO REVOLUTION

From 1774 to 1776 independence increasingly came to be seen as the only solution to the perceived misrule and corruption emanating from Great Britain. In turn, discourse shifted from the distinction between free and arbitrary rule to a more detailed consideration of forms of government and the foundations of sovereignty (Stourzh 1970: 40–43). The republican tradition of thought was particularly influential, quickly assuming a prominent role in the self-identification of the revolutionaries. In this regard, Cecelia Kenyon suggests that

> before 1776, the prevailing opinion in America had been that the ends of government ... could be secured within the framework of monarchy.... After 1776, they tended to associate all the characteristics of good government with republicanism, and with republicanism only. (Kenyon 1962: 165)

Due to its centrality in eighteenth-century political discourse, republicanism had multiple and contested meanings, but on a basic level it was connected with popular sovereignty, and operated as a counter-concept to monarchy.

Thomas Paine's *Common Sense*, published at the start of 1776, would be central as both a catalyst and a symbol of America's movement towards independence and its adoption of republicanism. It perfectly captured the moment, helping to forge the opinion that breaking with Britain was necessary. *Common Sense* was essentially a demolition job, an anti-monarchical polemic that forcefully expounded the need for independence. By arguing that British outrages prevented the possibility of reconciliation, he sought to locate responsibility for America moving towards independence with the British, and specifically their king. In making his case, Paine argued that remaining under the sway of a monarchy would drag America into the perpetual wars that plagued Europe. 'It is the true interest of America to steer clear of European contentions, which she never can do, while [dependent] on Britain.' Paine stressed the need for America to separate itself because Europe was filled with warmongering monarchies. In contrast, Paine presented republics as peaceful and argued that this was the form that America should adopt. He proposed that 'the republics of Europe are all (and we may say always) in peace. Holland and Switzerland are without wars, foreign or domestic: Monarchical governments, it is true, are never long at rest' (Paine 1988: 90). One way of shaping the meaning of a concept is by defining it in reference to a counter-concept, which is what Paine did in opposing Europe and America, monarchy and republic.

Paine fits closely with the figure of the innovating ideologist, and there are two dimensions of his influential polemics worth emphasising here. First, he comprehended and framed the conflict within a larger international context. America needed to become an independent member of international society, otherwise it would be condemned to the threat of war by virtue of its ties to Great Britain. For Paine, Great Britain was not a democracy cloaked in royal robes as Montesquieu had suggested, but an absolute monarchy masquerading as a republic. If America did not separate itself, it would be constantly caught up in British balance-of-power politics and the perpetual fighting that defined the European world of monarchies. Second, Paine insisted that independence must be followed by the foundation of republics. America needed to avoid the monarchical form that plagued Europe with continuous warfare and corruption. Only through republicanism could America be assured of peaceful relations and prosperity.

Moves towards independence unavoidably entailed a rejection of the British monarchy, as Paine made abundantly clear. This pushed the Americans towards defining themselves as republicans, almost by default: 'once the decision for independence was made, there seems to have been no serious question that any other form of government was either possible or desirable' (Kenyon 1962: 165). This stemmed from the widely understood notion that a republic was a polity that was not governed by a hereditary monarch. As Linda Kerber puts it, 'usually republicanism was simply what monarchism was not' (Kerber 1985: 475). This understanding strongly reflected the influence of Montesquieu, who had defined a republic simply as any regime where power was held by more than one individual. This conception was clearly reflected in John Adams's definition of a republic as 'a government whose sovereignty is vested in more than one man' (quoted in Everdell 1983: 6). Montesquieu distinguished between two forms of republic: an aristocracy and a democracy. In this regard, 'democracy' had a reasonably fixed meaning – it was a direct form of rule found in the ancient polities of Greece – whereas 'republic' was a much broader and more contested term. 'Republic' signified a basic principle of sovereignty tied to the people, which remained compatible with a range of governmental forms, while 'democracy' entailed a direct form of government. This meant democracy was not of much interest to the Americans, but there was widespread consensus that sovereignty should be located with the people, which is what republicanism conveyed.

Despite the value placed in republicanism by the revolutionaries, monarchies – either mixed or absolute – undeniably remained the standard in international politics. The ancient republics had mostly fared poorly in historical judgement, while the more recent republics in the city-states of Italy, the cantons of Switzerland, the Dutch free states and Poland had done little to inspire confidence. The founders were very cognisant of these contemporary cases that provided 'graphic examples of the disunity, absence of executive authority, and incapacity' of republics (Ghelfi 1968: 163). Paine's generous depiction was in stark contrast to the much more common perception of republics as sites of turmoil, instability and weakness. From the minor republics in Italy to their great forebear in Rome, all suffered similar fates: corruption and decline. This was not a particularly encouraging record for the Americans. As one anonymous author in 1776 concluded, 'history ancient or modern will make few Republicans' (W. P. Adams 1970:

414–15). Furthermore, the small community necessary to sustain the high levels of citizen participation and virtue required in republics was distinctly at odds with the trend towards larger states, and seemingly made republicanism a poor fit for the expansive territory of America. Simply put, republicanism did not appear a particularly wise or secure foundation on which to establish new states that would have to survive in a competitive international environment dominated by powerful monarchies (Bukovansky 2002: chs 3–4). These dangers of adopting republicanism were a recurrent theme in conservative writings up to 1776 (W. P. Adams 1970). It was only following Paine's *Common Sense* that most Americans began to fully embrace republicanism, regardless of the warnings from history and Europe. Commenting on this shift, Thomas Jefferson observed in the summer of 1777 that Americans 'seem to have deposited the monarchical and taken up the republican government with as much ease as would have attended their throwing off an old and putting on a new suit of clothes' (quoted in Wood 1969: 92). These were clothes that remained most unfashionable in Europe, however.

The concept of republic further suggested a general ruling principle about the ends of government. Understood in this sense, the term was much closer to the Latin it was derived from, *res publica*. When taken as a principle of rule, it was possible for a republic to be compatible with any form of government, bar absolute monarchy. This served as the basis for its use in another sense, as representing a mixed constitution, in so far as it was still identified as being most able to provide the common or public good (*res publica*). The constitution could be functionally mixed – a separation of powers between the executive, legislative and judicial – or socially mixed – a balance of social orders between the one, the few and the many (Pocock 1975: 61–5). From this perspective, American independence did not have to mean an outright rejection of the British model. A system based on social orders was not possible, but a functional mix was. This is what would emerge later when a stronger union was forged in 1787.

Both democracy and republic rested on popular sovereignty, but the two entailed different governing forms: democracies were unmixed, while republics were associated with a mixed constitution. The former was framed by connotations of chaos, disorder and turbulence: the people as the mob. The latter became imbued with a sense of stability, strength and virtue: the people as citizens (Shoemaker 1966: 88). In this vision, the republican nature of America would separate the new states not only from the ancient democracies, but also from the corrupt monarchical regimes that dominated international affairs. In Europe the republican self-labelling of America was accepted, but the suggestion that they were especially different from previous republics was received with great scepticism.


## INDEPENDENCE

In breaking free of British rule and declaring independence, the revolutionaries sought to establish a confederacy of republics. The relative *tabula rasa* on which the colonies had been built, combined with the disrepute monarchy had fallen into in America, meant that founding these new states on popular sovereignty was the most logical outcome. In this sense, even if democracy as *forma regiminis* (governmental form) was not central to the events taking place, clearly democracy as *forma imperii* (state form) was. The most important statement of the doctrine of popular sovereignty to emerge from revolutionary America was the Declaration of Independence. It announced in simple, assured language that governments derive their powers 'from the Consent of the Governed' (Continental Congress 2007: 165). In itself this proposition was not a new claim. Few rulers were bold enough to justify their power solely on rights of conquest, and most included some founding moment taken to embody the consent of the people. In the European context, consent was generally understood in a Hobbesian sense of the people contracting away their power. Once the people chose to invest the sovereign with power, they relinquished that power and were placed under the rule of the sovereign. This led to rule being legitimated in terms of historical right and custom, not in reference to (ongoing) consent. A British pamphleteer writing in 1776 summed up this conception of legitimacy: 'Government is (certainly) an institution for the benefit of the people governed, that is for the whole people, but the whole of people have not a right to model Government as they please' (quoted in Reid 1989: 21). In contrast, in America consent played a much more direct and active role. In a Lockean vein, the people construct a sovereign to rule over them, but they do not cede all their rights in the process. This was reflected in the declaration, which asserted that 'whenever any Form of Government becomes destructive of these Ends ['Life, Liberty, and the pursuit of Happiness'], it is the Right of the People to alter or to abolish it, and to institute new Government' (Continental Congress 2007: 165). The people never fully relinquish their power, retaining a right to alter the government if those in power become corrupted. The artificiality, or perhaps more accurately, the 'constructed-ness' of government was emphasised, with the consent of the people playing a more active and immediate role.

Placing popular sovereignty at the heart of the Declaration of Independence may have made sense in the American context, but it was an awkward way of framing a document that was also meant for international consumption. In this regard, it is important to appreciate that its main purpose was asserting membership in international society. The declaration should in this sense be understood as 'a document performed in the discourse of the *jus gentium* [the law of nations] rather than *jus civile* [the civil law]' (Pocock 1995: 281). In the opening and closing paragraphs it is evident that this was an international declaration, in the same way as a state would declare war. It commences with the new United States seeking to 'assume among the Powers of the Earth, the separate and equal Station to which the Laws of Nature and of Nature's God entitle them' (Continental Congress 2007: 165). What the revolutionaries took this to mean can be found in the document's conclusion: 'As FREE AND INDEPENDENT STATES, they have full Power to levy War, conclude Peace, contract Alliances, establish Commerce, and to do all other Acts and Things which INDEPENDENT STATES may of right do' (Continental Congress 2007: 170–1). This statement explicitly identifies the link between independence and external sovereignty, which, as David Armitage notes, 'was quite novel at the moment Americans declared their independence' (Armitage 2007: 137). What the document effectively represented was a claim to be considered as a member of the 'club' of sovereign states.

Unlike the French and Russian revolutionaries that would follow them, the Americans were not directly anti-systemic in intent: they were not trying to alter international society, but simply be accepted into it. Indeed, this could not have been otherwise: for America to be become fully independent and sovereign it needed to be recognised as such by other states. As David Armstrong explains, 'their revolution was fought to win the right for their country to exist as a sovereign state. Such a status was inseparable from acceptance of the juridical structure that alone made sovereign statehood legitimate: the society of states' (Armstrong 1993: 75). As such, the Americans largely sought to conform to what they understood as correct diplomatic behaviour. In January 1777, the American statesman James Wilson stressed that 'in our Transactions with European states, it is certainly of Importance neither to transgress, nor to fall short of those Maxims, by which they regulate their Conduct towards one another' (quoted in Armitage 2007: 65). Most Americans neither hoped nor expected that their revolution would spread to Europe and bring about the overthrow of monarchies (Rainbolt 1973). Schooled in traditional power politics, the revolutionaries were acutely aware that as a new, weak state on the periphery they would have to survive in a world dominated by powerful monarchies.

Considering this conservative desire to simply be accepted by other members of international society, the strong assertion that governments derive their powers 'from the consent of the governed' was an uncomfortable fit, as it directly challenged the prevailing standard of monarchical sovereignty. There was, however, a rather straightforward explanation: the document was also meant for domestic consumption. In claiming independence, America rejected the British monarchy and embraced republicanism, which necessarily entailed emphasising the constitutive role of the people. In this regard, the declaration is particularly significant because when the United States sought entry into the existing society of states, it did so while advancing an opposed conception of sovereignty, one that levelled an implicit challenge to the monarchical powers in Europe. As Peter Onuf notes, 'the Revolution is as important for offering a new definition and model for the constituent part ... as it is for promoting change in the *international* system' (P. Onuf 1998: 73; original emphasis). The declaration effectively represented one of the first major breaches in the old dynastic international order. According to Martin Wight, with it 'the floodgates were opened' (Wight 1977: 160; see also Armitage 2007: 139–44).

The declaration was a powerful speech act in itself, but it could only have the desired effect if it was listened to and accepted by other states, and especially the great powers. And so the revolutionaries were rather alarmed when it was largely met by silence from Europe. Not long after the declaration the Continental Congress instructed its commissioners in Paris 'to obtain as early as possible a publick acknowledgement of the Independancy of these States of the Crown and Parliament of Great Britain by the Court of France' (quoted in Armitage 2007: 81). This would not happen until February 1778, at which time the French entered into an alliance with the United States, which was a significant step towards independence as it indicated great-power recognition. The treaty of alliance stated that one of its purposes was 'to maintain the liberty, Sovereignty and independence absolute and unlimited of the said United States' (quoted in Armitage 2007: 83). The international standing of the United States was not fully confirmed until the conclusion of the American Revolutionary War in 1783, when the Treaty of Paris explicitly included recognition by its former colonial master. The first article of the treaty announced that, 'His *Britannick* Majesty acknowledges the said *United States* ... to be Free, Sovereign, and Independent States' (quoted in Armitage 2007: 87; original emphasis).

The United States secured its independence and membership of international society, but it also lost its one major bargaining chip in the European balance-of-power game. A confederacy of weak, fledgling republics on the periphery was of little interest, either as a threat or as a potential resource, to the dominant monarchical powers. The Marquis de Condorcet would observe in 1786 that American 'independence is recognized and assured', but the confederacy was also regarded 'with indifference' (quoted in Armitage 2007: 88). This lack of interest was reinforced by the republican character of the new confederacy. Absolute or mixed monarchies remained the standard, dictated both by custom and practice, and the great powers of Europe found little to worry about in the United States. Reflecting this opinion was John Andrews's assessment in 1783: 'A republican form of government is utterly inconsistent with the temper, disposition, and interest, of a great and powerful people' (quoted in Ghelfi 1968: 62). The weakness of the Italian city-states, the tiny Swiss cantons, the Dutch free republics and Poland strongly suggested that these new republics on the other side of the Atlantic would not last long. The Prussian monarch presumed that the former colonies would soon 'rejoin England and their former footing'. His Parisian ambassador concurred, describing the United States as, 'a people poor, exhausted, and afflicted with the vices of corrupt nations' (Morris 1965: 458–59). The early years of independence seemed to confirm the Prussians' scepticism.


## THE REALITIES OF INDEPENDENCE

By the middle of the 1780s it appeared that the American confederacy was not going to escape history. There was a growing belief that the republican experiment was in serious trouble. As Gerald

Ghelfi observes, 'throughout the literature of this decade Europeans constantly drew parallels between the causes which led ancient or modern republics to their ruin and the existence of similar "defects" in the Confederation' (Ghelfi 1968: 102). Not long after the *de jure* sovereignty of the United States was recognised, its *de facto* sovereignty was increasingly called into question. In this regard, the reports written by the Marquis de Lafayette after his attempts to lobby on America's behalf in the courts of Europe are particularly illustrative. He felt that perceptions of weakness were affecting the standing of the new confederacy, 'which delights her enemies, harms her interests even with her friends, and provides the opponents of liberty with anti-republican arguments' (quoted in Echeverria 1957: 127). Lafayette further noted that 'it is foolishly thought by some that democratical constitutions, will not, cannot last; that the States will quarrel with each other; that a King, or at least a nobility, are indispensable for the prosperity of a nation' (quoted in Ghelfi 1968: 126). Not only does this indicate that the United States was perceived as democratic, it illustrates the prevailing belief that popular states were not viable, with monarchies remaining the standard.

The low esteem the United States was held in stemmed not only from predominant opinions about republics, but also from the incapacity of the Continental Congress to act in a decisive fashion internationally, which merely confirmed these prejudices. The American confederacy was increasingly incapacitated by individual states jealously guarding their sovereignty. As Peter Onuf notes, 'the paradox of the Declaration [of Independence] is that the strong assertion of national *identity* should entail such a weakly articulated national *government*' (P. Onuf 1998: 80; original emphasis). This contradiction was becoming untenable, at least in its existing guise. George Washington judged that if more powers were not granted to the Congress, the United States would 'become contemptible in the Eyes of Europe if we are not made the sport of their Politicks' (quoted in Ghelfi 1968: 133). The poor standing of the United States was illustrated in the difficulty it had securing loans and forging treaties (Ghelfi 1968: 130). Dutch bankers offered four financial lifelines to the United States during the 1780s, with progressively higher interest rates, reflecting a belief that the new republics were becoming an increasingly risky investment. In order to strengthen their international standing the Continental Congress appointed Adams, Franklin and Jefferson to seek out treaties with as many countries as possible, a task that proved near impossible due to perceptions of American incapacity. The Prussian king felt he had nothing to gain from a treaty, noting that 'this so-called independence of the American colonies will not amount to much'. Britain was equally unconvinced, with the Earl of Sheffield concluding that 'it will not be an easy matter to bring the American States to act as a nation; they are not to be feared as such by us' (quoted in Ghelfi 1968: 136).

When considering the standing of the United States, French perceptions are especially instructive, as Paris was the source for most opinion on America in Europe, and it had also been the most sympathetic to the American cause (Venturi 1991: 4). The French position was very similar to that of Prussia and Britain. The minister to the United States, the Comte de Moustier, informed his king that the confederacy was hopelessly disorganised and suggested that this 'phantom of democracy' would inevitably degenerate into despotism (quoted in Echeverria 1957: 137). By 1787, the French government abandoned hope that the United States would hold together. The advice given by de Moustier is revealing:

> It appears, sir, that in all the American provinces there is more or less tendency toward democracy that in many this extreme form of government will finally prevail. The result will be that the confederation will have little stability, and that by degrees the different states will subsist in perfect independence of each other. This revolution will not be regretted by us. We have never pretended to make of America a useful ally; we have had no other object than to deprive Great Britain of that vast continent. Therefore we can regard with indifference both the movements which agitate certain provinces and the fermentation which prevails in Congress. (Quoted in Echeverria 1957: 138)

There was clearly no concern here about popular doctrines in America setting a dangerous example. Rather, the confederacy was deemed unthreatening, if not irrelevant, for France and Europe.

Talk of chaos, anarchy and decline in the United States was not limited to diplomatic opinion. It was also common throughout the European press, which made frequent comparisons with the unfavourable example of the tumultuous Dutch free republics (Venturi 1991: 59, 97, 126). After Thomas Jefferson was appointed as the American plenipotentiary minister in France in autumn of 1784, his job was one of public relations as much as diplomacy. As Franco Venturi notes, 'Jefferson's effort was directed toward international opinion … to persuade the world that the political creature born beyond the ocean was alive and well' (Venturi 1991: 110). This was a difficult task, especially as many Americans themselves were becoming more uncertain. In this regard, the Shays' Rebellion in 1786 was a catalyst in strengthening perceptions that the confederacy was in a state of crisis. Shortly after the rebellion, John Jay, the American secretary for foreign affairs, summed up the problem: 'To be respectable abroad it is necessary to be so at Home, and that will not be the Case until our public Faith acquires more Confidence, and our Government more Strength' (Ghelfi 1968: 134). Lafayette, America's greatest supporter in Europe, conceded that perceptions of weakness and incapacity 'did not seem to me quite destitute of a foundation' (Ghelfi 1968: 126). Later, in the fifteenth *Federalist*, Alexander Hamilton bluntly described the situation:

> We may indeed, with propriety, be said to have reached almost the last stage of national humiliation.… The imbecility of our government even forbids them ['foreign powers'] to treat with us: our ambassadors abroad are the mere pageants of mimic sovereignty. (Carey and McClellan 2001: 69)

Within the confederacy there was also a growing concern that its people were perhaps not so special as to possess the high level of virtue presumed necessary to sustain republics. Those agitating for a solution feared that all the vices that republics must avoid to survive – faction, corruption, self-interest – were far too prevalent. The source of these problems was regularly located in the overly democratic nature of state constitutions. In trying to guard against the dangers of executive tyranny, too much power had been handed to the people, who were subsequently failing the vital test of virtue. That a natural aristocracy did not appear meant that the concentration of power in the legislative branch was most troublesome (Pocock 1975: 516–17). The perceived results of the legislatures were not anarchy or licentiousness – the acknowledged and expected vices of a democratic system – but unexpectedly a kind of tyranny. Historical wisdom suggested that this was supposed to be found in the excesses of monarchies, not democracies. The classically minded John Adams complained that 'a democratic despotism is a contradiction in terms' (quoted in Wood 1969: 62–3). By contrast, Jefferson argued that a concentration of power was 'precisely the definition of despotic government', even if that concentration was found in the legislative branch chosen by the people. This was because the end results were the same: 'one hundred and seventy-three despots' were just 'as oppressive as one'. Despotism, long regarded as the vice of monarchy, now seemed to afflict the United States, which had purposely been founded on the principle of popular sovereignty partly to avoid such a danger. This growing dissatisfaction was summed up in Jefferson's lament that 'an elective despotism was not the government we fought for' (quoted in Corwin 1925: 519).

Failings at home and weakness abroad combined to create a palpable sense of crisis in the 'United' States. Independence was not supposed to result in 'mimic sovereignty' and 'democratic despotism'. These failings raised fears that Europe would soon try to carve up the United States as it had Poland. Disunion and weakness left it open to the designs of the great powers, whose appetite for conquest never appeared to be sated. Another possible scenario was that America would, in the words of Hamilton,

> be gradually entangled in all the pernicious labyrinths of European politics and wars; and by the destructive contentions of the parts, into which she was divided, would be likely to become a prey to the artifices and machinations of powers equally the enemies of them all. (Carey and McClellan 2001: 31)

Beyond the dangers of being dragged into the European system, there was the related threat of America *becoming* Europe. The fear was that without a strong national government, the confederacy would break down into a regional international society. Individual states closely guarding their freedom created the risk that the United States might descend into a Hobbesian state of nature composed of 'a number of unsocial, jealous and alien sovereignties', in Jay's words (Carey and McClellan 2001: 6).

Those that agitated for a stronger union worried that without one the United States was destined to suffer from the same systemic forces that brought constant conflict in Europe and the diminution of liberties within those states (Hendrickson 2003: 13). Hamilton was particularly sceptical about the possibility of sovereign states within America remaining at peace in an anarchical environment: 'To look for

a continuation of harmony between a number of independent uncon-
nected sovereignties, situated in the same neighbourhood, would be to
disregard the uniform course of human events' (Carey and McClellan
2001: 21). In stark contrast to Thomas Paine's optimism that republics
would enable more peaceful international relations, Hamilton denied
any difference: 'Have republics in practice been less addicted to war
than monarchies? Are not the former administered by men as well as
the latter? Are there not aversions, predilections, rivalships, and desires
of unjust acquisition, that affect nations, as well as kings?' (Carey and
McClellan 2001: 23–4). If a stronger union was not forged, and instead
a regional international society emerged as the confederacy fell apart,
the great fear was that the American republics would follow Europe
into despotism. The constant demands of war would likely cause an
increase in executive powers at the expensive of liberties and the legislature (Carey and McClellan 2001: 26–31).

A fear of being attacked or becoming Europe combined with a sense
of crisis emerging from the overly democratic state constitutions and
the inability of the weak Congress brought matters to a head, leading to
the Constitutional Convention in 1787. Observing this state of affairs,
Jay wrote that 'experience has pointed out errors in our national government which call for correction, and which threaten to blast the fruit
we expected from the tree of liberty' (quoted in Ghelfi 1968: 162). The
United States faced the prospect of strengthening the union or risking
its dissolution. The basic problem stemmed from the location of sovereignty within the existing confederacy. The belief that sovereignty
was indivisible meant that it could not be shared between the states
and the union. Ultimately sovereignty had to reside with one or the
other. During the discussions at Philadelphia and subsequent debates
over ratification, significant reflection took place on forms of state and
methods of rule, resulting in plans for the forging of a stronger union.
The ultimate solution was one that drew on the European model of
statehood without abandoning America's experiment with popular
sovereignty. It would truly be a 'republican remedy' to the diseases that
beset the United States (Carey and McClellan 2001: 49).


## REPUBLICAN REMEDIES

In forging a stronger United States the founding fathers were faced
with a host of difficult issues. The most challenging revolved around

sovereignty and the nature of the union. If the American confederacy was to hold, sovereignty could not ultimately lie with the individual states. Should it then be located at the national level? But surely such a concentration of power would lead to despotism and the abandonment of republicanism? There also remained considerable doubts about the viability of a republic existing across such a great territory. As Adam Ferguson explained, 'monarchies are generally found, where the state is enlarged in population and in territory, beyond the numbers and dimensions that are consistent with republic government' (quoted in Ghelfi 1968: 35). This opinion was reflected in diplomatic correspondence. One British agent in New York wrote that 'a Republican system, however beautiful in theory, is not calculated for an extensive country' (quoted in Ghelfi 1968: 35). The Prussian monarch offered a similar assessment: 'The extent of the country would alone be a sufficient obstacle to America's political success, since a republican government had never been known to exist for any length of time where the territory was not limited and concentered' (quoted in Ghelfi 1968: 36). Could the Americans prove these sceptics wrong? How could popular rule operate in such a large territory, while guarding against republican vices and democratic dangers?

The proposed constitution that emerged from Philadelphia in 1787 was a remarkable document, which managed to arrive at a viable solution to these challenges the United States then faced. The constitution re-envisaged the popular base of the United States. In it, the people were introduced as the source of sovereignty, while at the same time, they were removed by having their role limited and restrained in the exercising of this sovereignty.

## Popular Sovereignty

The sense of impotency abroad and discord at home was understood as a failure of the existing constitutional structure. A federal government stronger than the ineffectual Continental Congress was regarded as necessary to fend off the dangers posed by Europe. Admitting this, the socio-political realities of America dictated against the straight transferral of sovereignty upwards to a new national government. The individual states were jealous of their independence, and many were highly sceptical about the wisdom of ceding their freedoms. Indeed, it would ultimately take a civil war half a century later to fully solidify the union. Along with more parochial concerns, there was a greater issue about whether a federal government was compatible with republicanism. As noted, history and theory dictated that republics could only exist in small polities, which suggested that the separate states needed to maintain their independence. Anti-federalists used Montesquieu to remind Americans of the impossibility of large republics, a historical lesson most famously demonstrated by Rome, which had lost its republican character with its expansion. They warned that a federal government would be too big to be republican. Federalists countered by emphasising that an anarchical system of 'jealous sovereignties' transplanted to America would soon bring with it the corruption and despotism that afflicted European states. For republicanism to work in America, the founders had to reconcile the need for a stronger union with the realities of states protective of their freedom as well as widespread scepticism about the viability of a great republic. Sovereignty had to be moved upward, but not completely, as it had to be shared between the state and federal level. This was achieved through an innovative revision of the doctrine of popular sovereignty.

Simply appealing to popular sovereignty was not enough to resolve the issue of sharing sovereignty between state and national levels, but it did offer a way of reconceptualising the problem. Peter and Nicholas Onuf explain that 'by invoking and implementing, "popular sovereignty," Federalists could challenge this monopoly [of political power by the states] and provide a theoretical rationale for a powerful yet limited government for the federal republic' (P. Onuf and N. Onuf 1993: 131). The crucial move in the constitution was replacing the phrase 'we the states' with 'we the people'. The federalists persuasively argued that the separate states did not represent separate peoples. This enabled them to suggest that those who were against the federal system on the grounds that sovereignty was indivisible fundamentally misunderstood where this power ultimately lay. Both federal and state levels were equally representative of one American people, which remained the constitutive power. As sovereignty resided with the people, and not the states, it was theirs to distribute as they saw fit. The American people retained sovereignty by being its constitutive basis. They did so in a more immediate manner than in Europe through constitutional conventions, which operated as the 'founding moment' where the people constituted and delegated sovereignty (Palmer 1959: 214). Securing ratification of the constitution allowed for the creation of a stronger federal government, able to go beyond 'mimic sovereignty' and operate effectively internationally.

The founders had to be careful that in identifying sovereignty as residing in the American people they did not actually cede too much power to them. As Daniel Deudney observes, the founders 'were committed to popular sovereignty, but saw democracy as a source of instability and insecurity' (Deudney 2007: 165). Reflecting this, they sought to distinguish between the centrality of the people in legitimating rule and the more limited role they should play in actually governing. They did this through emphasising the distinction between the people as the constitutive power and the people as the constituted power (Pocock 1975: 517–18). The people were sovereign, they remained the constitutive power, and in turn, they delegated the constituted (legislative and executive) power to their representatives, who were of the people but separate from them. Sovereignty remained absolute, as the people were the constitutive basis of the United States and they retained this power in a more active and vigilant sense than in Europe, while legislative and executive powers were redistributed between state and federal levels. Sovereignty did not rest on a pact between ruler and ruled, as the people performed both of these functions. Without further revisions this suggested, in the words of James Otis, 'a government of all over all' (quoted in Wood 1969: 223), which is certainly not what the founders wanted. To avoid this scenario it was necessary to rethink another crucial concept – representation – which would reconcile these two roles played by the people.

### Representation

While a long tradition of political thought warned against the extensive exercise of power by the people, the immediate experience of the colonial period had left the framers of new state constitutions more wary of the one than the many. Not long after independence, as noted, fears instead appeared about the despotism of the many, with a belief that state constitutions were overly democratic. Drawing on contemporary sources, Gordon Wood highlights the shift in the discourse:

> 'It is a favourite maxim of despotick power, that mankind are not made to govern themselves' – a maxim which the Americans had spurned in 1776. 'But alas!' many were now saying, 'the

experience of ages too highly favours the truth of the maxim;
and what renders the reflection still more melancholy is, that the
people themselves have, in almost every instance, been the ready
instruments of their own ruin.' (Wood 1969: 397)

This is the context within which a system of representation was further
developed during the Constitutional Convention and subsequent ratification debates. In the formulation successfully propagated by the
Federalists, representation would ensure that popular sovereignty did
not entail popular rule in the form of democracy. In this regard, Wood
is not exaggerating when he states that 'no political conception was
more important to Americans in the entire Revolutionary era than representation' (Wood 1969: 164).

Representation, as James Madison so aptly put it, would be the 'pivot'
on which the American republic would turn (Carey and McClellan 2001:
328–9). It was hardly a new theory when it was afforded such a central
role in the constitution of the United States. Earlier versions could be
found in medieval times and it was notably present in the British mixed
constitution. Yet a mixed constitution based on social orders could not
exist in America as there was nothing to mix. Instead, the branches of
government that represented the one, the few and the many in Britain
came in the United States to be different representations of the same
collective people. Bicameral parliaments did not have two houses representing different social classes, but were a double representation of
the same people (Wood 1969: 248–50). The result was, as Wood notes,
that 'the American states were neither simple democracies nor traditional mixed governments. They had become in all branches governments by representation' (Wood 1969: 387). Power was not exercised
directly. There was a distinction between ruler and ruled that did not
traditionally exist in democracies, where the same collective people had
held power and exercised it. In the United States, the people remained
the locus of sovereignty, as in a democracy, but subsequently alien-
ated their powers to elected representatives. Representation thereby
allowed for the creation and maintenance of a ruling elite that would
govern, one selected by merit and regularly answerable to the people.
In this regard, Manin notes, 'representative government was instituted
in full awareness that elected representatives would and should be
distinguished citizens, socially different from those who elected them'
(Manin 1996: 94). And in a large republic there was a bigger talent pool

to draw leaders from. In this system of representative government the tensions between the necessities of popular consent and the dangers of popular rule were, to some degree, reconciled. Representation enabled the former, while limiting the latter.

The centrality of representation in defining the strengthened United States was definitively outlined in Madison's tenth *Federalist* paper, a work that marks a peak in both political theorising and rhetoric during the founding period. This was a particularly clear and successful case of ideological innovation in which Madison renovated the concept of republic in such a way that representation became central and a virtuous citizenry was no longer necessary, something that previously would have been a contradiction in terms. Representation became the defining feature of a republic, separating the American state from both the monarchies of Europe and the democracies of ancient Greece. The definition of democracy Madison provided was the standard one identified earlier: 'a society consisting of a small number of citizens, who assemble and administer the government in person' (Carey and McClellan 2001: 46). Reflecting commonplace interpretations, he found the historical record particularly troubling: 'Such democracies have ever been spectacles of turbulence and contention; have ever been found incompatible with personal security, or the rights of property; and have, in general, been as short in their lives, as they have been violent in their deaths' (Carey and McClellan 2001: 46). While Madison was working well within dominant understandings of democracy, he departed from established thought in offering a drastic reformulation of republic. As noted earlier, republics and democracies were often seen as similar, if not as synonymous, because of a shared popular base. Madison, however, drew a sharp distinction between the two. The difference was that a republic is 'a government in which the scheme of representation takes place' (Carey and McClellan 2001: 46). In the fourteenth *Federalist* he repeated this claim in an even more explicit fashion: 'In a democracy, the people meet and exercise the government in person: in a republic, they assemble and administer it by their representatives and agents' (Carey and McClellan 2001: 63).

Identifying representation as the characteristic that separated a republic from a democracy contrasted drastically with common usage in both America and Europe. Following this definition there were no republics in ancient times, a most untenable position. Reflecting on this, the Onufs ask, 'Why would Madison have taken a position as artificial, even silly, as this?' (P. Onuf and N. Onuf 1993: 79). The likely answer is the rhetorical capital gained from implying that Madison's opponents were democrats (P. Onuf and N. Onuf 1993: 79). Madison's distinction stemmed more from political exigencies than theoretical insights, as he was trying to strengthen the *Federalist* position against those sceptical of the new constitution. Indeed, John Adams later reprimanded Madison for his rhetorical manoeuvring: 'His distinction between a republic and a democracy ... cannot be justified. A democracy is really a republic as an oak is a tree, or a temple a building' (quoted in Stourzh 1970: 55). In following the distinctions outlined by Montesquieu, Adams saw the two concepts as related because both were based on popular sovereignty. Madison viewed matters differently, complaining of 'the confounding of a republic with a democracy; and applying to the former, reasonings drawn from the nature of the latter' (Carey and McClellan 2001: 63). For Madison, the crucial difference was in how popular rule was exercised. In one, popular power operated but it was controlled and channelled through representation, which created a virtuous balance of liberty and stability. In the other, the unrestrained will of the *dēmos* meant a constant 'turbulent existence', where the people suffered from the 'tyranny of their own passions' (Carey and McClellan 2001: 327–8). Simply put, in Madison's formulation what separated republic and democracy was the nature and consequences of popular rule. Representation offered the possibility for a state to be founded on popular sovereignty and ruled by the people, but not in the direct and dangerous manner found in democracies.

For supporters of the new constitution, it was the system of representation that would distinguish the American republic from the historical record. In providing the theoretical foundations for the new federation, Madison was most explicit in identifying representation as the 'pivot' separating popular sovereignty from democratic rule, and America from Athens. This was a position Paine would later adopt even more forcefully in *Rights of Man*. The centrality of representation identified the American experiment as unique, and the historical record as largely irrelevant,

> as most of the popular governments of antiquity were of the democratic species; and even in modern Europe, to which we owe the great principle of representation, no example is seen of a government wholly popular, and founded, at the same time, wholly on that principle. (Carey and McClellan 2001: 63–4)

Madison argued that what made the United States different, and likely to escape the historical tendency of republican failure, was that through representation it was possible to have both popular sovereignty and a form of popular rule, without suffering from the dangers that come from the directness of democracy. In the thirty-ninth *Federalist* he clearly distinguished between the two: 'It is *essential* to such a government, that it be derived from the great body of the society ... It is *sufficient* for such a government, that the persons administering it be appointed, either directly or indirectly, by the people' (Carey and McClellan 2001: 194–5; original emphasis). The people played a much more active part in governing compared with the Hobbesian model of sovereignty found in Europe, but representation still served to restrict the role they would play.

Representation offered a way for the United States to enjoy the advantages of popular rule, free from the wars and corruption that marked monarchical regimes, without succumbing to the failings that defined democracy in ancient Greece. From a more distant historical vantage point, it is valuable to note that at this time representative government was largely defined against democracy, which was still seen as a direct form of rule. The former was praised and lauded, the latter remained in disrepute. Prevailing opinion at the Convention still largely rejected the idea of democracy.[3] John Adams was most explicit in his judgement: 'Remember, democracy never lasts long. It soon wastes, exhausts, and murders itself. There never was a democracy yet that did not commit suicide.' Benjamin Rush echoed this viewpoint: 'A simple democracy has been aptly compared ... to a volcano that contained within its bowels the fiery materials of its own destruction' (quoted in Lipson 1964: 45). Democracy was widely seen as inappropriate for the new republic. Indeed for many, democracy was not only ill suited to modern eighteenth-century states, it had not even been appropriate for the ancient Greeks (J. Roberts 1994). Through the principle of representation the United States could be based on popular sovereignty, while distancing itself temporally and theoretically from democracy. Representation divided the people's two bodies: the constitutive power – the people as sovereign – was separated from the constituted power – the representatives of the people exercising power in the executive, legislative and judicial branches. This system was a clear improvement on ancient democracy: 'The public voice, pronounced by the representatives of the people, will be more consonant to the public good than if pronounced by the people themselves, convened for the purpose' (Carey and McClellan 2001: 46).

## FEAR AND FAITH

During the Constitutional Convention and the debates that followed the people were simultaneously regarded as both a source of strength and a threat to the viability of the United States. On the one hand, the people were identified as the constitutive base of the new republic. The United States separated itself from the absolute monarchies of Europe and the corrupted British mixed regime by constructing itself on the active and ongoing consent of the people. Alexander Hamilton put it in these terms: 'The fabric of American empire ought to rest on the solid basis of the consent of the people. The streams of national power ought to flow immediately from that pure original fountain of all legitimate authority' (Carey and McClellan 2001: 112). This was a fundamentally different conception of sovereignty to that which prevailed elsewhere in international society at the time. On the other hand, the correct mixture of liberty, stability and strong government that the Americans sought could not be secured through the people ruling directly, as in a democracy. Through the essentially aristocratic principle of representation, the role of the people would be limited and controlled, preventing popular sovereignty spilling over into direct rule. James Madison was clear on this point:

> The principle of representation was neither unknown to the ancients, nor wholly overlooked in their political constitutions. The true distinction between these and the American governments, lies *in the total exclusion of the people, in their collective capacity,* from any share in the *latter,* and not in the *total exclusion of the representatives of the people* from the administration of the *former.* The distinction, however, thus qualified, must be admitted to leave a most advantageous superiority in favour of the United States. (Carey and McClellan 2001: 329; original emphasis)

The prudential reasons that warned against democracy, combined with the practical necessities of enacting a popular form of rule in a great territory, made representation fundamental to the new constitution of the United States.

The beauty of representation was that it effectively allowed for rule of the people without rule by the mob. This point was expressed with great clarity at the time by Jean Louis Delolme: 'A *representative* Constitution places the remedy in the hands of those who feel the disorder, but a *popular* Constitution places the remedy in the hands of those who cause it' (quoted in Ghelfi 1968: 191; original emphasis). In activating popular consent while carefully limiting the actual input of the people in governing, representation truly acted as the 'pivot' of the new constitution. The principle that was supposed to enable popular sovereignty through overcoming the practical difficulties of extensive republics also dealt with the qualitative shortcomings of democracies. The resolution to the problems of the failing confederacy was thus a distinctly dialectical one, combining a unique mix of faith and fear in the people.

## CONCLUSION

The founding of the United States did not, at first, significantly alter conceptions of democracy as a governmental form, but as a form of state – namely popular sovereignty – it was asserted in a very powerful manner. As Alexis de Tocqueville would soon observe, 'if there is a single country in the world where the doctrine of the sovereignty of the people can be properly appreciated ... that country is undoubtedly America' (Tocqueville 2003: 68). Despite being founded on a conception of sovereignty that differed from the great powers of Europe, the United States was not perceived as a challenge to their legitimacy or standing. European monarchs, confident in their claims to rule, were not threatened by a weak, peripheral state that had yet to prove that its republican experiment would not end in failure. Furthermore, the Americans were not anti-systemic in intent, as later revolutionary actors in France and Russia would be. They were not trying to overturn international society; quite the opposite: they sought membership and acceptance. At the same stage, as was most clearly seen in the Declaration of Independence, the Americans were not simply conforming to existing understandings of statehood. This was further evidenced in the adoption of a republican constitution founded on popular sovereignty, and in instituting a form of government where the people played a much greater role than in Europe. In so doing, the Americans were – rather inadvertently – introducing a new, and revolutionary, conception of sovereignty into international society. In this regard, David Armstrong describes America's role well, noting how its emergence contributed to 'the dilution of the specific principle of international legitimacy of the eighteenth century' (Armstrong 1993: 76). Such an example had potential to become more challenging as revolutionary sentiment swelled on the other side of the Atlantic (Venturi 1991: 137).

In considering the role played by the founding of the United States in the emergence of democracy in international politics, it is also necessary to take a longer view. On the fiftieth anniversary of American independence, Thomas Jefferson wrote that the Declaration of Independence was 'an instrument, pregnant with our own and the fate of the world' (quoted in Armitage 2007: 1). This was an accurate assessment by the man who drafted the document. The revolution was a determinative step in the transition towards a society of sovereign states spanning the globe (Armitage 2007: 103). The success of the United States in its attempts to found and maintain a state based on, and animated by, the consent of the people was most consequential in the rise of popular sovereignty in the nineteenth and twentieth centuries. Furthermore, even if the concept of democracy was generally denounced, ignored or repudiated, many key dimensions of the modern representative form of democracy that would later emerge were initially explored in powerful ways in the United States. In this regard, Bernard Manin notes the remarkable situation that 'what today we call representative democracy has its origins in a system of institutions ... that was in no way initially perceived as a form of democracy' (Manin 1996: 1). James Madison announced the representative system as being a republic, not a democracy, but in time this difference would fade, as representation became identified as a fundamental component of modern democracy. This is one example of the revisions that took place in the United States, helping to lay the foundations for later conceptual shifts in democracy. And if it would take longer for the full impact of America's founding to become apparent, this was, in part, due to the outbreak of a great revolution on the other side of the Atlantic.

## Notes

1 The founders were schooled in the classics, and these texts were widely read, cited and used during the founding period (Ghelfi 1968: ch. 3; Wolverton 2005).

2 Rule by one could be either monarchy or tyranny, rule by the few either aristocracy or oligarchy, rule by the many either *politeia* or democracy.
3 Hamilton was perhaps alone in coining the phrase 'representative democracy', but did so in private correspondence and did not use the term repeatedly.

*Chapter 4*

# THE CRUCIBLE OF DEMOCRACY: THE FRENCH REVOLUTION

Know that you are kings and more than kings. Can you not feel the blood of sovereignty circulating in your veins?
Unknown French revolutionary (1792) (quoted in Sorel 1969: 256)

Let us fling down to the kings the head of a king as gage of battle.
Danton (1793) (quoted in Coupland 1940: xxvii)

We are at war with armed opinions.
William Pitt (1799) (Pitt 1940: 244)

## INTRODUCTION

The French Revolution and the subsequent wars that engulfed Europe represent the intersection of fundamental changes in the nature of international politics with the modern appearance of democracy as a political force. During this quarter-century of violence and upheaval many of the last vestiges of Christendom were swept away and some of the final pieces were added to the modern states system. These changes took place in unison with and in response to the popular doctrines that first emerged from revolutionary France. With the French Revolution a powerful articulation of ideas and principles that directly challenged the foundations of the existing society of states emerged from one of its greatest powers. The fundamental significance of these events for this book is conveyed by François Furet's observation that 'the central mystery of the French Revolution' remains 'the origin of democracy' (Furet 1981: 204).

The French Revolution has been a constant source of fascination over the past 200 years, and this chapter is strictly limited to exploring the conceptual shifts in democracy and popular sovereignty within France, and how these interacted with wider dynamics in international politics. There are two interrelated movements that are considered. First is the way democracy was employed by the revolutionaries and their opponents, and how this helped to shape its meaning. Compared with the American Revolution, significant contestation and re-evaluation of the concept did occur in France, which resulted in democracy being reactivated in political discourse. As John Dunn observes, 'with the French Revolution, democracy as a word and an idea acquired a political momentum that it has never since wholly lost' (Dunn 2005: 17). Second, there was a powerful theoretical and practical elaboration of popular sovereignty, a form of statehood that directly challenged the foundations on which monarchical powers and international society were then established. When considering the way popular sovereignty was understood and enacted, a fundamental point is that it is 'impossible to talk about *the* Revolution's conception of popular sovereignty in the singular' (Hont 2005: 139; original emphasis). Rather, two versions can be found and will be considered here: a represented or mediated version, best exemplified in the praxis of Abbé Sieyès; and a direct one, most closely associated with Robespierre and the Jacobins. Throughout the chapter close attention is paid to the overlap and interaction between 'internal' and 'external' changes in France, reflecting Fred Halliday's observation that revolutions 'are, above all, challenges to sovereignty *in both its dimensions*' (Halliday 1999: 11; original emphasis). Internally, the French revolutionaries questioned the legitimacy of the state by attacking the most basic foundations on which it rested. Externally, prevailing conceptions of sovereignty were challenged, as was the very nature of international society.

## THE *ANCIEN RÉGIME* IN FRANCE AND EUROPE

Before the revolution France was the embodiment of the monarchical principle of sovereignty. The Sun King, Louis XIV, famously announced its most basic meaning: *'L'État, c'est moi.'* Sovereignty was indivisible, located in the person of the king. All power derived from the monarch, 'the king was the fountainhead of all public authority, all magistracy, all legislation' (Furet 1992: 3–4). The only law that stood above that of the sovereign was divine. Louis XV powerfully restated this conception of absolute sovereignty in dressing down 'his' *parlements*:

> Legislative power is mine alone, without subordination or
> division.... Public order in its entirety emanates from me. I
> am its supreme guardian. My people are one with me, and the
> rights and interests of the nation – which some dare to make
> into a body separate from the monarch – are of necessity united
> with my own and rest entirely in my hands. (Quoted in Furet
> 1992: 5)

This understanding was shared by his successor, Louis XVI. A particularly instructive demonstration of this understanding of sovereignty
was his retort to a suggestion from the Parisian *parlement* that an act of
his was illegal: 'It is legal because I wish it' (quoted in Furet 1992: 43).

Given the exalted standing of the French monarchy it is unsurprising that democracy was little considered before the revolution. The
French word *démocratie*, originally taken from Latin translations of
Aristotle, remained an antiquarian term signifying an obsolete form of
rule that only existed in ancient times (Costopoulos and Rosanvallon
1995: 140–1). The concept carried with it the connotations identified in
the previous chapter: chaos, instability and irrelevance. The *philosophes*
were largely dismissive of democracy, if they even considered it. Despite
their differences, Montesquieu and Jean-Jacques Rousseau offered
similar descriptions, seeing it as a form of self-government where the
people directly exercise power, holding both executive and legislative functions (Costopoulos and Rosanvallon 1995: 141–3). And Abbé
Mably was hardly exceptional in regarding democracy and anarchy as
synonyms (Dupuis-Deri 2002: 106). In the entry on democracy in the
famed *Encyclopédie*, a classical interpretation could be found: 'It is the
fate of this government, admirable in principle, to become almost ines-
capably the prey of a few citizens' ambition, or the ambition of foreigners, and thus to pass from a precious liberty to the heaviest servitude'
(quoted in Dupuis-Deri 2002: 106–7). This judgement reflected that
the primary concern for most *philosophes* was the threat of despotism,
to which democracy represented a greater danger than even absolute
monarchy.

The position of the French monarchy was regarded as unassail-
able not only due to its strong domestic foundations, but also because
dynastic regimes remained the international standard. The few republican states that existed were small and ineffectual, and as considered
in the last chapter, the American experiment had yet to impress. Most

major powers were monarchies, but there was considerable variation between them, ranging from the absolute version found in France through to the restrained British model. Indeed, international society was more heterogeneous than a focus on the most powerful states might imply. Pre-revolutionary Europe still had many feudal elements to it, with a rather broad mixture of polities remaining (Sorel 1969: 39–40). Considerable homogeneity did exist, however, in social structures, with almost all polities being hierarchically ordered. This had two major consequences. First, as Andreas Osiander suggests, kingship 'was simply the outgrowth' of these common hierarchical orders (Osiander 1994: 209; Bukovansky 2002: 77–82). It was the social structure of monarchical states that was arguably most important to their continuity, something Prince Metternich would later be acutely aware of. Second, diplomacy was conducted primarily by the nobility and aristocracy. Indeed, diplomats more readily identified with each other than with the people they represented (Bukovansky 2002: 62). The result was that diplomacy in international society resembled court culture, with a strong emphasis on less tangible interests such as glory and prestige. Thus, while there was a degree of heterogeneity in the state forms found in Europe, this diversity was tempered by the high level of homogeneity in their social makeup.

There may have been a range of constitutional forms in existence, but there was little doubt about which were better than others. As Mlada Bukovansky notes, 'implicit in the rules of the game … were ideas about the identities of the major players – their constitutions were monarchical and dynastic rather than republican' (Bukovansky 1999: 204–5). Great powers were monarchies, with Louis XIV's France being the prototype. In contrast, democracy was simply not considered possible or viable for modern states. In this regard, Edmund Burke's reflections on revolutionary France's attempts to be a 'pure democracy' are instructive:

> I reprobate no form of government merely upon abstract principles. There may be situations in which the purely democratic form will become necessary. There may be some (very few, and very particularly circumstanced) where it would be clearly desireable. This I do not take to be the case of France, or of any other great country. Until now, we have seen no examples of considerable democracies. (Burke 1999: 94)

Burke's observations are illustrative of a general perception that France's status as a great power necessitated that it remain a monarchy. Recognising this context sheds light on the way the events of 1789 unfolded within France, and how they were received by the rest of Europe: the framework of monarchy continued to dominate expectations, and the idea of France becoming a republic was simply not considered as a possibility for some time.

Eighteenth-century international society was dominated by monarchies that engaged in balance-of-power politics and *raison d'état* thinking. The result was a system of shifting alliances, with constitutional forms not being determinative of partners. Conflict was mainly dynastic and territorial. As Martin Wight observes, 'from the time of Louis XIV down to the French revolution the fundamentals of international society were not challenged. This is the classic age of power politics without doctrinal overtones' (Wight 1978: 83). The prevailing wisdom of *raison d'état* meant that domestic revolts, revolutions, the overthrow of monarchs and even regicide were largely responded to in reference to state interests. Representative were the policies of Louis XVI: backing monarchy in Sweden and Poland, fighting for republicanism in America, intervening against democrats in Geneva (Sorel 1969: 92). This could only be considered consistent if understood in terms of *raison d'état*. As revolution broke out in France, it was from this perspective that Europe interpreted developments.

## 1789 AND THE CHALLENGE OF ABBÉ SIEYÈS

Decades of blunders, failed attempts at reform, short-sightedness, ineffectual leadership, aristocratic greed, international pressures and simple bad luck all collectively worked to bring France to a state of crisis by the 1780s. It remained an absolute monarchy, but it was more so in appearance than in substance: in reality it was heavily mixed with aristocratic rule. The end result was a hybrid beast, neither 'absolute monarchy or aristocracy, but something born of the decadence of the two principles and still surviving on their complicity, at the expense of the people' (Furet 1992: 32). The situation became increasingly untenable as national debt continued to mount at an alarming rate due to an inability to control the spending of the court, a problem further compounded by the costly support of the American revolutionaries. The complex causes that triggered the revolution are well beyond the scope of this chapter. What matters, however, is that in August 1788 this potent cocktail of domestic and international failings resulted in Louis XVI calling for the Estates-General to convene.

A wealth of political tracts flooded France in the interregnum between the calling of the Estates-General and its scheduled opening on 1 May 1789. Among this deluge three particularly influential statements appeared from a previously unknown Abbé Sieyès. Of these, the most significant was the widely read *Qu'est-ce que le Tiers État? (What Is the Third Estate?)*, published in January 1789. Like Paine's *Common Sense* in the American Revolution, Sieyès's intervention was a deftly weighted mix of polemic and praxis, acting both to crystallise and to catalyse emerging revolutionary sentiment. Sieyès would become central to the course of events of 1789, due both to his writings and to his leadership in the National Assembly. What one finds in Sieyès's thought is what could then be found in France: a radical, revolutionary challenge to the *ancien régime*. Indeed, it is not a great overstatement to propose that Sieyès was '*the* man of 1789', as 'his theory represents the idea of the revolution itself in its first, momentous stages' (Forsyth 1987: 3; original emphasis). What made him so pivotal – a true ideological innovator – was that he provided the means for fundamentally reconstituting the foundations of the French state on a popular basis, through furnishing 'practicable, realizable ideas' centred on popular sovereignty and representation (Forsyth 1987: 216–17). These innovations would ultimately reverberate well beyond the borders of France. As Murray Forsyth observes, Sieyès is 'the most perfect representative in thought of the ideas that the Revolution transmitted to Europe ... regarding the ends and organization of the state' (Forsyth 1987: 3–4). For these reasons, it is valuable to consider his thought in more detail.

Sieyès outlined a theory of popular sovereignty that radically challenged the basis on which the French monarchy had been founded. While his ferocious assault was aimed at the nobility and clergy, the nature of his claims also unavoidably undermined the monarchy. Building on the social-contract tradition – of Thomas Hobbes especially – Sieyès identified sovereignty as residing not in the king, but in the nation. Compared with the absolute conception of sovereignty that had long prevailed in France, this was a significant reinterpretation as it left the monarch as a delegate of power, rather than its source. In placing sovereignty in the nation, this grouping was not conceived of in a cultural or ethnic fashion.[1] The nation was neither a pre-political form of community, nor derivative of the king's *dignitas*, but defined through its socio-political unity. It did not emerge from an agreement between the monarch and a number of social orders. The nation was a historical fact and political reality created by the coming together of previously atomised individuals. As such, the unity that defined the nation was deeply political: 'a nation is made *one* by virtue of a common system of law and a common representation' (Sieyès 2003: 99; original emphasis). It was this understanding that Sieyès successfully promoted in revolutionary discourse (Forsyth 1981; Hont 1994; Hont 2005). Sieyès failed, however, to provide a satisfactory explanation for the external boundaries of the nation, instead taking them simply as *de facto* (Hont 1994: 187). And this was where his conception of the nation was liable to merge into a pre-political, cultural understanding, as shared traits such as ethnicity are one way of clearly demarcating inside and outside.

The nation, identified as a historical and political reality, was the ultimate source of sovereignty, and thus logically prior to the form of government instituted. Sieyès expressed this very clearly: 'The nation exists prior to everything; it is the origin of everything' (Sieyès 2003: 136). Flowing from this, the nation is the 'constitutive power', which 'is the one who makes the constitution and establishes a new political and legal order' (Kalyvas 2005: 226). Sieyès explicitly distinguished between the 'constitutive power' and the new order it founds, the 'constituted power'. This separation was central to his thought and the mediated conception of popular sovereignty it would give rise to. The constitutive power exists prior to any government, and in this sense, 'it is the origin of all legality' (Sieyès 2003: 137). Positive laws flow from the constitution, which is granted by the constitutive power. As such, the legal system and the government founded form the constituted power. These remain derivative of the constitutive power, the ultimate source of sovereignty.

Sieyès's distinction between the constitutive and constituted powers provided the crucial link in the disaggregation of democracy into a form of state and a form of rule. In the latter sense, democracy is the constituted power, emerging from the exercise of the nation's prerogative as the constitutive power, which is what popular sovereignty entails. As seen, this separation was present in the American Revolution, but Sieyès gave it greater force and conceptual clarity. Through identifying the nation as the constitutive power, the government and the state were fully secularised, as the constitution was explicitly a human construction (Kalyvas 2005: 229). The constitutive power was the nation: a collective, unitary body from which all constituted power emanated. Sieyès explained: 'To assume that there is a contract between a people and its government is a false and dangerous idea. A nation does not make a contract with those it mandates; it *entrusts* the exercise of its powers' (Sieyès 2003: 120; original emphasis). This reformulation had potentially far-reaching consequences, as Keith Michael Baker observes: 'The logic of *Qu'est-ce que le Tiers Etat?* threatened the entire standing order of international relations no less radically than it subverted the institutional order of the French monarchy' (Baker 1989: 850). In this interpretation, the monarch was no longer sovereign, but merely a delegate of the people's sovereignty. This represented a radically different understanding to that which prevailed in international society.

Sieyès challenged where sovereignty resided – arguing it ultimately lay with the people, not the king – but he did not question its nature as unitary and indivisible. The dictum of '*l'État, c'est moi*' was effectively replaced with '*l'État, c'est le peuple*'. What this meant was that once a nation was formed of individuals, a general will had to emerge. 'Power resides solely in the whole. A community has to have a common will. Without this *unity* of will, it would not be able to make itself a willing and acting whole,' Sieyès explained (Sieyès 2003: 134; original emphasis). In any modern nation this will manifest itself indirectly, through representatives. Once polities became too large and numerous in population, '*government by proxy*' had to be introduced, whereby 'there is no longer a *real* common will that acts, but a *representative* common will' (Sieyès 2003: 134–5; original emphasis). Whereas Rousseau denied that representation of the general will was possible, Sieyès argued that it could, and should, be represented. As well as being practically necessary, it was also a more rational system. According to Sieyès, 'it is for the common utility that they [the people] nominate representatives more capable than themselves of knowing the general interest and of interpreting their own will in this respect' (quoted in Forsyth 1987: 138). The parallels with Madison are apparent: representation would enable a modern system of popular sovereignty and rule without it becoming a democracy. Notably, for Sieyès democracy still meant direct rule in a polity of limited size, and as such, the only way it was possible was by federalising France, an idea to which he was strongly opposed: 'France is not, and cannot be a *democracy*; it must not become a *federal state*, composed of a multitude of republics, united by some kind of political tie. France is and must be a *single whole*'.[2] Sieyès argued that modern states needed to be large and united, as this allowed for the pooling of resources to advance the arts and sciences and greater capacity for defence against others, and also protected against the perpetual wars that smaller, neighbouring states were prone to (Forsyth 1987: 140). On these grounds, democracy was seen as hopelessly inadequate.

Sieyès may have dismissed democracy as a form of rule, but his interventions were crucial in laying the conceptual groundwork for what Condorcet called, as early as 1789, 'representative democracy' (Urbinati 2006: ch. 6). These foundations were laid not through revising the concept of democracy itself, but by offering the most systemic and complete theory of representative government yet devised. The *dignitas* of the nation replaced that of the king, and the representative system activated and realised the ultimate power that resided in the people.

## THE ESTATES-GENERAL AND THE NATIONAL ASSEMBLY

The revolt of the *parlements*, the airing of grievances through the *cahiers des doléances*, the explosion of new thought in political tracts, and the sense of increased participation through voting for representatives for the Estates-General, all exacerbated by poor harvests, gave an increased sense of urgency and gravity to the convening of the Estates. The gathering of France's three orders had quickly outgrown its original purpose of finding a solution to the debt crisis, and had instead come to represent an opportunity to liberalise the French state. When the Estates-General opened in May 1789 it was immediately deadlocked by the Third Estate's insistence that the three orders should meet together and that voting be by head, not by order. A resolution to the standoff was forced when, at the urging of Sieyès, the Third Estate reconstituted itself as the National Assembly on 17 June. After the king acceded to this bold move just ten days later, a new power was created.

Shortly after the National Assembly was constituted, the famous 'Tennis Court Oath' took place, where delegates vowed to continue meeting until they gave France a constitution. In so doing, the Assembly claimed for itself the constitutive powers to reform the French state, reflected in the new name adopted weeks later, the 'National Constituent Assembly'. These developments powerfully enacted the thinking of Sieyès, effectively moving sovereignty from the monarch to the people, as represented by the Assembly. Changes continued apace, with August 1789 being an especially busy month for the new Assembly. It commenced on 4 August with decrees abolishing feudalism, effectively demolishing the social basis of the *ancien régime* in France. These sweeping reforms – abolishing privileges and instituting civil equality – also established the revolutionaries as a major threat to the hierarchical social structure on which international society was then based. France abolished a composite body of social orders united and represented by a monarch, and refounded itself on the radically opposed principle of popular sovereignty. In reconstituting the state from a collection of individuals – who together formed the nation – it was necessary to consider first principles: to set out what rights, and perhaps also what duties, these individuals possessed (Furet 1992: 73). This would lead to the Declaration of Rights and Man and Citizen, which had its last article adopted by the Assembly on 26 August to complete a productive month.

The Declaration of Rights and Man and Citizen was further evidence that the revolution was pregnant with consequences for international society. Its universalist claims challenged the boundaries and the sovereign rights of Europe's rulers. And by framing the declaration in terms of *principles*, it threatened an international order built on historic right and custom. This was one of Burke's major reasons for attacking the 'abstractions' of the revolutionaries. He rhetorically asked: 'Is it because liberty in the abstract may be classed amongst the blessings of mankind, that I am seriously to felicitate a madman, who has escaped from the protecting restraint and wholesome darkness of his cell, on his restoration to the enjoyment of light and liberty?' (Burke 1999: 45). The example he used was hardly accidental, as it conjured up images of anarchy and violence then associated with popular rule. This reflects that it was not just abstract principles, but specifically popular principles that exacerbated the threat posed by the French revolutionaries. The declaration reinforced what Sieyès and the Assembly had already made clear: sovereignty no longer resided in the French monarch. Article 3 announced that 'the source of all sovereignty resides essentially in the nation; no group, no individual may exercise authority not emanating expressly there-from' (National Assembly of France 1789). The general will emanated from the nation, and this will defined the nature of the positive laws that existed in the French state, as Article 6 outlined: 'Law is the expression of the general will; all citizens have the right to concur personally, or through their representatives in its formation' (National Assembly of France 1789). A noteworthy feature is that the declaration was ambiguous as to whether the general will was formed directly or was represented. As Pierre Rosanvallon observes, 'the sacralization of the general will does not necessarily involve popular power, in other words. The equivocation is fundamental and foundational' (Rosanvallon 2002: 696).

## FRANCE AND EUROPE: THE QUIET BEFORE THE STORM

During the opening stages of the revolution the French were understandably preoccupied with the momentous changes taking place. Reactions from other states ranged from mild concern, through indifference, to barely concealed pleasure at France's fall. Events were viewed through the dominant *raison d'état* lens, which explains the 'relative sangfroid' that defined Europe's collective reaction (Hobsbawm 1962: 116). The internal chaos and upheaval effectively removed France from balance-of-power calculations, which meant the major players could focus on other matters. As J. H. Clapham observes, 'the prevailing opinion in European diplomatic circles was that to prevent France from destroying her own supremacy would be short-sighted and impolitic' (Clapham 1899: 18). Moreover, the fate of Poland and the impact that any partitions would have on the overall balance of power was of greater concern. The revolutionary principles emerging from Paris were yet to be perceived as a serious challenge. The man in charge of Austria's foreign policy, the Prince of Kaunitz, was most explicit about this: 'The alleged danger of the possible effects that the bad example of the French could have on other peoples is nothing but a wild-eyed panic, a chimera contradicted by the facts' (quoted in Walt 1996: 73). The Austrian's judgement reflected the confidence of *ancien régime* Europe. Nonetheless, the popular doctrines being espoused and enacted in France were a major challenge to the foundations of international society, even if most lagged behind Burke in recognising this threat.

In comparison to the monumental changes of 1789, and the turmoil that would soon engulf France and eventually most of the continent, the intervening years of 1790–1 appear relatively quiet. Changes within France continued apace as the rest of Europe largely watched on: some with concern, others with hope, and most with a fading degree of ambivalence. Writing early in 1790 Lord Sheffield, the British foreign secretary, observed:

> At present there seems no symptom of attaining anything worthy the description of government in France. I cannot conceive it possible that a revolution, so managed as it is, can proceed smoothly. Progressive distress must produce a crisis, and probably a grand burst. (Quoted in Burley 1989: 94)

Trouble was brewing within France, as well with Europe. One of the first clear signs that the revolutionary principles would have direct and immediate consequences for international society was the Nootka Sound crisis in 1790. Facing possible war with England, Spain sought French naval support in accordance with the family compact between the Bourbon rulers. Even though the king retained prerogative over matters of war and peace, his foreign minister had to call on the National Assembly for funds to ready the fourteen ships that Louis had promised. The Assembly refused to allow the king to send the ships. In rejecting France's obligations under the family compact, the revolutionaries were indicating they would not be bound by existing international law, as they did not accept the legitimacy of pacts made by monarchs, and not by peoples. This position was reinforced by the Assembly's handing of the situation in Alsace, where the abolition of feudal privileges threatened the rights of a number of German princes, whose claims dated back to the treaties of Westphalia. In refuting their claims, the National Assembly decreed that 'treaties made without the consent of the people of Alsace could not bestow legality on rights to which they had not given their consent.... In short, it is not the treaties of princes which regulate the rights of nations' (quoted in Blanning 1986: 74–5). The revolutionary French were now defiantly asserting a new principle of legitimacy – one based on popular sovereignty – that openly challenged an international order built on monarchy and hereditary right.

A further consequence of the Nootka Sound debate was the Assembly issuing the 'Declaration of Peace to the World'. It pledged that 'the French nation renounces the undertaking of any war with a view to making conquests, and it will never use its forces against the liberty of any people' (National Assembly of France 1951: 285). This declaration reflected a fundamentally different *Weltanschauung* to that which prevailed among European sovereigns and diplomats. The revolutionaries believed that peace would result when sovereignty was placed in the hands of the nation, as warfare was the practice of kings, not of peoples. A deputy from Poitou expressed this position with great clarity:

> All unjust aggression is contrary to natural law; a nation has no more right to attack another nation than an individual has to attack another individual. A nation cannot therefore give a king the right to aggression that it does not have itself; the principle should above all be sacred for free nations. Were all nations free as we wish to be, there would be no more war. (Quoted in Keitner 2007: 101)

The problem was that not all nations were free by French standards, which left open the possibility that France might need to 'assist' other nations to be free. 'The belligerent implications', as Chimène Keitner observes, 'were not immediately recognized by its proponents' (Keitner 2007: 101).

The repudiation of the family pact with Spain, combined with the handling of the situations in Alsace and Avignon,[3] were the first direct indications that change within France might be incompatible with international society as then constituted. Nonetheless, states continued to view the words and actions of the revolutionaries through the lens of *raison d'état*, which prevented a recognition of the genuineness of French universalism and the full ramifications of the doctrine of popular sovereignty they espoused. The revolution would become a more pressing concern when King Louis and Marie-Antoinette attempted to flee France.

## THE FLIGHT TO VARENNES

The place of the French king in the new order being constructed was an ongoing thorn in the side of the revolutionaries. The National Constituent Assembly's awkward attempt to turn the previously absolute monarch into a representative of the nation reflected a continuing inability to conceive of France without a monarch. Despite advocating a theory of popular sovereignty that fundamentally undermined the position of the king, Sieyès sought in vain to reconcile it with a form of elective monarchy, something Thomas Paine strongly critiqued him for (Sieyès 2003: 166–73). Like most of his fellow revolutionaries, Sieyès was not yet willing to dispense with the hapless king. Louis himself did not help matters, charting the worst possible middle course: monarchical sensibilities left him incapable of reconciling himself with the revolutionaries' programme, yet the weakness of his person prevented him from taking the steps necessary to restore the Bourbon throne. His farcical attempt to flee the country reflected this perfectly. Having complained secretly in letters to the Spanish king since October 1789, Louis finally decided to make a stand, hoping that from outside France he would be able to crystallise opposition against the revolution. When escaping Louis did so in a large coach suitably fitted for a king, making no real attempt to conceal his identity, or even to proceed in haste. The party made it as far as Varennes, near the border with the Austrian Netherlands, before being stopped and forced to return to Paris in humiliation, where the king and his family were again placed under heavy guard at the Tuileries.

The doubts many held about the real views and intentions of Louis, Marie-Antoinette and their associates had been confirmed. Following Varennes the king's standing was irretrievably damaged, and claims that he was a representative of the nation were no longer tenable. In seeking refuge beyond its borders and with his fellow monarchs, Louis separated himself from the French nation. With his poorly executed attempt to flee Louis destroyed the strained attempts of moderates to construct a constitutional monarchy, and instead created the possibility of a France without a king. Shortly after Varennes the British envoy, Earl Gower, observed: 'If this country ceases to be a monarchy it will be entirely the fault of Louis XVI' (quoted in Black 1999: 519). Immediately on hearing the news of the attempted escape, Paine nailed a placard to the door of the National Constituent Assembly that denounced the king in typically strong fashion: 'Whether fool or hypocrite, idiot or traitor, he has proved himself equally unworthy of the important functions that had been delegated to him' (J. S. Hall 1951: 215). Even at this stage, though, Paine's calls for a republic remained premature, and the Assembly instead suspended the king. The massacre at the Champs de Mars, involving the suppression of crowds rioting over this tepid response, indicated that growing republican sentiment among the Parisian crowd did not yet extend to the Assembly, which remained unable to abandon the monarch entirely.

The repercussions of Louis's bungled escape were felt well beyond French borders. The plight of the hapless king garnered more attention from other sovereigns, who were starting to comprehend that the revolutionary changes were far greater in scope and significance than they had previously realised. Notably, Leopold II, the new emperor of Austria, kept a close watch on developments, as his sister – Marie-Antoinette – was married to Louis. Shortly after their capture at Varennes Leopold issued the 'Padua Circular', which built on discussions between Austria, Spain and Prussia, and indicated concern over the fate of the French king. A month later, Leopold and Frederick William II of Prussia subsequently issued the 'Declaration of Pillnitz'. It announced that 'they regard the present position of His Majesty the King of France as a matter of common concern to all sovereigns in Europe', and that concerted action was needed to restore Louis (J. S. Hall 1951: 223). Included in the declaration was the proviso that international cooperation was an essential condition, which made action highly unlikely due to the unwillingness of the British to get involved (Blanning 1986: 87). Despite this careful phrasing, the actions of Austria and Prussia betrayed an inability to comprehend the revolutionary mindset, specifically how the declaration clashed with the emerging doctrine of popular sovereignty and its corollary of non-intervention. Likewise, the French Assembly was unwilling to acknowledge that the highly conditional nature of the document meant the strong words of Leopold and Frederick William held little real consequence. The result, as James Der Derian carefully explains, was that 'France's sense of isolation and estrangement had grown proportionally with the perception of a strengthened monarchical solidarity. This reciprocal estrangement had spread throughout Europe' (Der Derian 1987: 174).

After more than two years of work the new constitution was completed in September 1791. Louis was reinstated after accepting it, decreeing prematurely that 'the revolution is over' (J. S. Hall 1951: 263). Reiterating the Declaration of the Rights of Man and Citizen, it definitively asserted the sovereignty of the people: 'Sovereignty is one, indivisible, inalienable, and imprescriptible. It appertains to the nation' (J. S. Hall 1951: 234). Sovereignty was seen as residing in the nation and being mediated through a system of representation, as Sieyès had envisaged. The constitution announced that 'the nation, from which alone all powers emanate, may exercise such powers only by delegation. The French constitution is representative' (J. S. Hall 1951:

234). Combining popular sovereignty with a system of representation distinguished the French constitution from the directness of Athenian democracy. As in the American case, this formulation fulfilled both revolutionary and conservative functions. In terms of the former, it confirmed that the king was no longer sovereign, but a delegate of the French nation, which now held absolute sovereignty. At the same stage, the form of representation instituted prevented this system from being overly democratic, as it tempered the direct influence of the people.[4] In effect, representation played an intermediary role through offering the possibility of enacting popular sovereignty without it leading to direct popular rule.

There were two immediate consequences from the 1791 constitution worth highlighting. First, Louis's public acceptance of the constitution made it difficult for Austria to justify intervening. As Emperor Leopold complained, it was impossible to 'reply that they did not believe what he [Louis] said' (quoted in Clapham 1899: 94–5). Returning to the theoretical discussion in Chapter 2, this is an example of the way language can shape the range of actions possible, enabling some and limiting others. Second, the newly formed Legislative Assembly was composed of the revolution's 'second generation'. The self-denying ordinance successfully championed by Robespierre prevented the re-election of deputies that had previously sat in the Constituent Assembly, which meant a fresh set of actors were brought to the centre of the revolutionary stage. The change in cast was an important facilitating factor in the radicalisation of politics that soon began to occur. The new Assembly would commence its work in a period of increasing instability and tension.


## THE DAWNING OF WAR AND THE SECOND REVOLUTION

War between revolutionary France and Europe appeared increasingly likely as 1792 commenced. From Paris, America's representative, Gouverneur Morris, observed: 'All Europe just now is like a mine ready to explode' (quoted in Burley 1989: 101). Within France the push for war had begun, driven by factional politics and jockeying for control of the revolution. A rather odd *de facto* alliance in favour of war soon emerged between the left and right. For the king and his supporters, it represented perhaps the last chance to restore the Bourbon throne to its former position. Meanwhile, the war party of the left was convinced of the need to directly confront the revolution's external enemies. Its leader, Jacques Pierre Brissot, thundered: 'The time has come for a new crusade, a crusade of universal freedom' (quoted in Lefebvre 2001: 211). This call to arms was driven by, and helped to further, an emergent 'universalistic nationalism'. On the one hand, Austria and Prussia's growing concerns with France's revolution directly clashed with the emergent doctrine of popular sovereignty, which entailed the nation's right to determine its own constitution. On the other hand, the Brissotins believed the French version of liberty was readily exportable, and the corrupt rulers of Europe would be quickly overthrown once local populations were exposed to the tenets of the revolution. In demanding that the band of *émigrés* on France's borders be dispersed, the Legislative Assembly warned that 'we will bring to them, not the sword and the torch, but liberty. It is up to them to calculate what the consequences of the awakening of nations might be' (quoted in Keitner 2007: 108). One of the few unconvinced by the seductive logic for war was Maximilien Robespierre, who feared it would threaten the revolution at home without succeeding in spreading its doctrines abroad. 'No one likes armed missionaries,' he famously surmised. He argued that the focus should remain on finishing the more immediate task at hand: 'Before losing yourselves in the politics and the states of the princes of Europe, start by turning your gaze to your internal position; restore order at home before carrying liberty abroad' (Robespierre 2007: 31). Robespierre's words of caution would fall on deaf ears, with those in favour of war prevailing.

After months of escalating rhetoric and growing tensions, war was declared by the French on 20 April 1792. The declaration was not addressed to the Holy Roman Empire or even Austria, but to one man: 'The National Assembly declares war on the King of Hungary and Bohemia' (J. S. Hall 1951: 288). The French were explicit that it was 'not a war of nation against nation, but the just defence of a free people against the unjust aggression of a king' (J. S. Hall 1951: 287). Here the logic of the revolution's changes was directly extended to foreign policy. The Assembly distinguished between the Austrian nation, against which they held no grudge, and the Austrian emperor, whom they regarded as a usurper of the Austrian nation's sovereignty and a threat to France. While this semantic separation between king and nation was rarely followed in practice, it 'did not impair the potency and resonance of … [this] new legitimating standard', or the innovative nature of this distinction (Keitner 2007: 108). The consequences of the French adoption of the doctrine of popular sovereignty now migrated to the international sphere, standing in direct opposition to monarchic forms that had long prevailed in international society.

The rhythm of war would now come to dictate the tempo of the revolution, and it soon moved far beyond the relatively moderate goals the first generation had sought to entrench in the 1791 constitution. Republicanism would grow apace with France's failing war effort. Economic hardships and a bad start to the war were blamed on the holder of the executive power, the duplicitous king, who looked even more suspect after vetoing an Assembly decree against refractory priests and then sacking ministers from the Girondin faction. On 20 June 1792 the Parisian crowd attempted to assert its sovereignty, marching on the Tuileries and unsuccessfully seeking the reinstatement of the Girondins. The degree to which the doctrine of popular sovereignty had been imbibed was evidenced in the words that accompanied the very physical presence of the crowd: 'The people is here; it silently awaits a response worthy of its sovereignty' (J. S. Hall 1951: 302). The following month, on 23 July, volunteer troops known as the *Fédérés* petitioned the Assembly to suspend the king, berating their representatives in similar terms: 'Some weeks have passed since you declared that the *Patrie* was in danger, and you show us no means of saving it.... We tell you that the source of our ills lies in the abuse which the head of the executive power had made of his authority' (J. S. Hall 1951: 305). Notable here is the wording that clearly separated the Assembly – 'you' – from the people – 'us'. The growing republican mood of the Parisian crowd outstripped that of the Assembly, which placed further strain on the representative system the first generation of revolutionaries had established. Emblematic of this breakdown in representation was the commune of Marseilles assailing the Assembly for its support of the king:

> How, then, could our constituents, your predecessors, establish upon such bases [the Declaration of the Rights of Man and Citizen] that monstrous pretension of a particular family to which the crown would be delegated hereditarily, by order of primogeniture? ... What infamy! The nation cannot subscribe to it. It once made vain claims; today it wants them to be effective. Since it is the sole sovereign, it has the incontestable right to approve or

reject the laws with which its representatives impose on it. (J. S. Hall 1951: 303)

Contradictions stemming from the attempt to mediate popular sovereignty through a system of representation were now coming to the fore.

A deciding factor in France finally dispensing with its monarchy was the Brunswick Manifesto, a document that reflected the inability of old-regime Europe to comprehend the revolutionary mindset. On the urging of Louis, Marie-Antoinette and the ever-persistent *émigrés*, the Duke of Brunswick issued a heavy-handed warning:

> If the least violence, the least outrage be done to Their Majesties, the King, the Queen, and the Royal Family, if their security, preservation, and liberty be not provided for immediately, they will exact an exemplary and ever-memorable revenge thereon by delivering the city of Paris to military punishment and total destruction … (J. S. Hall 1951: 310)

Instead of shoring up the precarious position of the embattled king, these threats enflamed public opinion in Paris, taken as further proof that Louis was in league with hostile foreign powers. The manifesto was read to the Assembly on 1 August and published two days later. Forty-seven sections in Paris subsequently called for the removal of the king, and the section of Faubourg Saint-Antoine gave the Assembly until 9 August to accept their petitions. The representatives of the French nation would still not move against Louis, and so on 10 August the Parisian crowd did, storming the Tuileries. The constitutive power came to life, determining that France would be a republic. With these actions it was not just the king that fell; the 'representative-ness' of the Assembly was also destroyed through the direct action of the Parisian crowd. These dramatic events led to the emergence of a revolutionary commune that shared power with the Assembly, which was suspended along with the monarch as a new National Convention was convened to respond to the dramatic changes of 10 August 1792.

The Convention opened on 21 September 1792 and its first piece of business was abolishing royalty. What the Parisian crowd had already decided was confirmed by its representatives: France would be a republic. One of Europe's greatest monarchies was replaced with the antiquarian form of a republic, something thought impossible for a powerful country like France. For three years the revolutionaries had tried to construct a constitutional monarchy from the ill-matched parts of popular sovereignty and a king schooled in absolutism. Pushed by the Parisian crowd, France finally took the last step on a path that had been laid out in the opening stages of the revolution: this was where the logic of Sieyès had long pointed. This left the newly founded republic with the awkward question of what to do with their former king. In debating whether he could be brought to trial, Louis Antoine de Saint-Just argued that Louis 'had no part in the contract which united the French people'. As he was outside the nation, no legal or moral obligation was owed to him. The deposed king was not a citizen but an 'enemy', which meant that 'we must not so much judge him as combat him' (Walzer 1974: 121). Supporting his ally, Robespierre argued that Louis could not be tried, as it left open the possibility of his innocence, which would thereby indict the revolution that overthrew him. Such reasoning was based on might, as it was the brute power of the people that determined Louis's fate. Robespierre's thinking was suggestive of the form of popular sovereignty that would emerge during 1793–4, where the will of the people was necessarily right. Louis was brought to trial, but it was hard to avoid Robespierre's logic. While the Assembly was near unanimous in voting that Louis was guilty, the subsequent decision to put him to death passed only by a small minority. On 21 January 1793, Louis went to the guillotine. Saint-Just's words rang true: 'This man must reign or die' (Walzer 1974: 123).

## CONSEQUENCES OF FRANCE BECOMING A REPUBLIC

With the regicide there was no turning back, a new era was born. France's dramatic transition to a republic had significant consequences. First and foremost, France was stepping into the unknown. It had yet to be seen whether it was possible for a large country to exist successfully as a republic, and history did not offer a favourable prognosis. This relates to a second observation, which is that republicanism entailed more than simply being free of a monarch. As Norman Hampson explains, 'the actual proclamation of a republic, in September 1792, meant much more than a deposition of a king. For men like Robespierre, it implied a qualitative change, government, not merely of the people, but of *vertu*' (Hampson 1988: 132). The consequences of this shift were to play out over the next two years during the Jacobin ascendancy. Soon only those that possessed virtue – the defining characteristic of republicans – were considered part of the French nation. The third consequence was that popular sovereignty, already important to revolutionary discourse, now became absolutely central. Having dispensed with the monarchy, the people were left as the sole source for the legitimation of power. This also led to a significant rise in the consideration of democracy as a constitutional form.

The regicide completed France's transition to being based solely on popular sovereignty. Since the people were not defined through exercising sovereignty directly as in ancient republics, nor through being part of a 'community of subjects' as in a monarchy, the question arose of how the French nation was constituted. Popular sovereignty necessitated the existence of a separate people, which then formed the constituted power, yet the doctrine was unable to provide an explanation for who is included and excluded in this pre-existing collective of people (Näsström 2007; F. Whelan 1983). The revolutionaries understood the nation as a political category, defined through its unity in a common government and participation in society. As the constitutive power, however, the people cannot be defined by their participation in political life: they are necessarily prior to it, as they first constitute the political realm. It is at this point that the revolutionary conception of the nation as a political body began to transmogrify into an understanding of the nation as a pre-political community, identified more in ethnic, cultural and/or temporal terms (Yack 2001: 525). As Eugene Kamenka explains,

> modern political nationalism arises in the course of stabilising or making possible the transition from autocratic to democratic or at least popular government. It is a recasting and re-formation of communities and of political boundaries in circumstances where the old basis of the polity has been radically undermined. (Kamenka 1976: 15)

This need to identify how the constitutive power was originally formed forged the bond between popular sovereignty and nationalism that emerged during the French Revolution. A pre-political, cultural conception of the nation would define the people that the doctrine of popular sovereignty could not itself account for.

Through the need to define the people who hold and exercise sovereignty, which led to the pre-political community as an answer, the foundations were laid for the modern nation-state. A link was forged between the state, understood as a juridical and political territorial unit, and the nation, as a cultural entity. As Bernard Yack notes, 'popular sovereignty doctrines teach us to think of states as masters of territory and peoples as masters of states' (Yack 2001: 527). This discussion suggests that in considering the appearance of nationalism as a powerful force in international politics in the nineteenth and twentieth centuries, it must be placed within the context of the emergence of popular sovereignty. 'The nationalization or culturalization of political community is', Yack suggests, 'an unintended consequence of the widespread acceptance of the doctrine of popular sovereignty' (Yack 2001: 524). The French Revolution is regularly taken as the catalyst in the creation of modern nationalism. The reading here supports a modified version of this argument. The French themselves largely understood the nation in political terms, most evidently in their broad conception of citizenship. They did not directly advocate a cultural understanding of the nation, but the doctrine of popular sovereignty they instituted ultimately relied on such a notion.

The regicide also had clear international ramifications. Most states had withdrawn their ambassadors after 10 August and France's break with Europe was completed when Louis was sent to the guillotine. The conflict would now be about not only conflicting interests, but opposed values and principles. Popular sovereignty was no longer an abstract cause for concern for other rulers; the revolutionaries were deadly serious when they proclaimed: 'You shall have no more kings!' (quoted in Ozouf 1989: 219). Shortly after the regicide Great Britain and Spain joined the war against France. That Britain moved against the revolutionaries was significant, given its previous policy of strict neutrality. As late as November 1792, foreign minister Lord Grenville congratulated the British cabinet for having 'the wit to keep ourselves out of this glorious enterprise.... We are not tempted by the hope of sharing the spoils in the division of France, nor by the prospect of crushing all democratical principles all over the world' (quoted in Walt 1996: 82). The change in policy was partly driven by France's provocative behaviour in the Low Countries, which the British regarded not only as a direct threat to its material interests, but also as demonstrating flagrant disregard for international law. Writing to Lord Auckland at the time, the British foreign minister explained why the situation was now sufficiently grave to warrant action:

> It is these views [of aggression and aggrandisement] rendered indefinitely more dangerous by the principles of Anarchy with which they are connected, both in their means, and in their ultimate object, that His Majesty is to oppose a vigorous and effectual resistance. (Quoted in MacLeod 1999: 37)

Sending Louis to the guillotine was a potent sign that the time for compromise was over. Beyond France's borders it soon led to a broadening and deepening of the revolutionary wars. At home civil unrest and external conflict pushed the revolution to its extremes. The pressures of war manifested themselves in a vicious circle of threatening principles and actions: the conflict exacerbated tensions in the revolution, resulting in increasingly radical behaviour by the French, which in turn made France appear even more threatening to the rest of Europe, thus further strengthening the counter-revolutionary cause, thereby enhancing the perceived danger facing France, again leading to further radicalisation, and the cycle repeating. The course of the revolution until Thermidor and the fall of the Jacobins largely followed this pattern. It was also during this period that a second version of popular sovereignty came to the fore: one much more direct, finding inspiration not in the moderns, but in the ancients.

## CONCEPTUAL SHIFTS IN DEMOCRACY

Following the establishment of the French republic there was a noticeable surge in the use and consideration of democracy. It was at this time that it began to appear as a pivotal concept in political discourse, in so far as it was becoming a term of contestation and contention, used to define one's position and that of others. At the Jacobin club Camille Desmoulins did nothing but confirm Europe's fears in proclaiming that 'the English people must be exterminated from Europe, unless they democratise themselves!' (quoted in Palmer 1964: 214). And when Prussia invaded Poland in January 1793, in a widely published circular the Prussian king claimed that he had done so in order to combat 'the spirit of French democraticism' (quoted in Palmer 1964: 94). This 'spirit' manifested itself most explicitly in the behaviour and words of the *enragés* and the *sans-culottes*, for whom the term's classical connotations of directness and equality made it of value. As the economic crisis worsened in France, Jean-Paul Rabaut feared that 'democratic government will not last long alongside a huge inequality in fortunes', and that aristocracy would soon rise from the ruins of France's nascent democratic republic (quoted in Dupuis-Deri 2002: 194). In seeking more radical changes the *sans-culottes* consciously strove to emphasise the classical elements of equality and levelling, but identified these as positive, in contrast to most thinkers at the time.

When considering how democracy was used during the revolution a particularly important intervention came from Thomas Paine, acting again as an ideological innovator in his highly influential *Rights of Man*. Taking 'democracy as the ground', Paine argued that the system of representation remedied 'the defects of simple democracy as to form, and the incapacity of the other two [monarchy and aristocracy] with respect to knowledge' (Paine 1988: 281). Mirroring Madison and Sieyès, Paine argued that the representative system was a more practicable and desirable method for enabling popular sovereignty. He went further by actively identifying democracy as something positive, undesirable only for practical reasons that left it unworkable for the modern territorial state. With the representative system it was possible to improve on 'simple democracy', while remaining true to its original spirit. Paine explained that, 'by ingrafting representation upon democracy, we arrive at a system of government capable of embracing and confederating all the various interests and every extent of territory and population' (Paine 1988: 281). A remarkably similar formulation appeared in a speech given to the National Convention in 1794 by one of Paine's arch-enemies, Robespierre. This is referred to by R. R. Palmer as nothing less than 'the *locus classicus*' for the concept of democracy during the revolution (Palmer 1959: 16). Speaking on behalf of the ruling Committee of Public Safety, Robespierre outlined the ultimate aims of the revolution. He proclaimed that 'only democratic or republican government' was capable of achieving the revolution's goals, and made it clear that 'these two words are synonymous, despite the abuses of vulgar language' (Robespierre 2007: 108–25). This was a powerful rhetorical move, attaching the once-disreputable 'democracy' to the laudatory 'republic'. Robespierre also went further than Paine by identifying democracy as a representative system of rule: 'Democracy is a state in which the sovereign people, guided by laws which are its own work, does for itself all that it can do properly, and through delegates all that it cannot do for itself' (Robespierre 2007: 111). Found in these opposing figures of Paine and Robespierre is a significant combination of two thoughts that are commonplace now, but were very innovative at the time: one was that democracy was something desirable; the other was that democracy was based on a system of representation (C. Hobson 2008b).

By now most of Europe tended to agree with Robespierre's description of France as a democracy, yet few would have supported his hope that the French would become 'the model for all nations' (Robespierre 2007: 110). As the strength of the revolutionary armies became evident, the coalition was expressly concerned with stopping France from imposing the doctrine of popular sovereignty elsewhere. Lord Auckland explained that 'war was not made to prevent France from giving herself the constitution that she might prefer; but to prevent her from giving to Great Britain, and to her allies, all the wretchedness and horrors of a wild democracy' (quoted in MacLeod 1999: 44). This depiction of France as a 'wild democracy' threatening Europe with canon and doctrine was one that became entrenched during the ascendance of the Jacobins. As Palmer notes, 'for the adherents of monarchy and aristocracy, the Reign of Terror had in fact been a piece of remarkable good fortune. It "proved" what they wanted to know' (Palmer 1964: 131). Ideational apologists of the *ancien régime*, such as Burke and de Maistre, interpreted the violence and chaos of the revolution as the logical outcome of trying to institute democracy in a large, modern state like France. Framing events in relation to the classical interpretation of democracy, Burke had warned that 'if I recollect rightly, Aristotle observes, that a democracy has many striking points of resemblance with a tyranny' (Burke 1999: 94). Countering the revolutionaries' claim that monarchy was despotic, he argued that in a democracy oppression 'will be carried on with much greater fury, than can almost even be apprehended from the dominion of a single sceptre' (Burke 1999: 94). This fear was echoed by Joseph de Maistre: 'Of all monarchs, the harshest, most despotic, and most intolerable, is the monarch *people*' (Maistre 1996: 163). For these apologists, revolutionary excesses were taken as further evidence that democracy was something that should be left to the history books.

## THE TERROR AND THE BREAKDOWN OF REPRESENTATION

Robespierre headed the Committee of Public Safety, which oversaw the 'Reign of Terror', a period that lasted from September 1793 until the fall of its leader and his allies in July 1794. During this period tens of thousands were put to death at the guillotine and in summary executions across the country. Central to the origins and nature of the Terror were fundamental tensions in the mediated form of popular sovereignty that had been instituted during the initial stages of the revolution. The order constructed by the first generation of revolutionaries stood on the threshold between the worlds of democracies ancient and modern. The appropriation of absolute sovereignty by the people, and the unity that the general will required, gravitated towards the direct exercise of sovereignty. Yet the practical realities of France – vast in territory and population and needing to stay so to be a great power – suggested a representative system, as Sieyès and others had successfully argued. Disaggregating popular sovereignty from popular rule was not necessarily so straightforward, however. Maistre pinpointed the tension that arose:

> The people is sovereign, they say; and over whom? Over itself apparently. The people is therefore subject. There is surely something equivocal here, if not an error, for the people that *commands* is not the people that *obeys*.... The people, they will say, exercises its sovereignty by means of its representatives. We begin to understand. The people is a sovereign that cannot exercise sovereignty. (Maistre 1996: 45; original emphasis)

Beyond practical reasons that suggested representation was necessary, for more moderate revolutionaries it was also meant to restrict the part played by the people. Sieyès and his peers saw representation as a more rational system as it placed an elite ruling class in power. Through representation, as Nadia Urbinati explains, there were '"two peoples" – "the producers" and "the auxiliaries": a class of citizens who make the laws for all and a class of citizens who obey them' (Urbinati 2006: 143). As the revolution progressed the continuous stress on the unity of the general will resulted in a breakdown in the separation between these two peoples.

What emerged during the Terror was, in essence, a contest between direct and representative forms of democracy. Who represented the French nation: the Parisian crowd or the National Convention? The problem Rousseau had stressed – the inability to represent the general will – would now play itself out in the politics of France. How could the general will be represented with certainty? How could one be sure that what was *re*-presented by the National Convention as the general will was indeed consonant with the 'real' general will? The answer, of course, was that it was impossible to do so, which created the problem of one representation being subverted or replaced by another that appeared to correspond more closely to the perceived general will. Keith Michael Baker explains that 'sovereignty represented could always be challenged in the name of sovereignty embodied in the people; claims to express the general will could always be indicted as particular' (Baker 2001: 46). Each decision of the Convention was left open to challenge on the grounds that it failed to correspond to the 'real' will of the people. From Varennes onwards, this is what happened as the Parisian crowd increasingly questioned the right of their representatives to speak for the nation, instead actively seeking to assert *their* sovereignty, with the storming of the Tuileries being a particularly striking example of this shift. As R. R. Palmer observes, 'when they said the people were sovereign, they mean it literally, and they meant themselves' (Palmer 1964: 103). Pierre-Victor Malouet was among the first to identify the risks inherent in this synthesis of absolute popular sovereignty and representation:

> You wanted … to bring people and sovereignty closer together, and you continually offer them the temptation of sovereignty, without immediately entrusting them with its exercise … By saying that sovereignty belongs to the people, but only delegating some powers, the enunciation of the principle is false as well as dangerous. (Quoted in Dupuis-Deri 2002: 128)

The chaos and violence of 1793–4 flowed, in part, from these contradictions that underlay the representative system that Sieyès and his fellow revolutionaries had established.

The centrality of the general will to the absolute version of popular sovereignty that was adopted created a greater need for a symbolic correspondence between the people and their representatives. Both the people and those that stood for them had to be virtuous. Blurring the difference between republicanism and democracy, Robespierre was clear that the 'fundamental principle of democratic or popular government' was 'virtue' (Robespierre 2007: 111, 113). In this rendering, if either the French people or their representatives failed the test of virtue, the republic was unlikely to survive. This demand for a virtuous nation interacted with the breakdown of representation to drive the Terror. The need to assure, in Robespierre's words, the 'great purity of the foundations of the French revolution' led to an exclusive understanding of the people, which manifested itself in a pernicious need to identify and 'stifle the internal and external enemies of the Republic' (Robespierre 2007: 114–15). Membership of the French nation continued to shrink to include only the virtuous, with all others identified as a threat. As the pressures of war combined with this republican demand for virtue, the heady universalism of the revolution's early days was replaced by a Manichaean worldview that separated the French nation from its enemies. This mindset was evident in both the overriding emphasis placed on the unity of the nation and the ruthlessness towards those seen as threats. No mercy was shown to the 'impure race … of rogues, of foreigners, of hypocritical counter-revolutionaries' (Robespierre 1794). The guillotine worked overtime in Paris, while representatives on mission crushed royalist revolts in Lyons and the Vendée. Similar treatment was accorded to France's external enemies. On 10 June 1794 it was declared that 'no British or Hanoverian prisoners will be taken'. While this policy was actually applied only in a number of situations, it was a clear example that the conflict had 'turned into something which went far beyond the normal aggressions of international politics' (Cobban 1960: 188). Death to enemies, and life for the revolution: compromise was no longer an option.

Reflecting on the Terror, Abbé Sieyès would later observe that 'people seem to think, with a kind of patriotic pride, that if the sovereignty of great kings was so powerful and so terrible, then the sovereignty of a great people had to be something greater still' (quoted in Forsyth 1987: 146). Describing the heady cocktail of ancient republicanism and modern absolutism that emerged during the ascent of the Jacobins, Sieyès termed this direct version of popular sovereignty a *'ré-totale'*. A *ré-totale* was popular sovereignty unmediated, emphasising the unity of the people. Sieyès contrasted this with what he and Paine understood as a *'ré-publique'*, a mediated form of sovereignty. Whereas this representative form did not rely on a strict unity of the people, a *ré-totale* did:

the government had to 'push down' on itself, in Robespierre's telling words (2007: 114), so as to eliminate or minimise the gap between the people and their representatives. The corollary to this emphasis on homogeneity, as Carl Schmitt (perhaps unsurprisingly) notes, is a need to identify and exclude those not part of the nation. The identity between ruler and ruled is constructed through its boundaries, with democracy resting 'on the quality of belonging to a *particular people*' (Schmitt 2008: 258; original emphasis; see also Schmitt 1985: 8–9). Through the revolutionaries' discovery, defence and promotion of this vision of popular sovereignty, an international environment of separate states was not challenged or overthrown, as the Jacobins originally hoped, but actually reinforced (Bukovansky 1999; Hont 1994).

## ABSOLUTE SOVEREIGNTY AND ABSOLUTE WAR

The emergence of the *ré-totale* of the Jacobins – a potent mixture of ancient republicanism, emergent nationalism, ruthless reason of state and exclusionary universalism – confirmed that compromise between France and international society was not an option. The principles of the revolution, which directly challenged the monarchies of Europe, had become so closely intertwined with the French state that the conflict had become one of non-negotiable identities. The increasingly radical nature of the revolution was even more troubling due to the surprising resilience and success of the French armies. After withstanding the initial push by the Austrians and Prussians, the activation of popular sovereignty in the form of the *levée en masse* had turned the French into a far more formidable fighting force than its opponents could have ever imagined. It was representative of revolutionary France being both behaviourally and ontologically threatening to international society.[5]

That the Jacobins pursued primarily defensive strategies while in power was to some extent inconsequential, as it was what they were, rather than what they did, which made them so threatening. The Jacobins embodied the most radical, unmediated form of popular sovereignty that modern Europe had seen, one which posed a direct, sustained challenge to an international society founded on monarchic right and custom. In a speech entitled 'The Jacobin Government of France', British prime minister William Pitt stated 'unequivocally' that 'the moment will never come, when I shall not think of any alternative preferable to that of making peace with France, upon the system of its present rulers' (Pitt 1940: 108). Prince Metternich drew a similar conclusion: 'Peace does not exist with a revolutionary system' (Metternich 1880: 205). What made peace impossible was precisely the dual challenge revolutionary France posed, attacking international society with both doctrine and canon.

The rule of Robespierre and the Jacobins came to an end with the Thermidorian Reaction of 27 July 1794. This marked the conclusion of the Terror, and with it the revolutionaries completed what François Furet calls their 'exploration' of 'the paradox of democracy', namely, the relationship between sovereignty and the people (Furet 1981: 77). From 1795 the French republic went on the march, destroying much of Europe and in the process shattering preconceptions about what republics were capable of. As important as the subsequent revolutionary and Napoleonic wars were, they were much less consequential in terms of the development of popular sovereignty and democracy. The major exception to this generalisation was the development and promulgation of the Napoleonic Code, as well as the creation of a modern administrative state apparatus to enforce it. As Francis Fukuyama notes, 'even in the absence of democracy, these constituted major advances that made government less arbitrary, more transparent, and more uniform in its treatment of citizens' (Fukuyama 2014b: 15–18). Another lasting consequence of the revolutionary and Napoleonic wars was the simplification of the international landscape with many of the remaining vestiges of Christendom being swept away. While the revolution and the ensuing wars irrevocably destroyed the *ancien régime* based on custom and precedent, the anarchical society composed of separate, sovereign states was actually reinforced. Reflecting on the revolutionaries' failed attempts, Linda and Marsha Frey observe that 'the French, who had envisaged the possibility of a law common to all mankind, had permanently and ironically destroyed that conception' (Frey and Frey 1993: 741; see also Hont 1994: 217–31). The revolutionary wars shaped the fortunes not only of democracy, but also of international society.

## CONCLUSION

The French Revolution represents the most significant turning point in the development of modern democracy and international relations. Certainly many important elements of popular sovereignty, democracy

and representation were already present before 1789. And it is undeniable that in 1815 'democracy' remained a term of opprobrium. The
attempt to implement popular sovereignty was seen by most as hor-
ribly misguided and was widely identified as the root cause for the
conflict that engulfed Europe for a quarter of a century. Nonetheless,
what makes the revolution such a pivotal moment is that it was when
democracy, both as a form of statehood and as a method of rule, was
fully activated in modern politics. Democracy appeared as a term of
identification and a point of contestation. It was no longer an antiquarian idea: it was alive and very much part of the political landscape. John
Dunn accurately identifies the significance of the revolution:

> When democracy re-emerged from those years of blood and con-
> fusion it had gained nothing in plausibility as a practical model of
> how France could hope to govern itself in peace, prosperity and
> good order. What it lost definitely was its reassuring air of practical
> irrelevance. (Dunn 2005: 111)

The consequences of France's rediscovery of democracy were felt
across the whole of international society. France's fleeting, yet powerful, existence as a 'military democracy', in the words of a prominent
British politician at the time (quoted in MacLeod 1999: 39), reflected
that the appearance of democracy was an international question, right
from the outset.

The revolutionaries fundamentally challenged, and in time helped
to change, the prevailing conception of statehood through proclaiming
and then enacting popular sovereignty. In so doing, the revolution produced two versions of popular sovereignty, understood here in terms of
Sieyès's distinction between *ré-publique* and *ré-totale*. The former was
an indirect form of sovereignty, where the people were sovereign but
their role in government was limited, mediated through representatives. This representative system was what the first generation of revolutionaries led by Sieyès had attempted to institute. Representation
enabled the consent and participation of the people in the exercise of
power, but it also acted as a filter by limiting and constraining the direct
role they could play. Yet this compromise of locating ultimate power in
the people without actually entrusting them with its full exercise broke
down, as the people – manifested in the immediate form of the Parisian
crowd – asserted their sovereignty in a very direct and real manner. The

result was the emergence of a second version of popular sovereignty, a *ré-totale*. This was a much more direct form, one constructed on a suspicion, if not outright denial, of representation. The term *ré-totale* conveys the emphasis placed on the absolute and unitary nature of the sovereign people and the general will, which was central to the way the Terror unfolded.

The multiple visions of democracy to emerge from the French Revolution meant its legacies were unavoidably diverse and contradictory. As will be seen, the immediate reaction was to view the revolution as an attempt to institute a *ré-totale*. The Jacobins and the Terror they unleashed came to represent the danger of trying to establish the ancient form of democracy in a modern world. At the same stage, it was the mediated *ré-publique* advocated by Sieyès and Paine, already taking shape in the United States, that would prove more consequential in the medium to long term. The question was left open: would popular sovereignty mean the United States or France? The statesmen that gathered in Vienna thought the latter was much more likely.

### Notes

1  The crediting of Sieyès as one of the progenitors of nationalism, as numerous commentators have done, misunderstands the sense in which he used the term (Forsyth 1987: 71–2; Hont 2005: 133–4).
2  Sieyès continues: 'Hence citizens who nominate representatives, renounce and must renounce the idea of making the law directly themselves.... If they dictate their wills, it would no longer be a representative state but a democratic one' (quoted in Forsyth 1987: 138).
3  Conflict broke out in Avignon, a papal territory, between revolutionaries and supporters of the *ancien régime* shortly after the revolution commenced. Following a number of petitions to the National Assembly, in May 1791 a vote to annex Avignon was narrowly defeated. A decision was made to occupy the area so as to restore order and consult with the population. This led to the first recorded plebiscite, which resulted in Avignon joining France in September 1791.
4  The manner in which representatives were to be chosen imposed strong 'filters' that limited the role played by the people. Most notable was the contentious distinction between 'active' and 'passive' citizens, with only the former having full voting rights.
5  This draws on a distinction that Jack Donnelly makes between 'behavioural' and 'ontological outlaws' (Donnelly 2006).

*Chapter 5*

# REACTION, REVOLUTION AND EMPIRE: THE NINETEENTH CENTURY

Democracy is like a rising tide; it only recoils to come back with greater force, and soon one sees that for all its fluctuation it is always gaining ground. The immediate future of European society is completely democratic: this can in no way be doubted.

Alexis de Tocqueville (1833) (Tocqueville 1958: 67)

What *is* Democracy; this huge inevitable Product of the Destinies, which is everywhere the portion of our Europe in these latter days? There lies the question for us. Whence comes it, this universal big black Democracy; whither tends it; what is the meaning of it?

Thomas Carlyle (1850: 13)

## INTRODUCTION

Following Napoleon's last hurrah at Waterloo in June 1815, Europe's great monarchies were still standing (some only just), but they now existed in a world that had undergone irreversible change. The ideas and principles of the revolution remained, even if their French standard-bearers had finally been defeated. This meant a simple restoration of the *ancien régime* was not possible. With historic right and custom undermined, international society would instead be explicitly founded on principles of legitimacy that were defined against the popular doctrines that had emerged from revolutionary France.

If many of the fundamental tenets of the revolution would eventually, in one form or another, succeed the old hierarchical order of the monarchy, aristocracy and church, in the immediate aftermath of French defeat, the forces of reaction were overwhelmingly in the ascent. The course of the revolution seemingly vindicated many of

106

the complaints against popular rule levelled throughout the centuries, with the excesses of the Terror providing clear evidence of the dangers of seeking to establish a democracy in the modern world. John Jay, one of the authors of the *Federalist* papers, summed up the prevailing sentiment in a letter to William Wilberforce: 'The French revolution has so discredited democracy ... that I doubt its giving you much more trouble' (quoted in Morantz 1971: 149). In the short term, this was a rather accurate assessment, although the situation slowly changed, spurred by developments in the United States and the 1848 revolutions. Given that democracy's meaning and significance altered during this period in a relatively gradual and piecemeal fashion, the structure and analysis of this chapter focuses more on these longer trends. It corresponds to Reinhart Koselleck's observation that often conceptual change is 'slower and more gradual than the pace of political events' (Koselleck 1996: 66).

## DEMOCRACY REVILED

With the French finally defeated, popular sovereignty was identified as the ultimate cause of the revolutionary and Napoleonic wars. The fleeting ascendance of the Jacobins, and subsequent rise of Napoleon, seemed to correspond closely to the warnings found in classical and contemporary works about the unstable and violent nature of popular states. Polybius's understanding of the cyclical nature of constitutions, whereby democracy deteriorated into anarchy, only to be rescued by a powerful leader, resonated especially strongly (Polybius 1927: book 6). While there were a number of attempts at ideological innovation from Thomas Paine, William Godwin and other radicals who sought to release democracy from the heavy legacy of Athens, the ancients still remained the dominant referent (Canfora 2006: 47; Costopoulos and Rosanvallon 1995: 148). The violence of the Terror would further stain the image of democracy. As Giuseppe Mazzini later lamented, people 'no sooner hear the name of democracy than the *phantom* of '93 rises immediately before them. With them democracy is a guillotine surmounted by a red cap' (Mazzini 2001: 4; original emphasis). For much of the nineteenth century democracy would be 'almost unanimously' linked to Jacobinism (Naess *et al.* 1956: 113), blamed (somewhat unfairly) for the revolutionary wars, and portrayed as a great menace to stability and peace. Negative interpretations of democracy were by no means the exclusive preserve of reactionary forces in Europe; they could also be found in the United States. 'Look at France!' Noah Webster concluded. 'There you have a picture of real democracy' (quoted in Morantz 1971: 149). John Adams surmised: 'Robespierre is a perfect exemplification of the character of the first bellwether in a democracy' (quoted in Bailyn 1967: 282), further warning that democracy 'when by chance it happens to get the upper hand for a short time, it will be revengefull bloody and cruel' (quoted in Levin 1992: 84). Much like the 'red menace' during the Cold War, democracy came to be identified as a constant, underlying threat both to the fledging republic of the United States and to the European states that had narrowly survived the revolutionary and Napoleonic wars.

The prevailing opinion during the restoration was that the result of applying the ancient form of democracy to the modern world had been the chaos, violence and tumult of the revolution. Ideological apologists drew a straight line between ancient Greece and revolutionary France, reiterating classical tropes about democracy degenerating into tyranny and despotism. Louis de Bonald and Joseph de Maistre were two prominent apologists who sought to counter the popular doctrines that had emerged. Reflecting on the French experience, Bonald concluded: 'Despotism and democracy are, fundamentally, the same government' (quoted in Christophersen 1966: 35). In his view, the evils of democracy were almost limitless. The levelling that democracy required was brought about through violence and revolution; it promoted, if not demanded, atheism; and it also spelled the end of reason, judgement and literature (Christophersen 1966: 37). Painted in this light, democracy was nothing less than a threat to the whole of European civilisation. Maistre reiterated similar themes: democracy as violent, unstable and 'government of the mob' (Maistre 1996: 155). In addition to these standard criticisms, he explicitly sought to refute Jean-Jacques Rousseau's *Social Contract*, which was widely blamed with providing the revolution's theoretical blueprint. Recalling Rousseau's judgement, Maistre pointedly said: 'It remains to be seen how a government that is made only *for gods*, is nevertheless proposed *to men* as the only legitimate form of government' (Maistre 1996: 152; original emphasis). Democracy was deployed as a counter-concept to monarchy, with the destructive characteristics of the former imbuing the latter with positive meaning:

> One can say in general that all men are born for monarchy. This is the oldest and the most universal form of government … Democracy above all is so rare and so transient, that we are allowed not to take it into account. (Maistre 1996: 119)

Monarchy recognised distinctions, protected religion and was best able to promote happiness, stability and civilisation. The interventions of Bonald and Maistre offer strong examples of the way apologists sought to counter popular doctrines by challenging and denying the conceptual innovations of the revolution.

Democracy's potential for despotism was noted not only by defenders of the *ancien régime*, but also by early liberal thinkers. A particularly relevant case is Immanuel Kant, who held a strongly classical understanding of democracy. Like James Madison and Abbé Sieyès, Kant dismissed democracy because he viewed it through an Athenian lens: it was 'necessarily *a despotism*' (original emphasis), as it was a direct form of rule where executive and legislative powers were not separated. In comparison, a republic was based on representation. Kant explained:

> If the mode of Government is to conform to the idea of Right, it must embody the representative system. For in this system alone is a really republican mode of Government possible; and without it, let the Constitution be what it may, it will be despotic and violent. (Kant 1970: 99–102)

Kant's concerns were shared by Benjamin Constant, another influential thinker in the development of liberalism. Constant distinguished between the world of ancient republics where liberty was brought about through participating jointly in the exercise of sovereignty, and the modern world where liberty entailed independence for the individual to pursue their private interests (Constant 1988: 316). The fatal mistake of the Jacobins had been in trying to institute a classical form of polity that was ill suited for the modern world. The revolution had, however, also offered representative government, unknown to the ancients, which was best able to provide the kind of liberty now desired (Constant 1988: 309, 325–6). Here Constant drew the same distinction as Kant: 'democracy is very different from representative government' (quoted in Christophersen 1966: 52). These influential examples indicate how democracy was perceived negatively by many early liberal thinkers, who regarded a constitutional, representative system as the best provider of liberty and freedom but something which was distinct from democracy.

Democracy remained in low esteem across most of the political spectrum, with only a few radicals explicitly identifying themselves and their cause with it. During the conservative reaction there was a tendency not to distinguish between the two forms of popular sovereignty that had emerged from the revolution: democracy was equated completely with the *ré-totale* of the Jacobins. The mediated version of popular sovereignty, the *ré-publique*, was obscured from view, and most liberal thinkers that did espouse it generally saw it as distinct from democratic rule. Even this more moderate form of popular sovereignty remained a threat to monarchical powers, which sought to rebuild an order based on hereditary rights and social hierarchy. In this regard, popular sovereignty and democracy may have been widely discredited, but they could not be ignored when the peacemakers met at Vienna.

## THE CONGRESS OF VIENNA:
## BUILDING A LEGITIMATE ORDER

After France's defeat the forces of reaction may have been in the ascent, but the key powerbrokers were acutely aware of their precarious position. As a result, a remarkably lenient peace was initially imposed, shaped by a fear that too harsh a settlement would cause the revival of Jacobinism, something which could spell the end of the *ancien régime* once and for all. This awareness was reflected by the Duke of Wellington: 'Revolutionary France is more likely to distress the world than France, however strong in her frontier, under a regular government; and this is the situation in which we ought to endeavour to place her' (quoted in Osiander 1994: 202). The challenge for the victorious great powers was putting Europe back together in a way that would secure their own interests while preventing the reappearance of a revolutionary France.

Peace with France had already been concluded in the first Treaty of Paris in May 1814, leaving the Congress of Vienna for dealing with more general questions about the nature and makeup of international society. The significance of this meeting was not lost on the participants, with Prince Metternich noting that 'it does not require any great political insight to see that this Congress could not model itself on any predecessor' (quoted in Langhorne 1986: 318). This was the first attempt to consciously construct and regulate relations between states, establishing a clear set of principles defining rightful membership of and behaviour in international society (Clark 2005; Ikenberry 2001; Langhorne 1986). As Martin Wight explains, previously 'the society of states needed neither definition nor explanation. It was what it was, and everybody knew its members' (Wight 1972: 5). The *ancien régime* had been legitimated by its spontaneity, through what it *was*, rather than what it *said*.[1] Rule was based on historical right: custom and precedent were the foundations of international society and its members. It is for this reason that Wight talks about the existence of a dynastic international order, without there being an explicit principle of dynastic sovereignty (Wight 1977: 153–4). Indeed, it was not a coincidence that Edmund Burke was one of the first to clearly espouse *principles* of conservatism, as these were somewhat of an anathema to its worldview. Having been attacked with doctrine, conservatives were now forced to answer on these terms.

The statesmen at Vienna were forced to incorporate principles of legitimacy as a way of managing the unchangeable realities brought about by the revolution. The prominent role legitimacy played in the settlement was largely due to the tireless campaigning of the French representative, Prince Talleyrand, who was most attuned to, and insistent on, the need for principles or legitimacy (he used these two terms interchangeably) as a central dimension of the new order being constructed. One need only casually glance through his correspondence during the Congress to observe how important legitimacy was to his thought and rhetoric (Pallain 1881). Talleyrand immodestly, though somewhat accurately, regarded this as his great contribution. On arriving in Vienna, he announced: 'I ask for nothing but I bring you something important – the sacred principle of legitimacy' (quoted in Nicolson 1946: 143). In promoting this 'sacred principle' Talleyrand was obviously not acting out of altruism. Given France's weak negotiating position, framing the discourse in terms of principles was a valuable bargaining tool against the other great powers (Nicolson 1946: 157). Even if the constant talk of legitimacy was self-serving, to be successful Talleyrand, like any innovating ideologist, had to tailor his arguments for acceptance by other parties, which influenced how he presented his case.

Monarchy was identified as the form of rule most capable of providing order at both the domestic and international levels. Along these

lines, Talleyrand argued that the Bourbon monarchy should be maintained for practical reasons, presenting it as the only real possibility
for stability within France. Talleyrand persuasively made his case to
Tsar Alexander: 'In order to establish something lasting which will be
accepted without protest, one must have a principle on which to act.…
As for a principle, there is only one – Louis XVIII is a principle' (Ferrero
1941: 89). What made Louis XVIII the best chance at 'establishing
something lasting' was the historical role the Bourbons played in the
constitution of the French state. The great threat was revolution, which
Talleyrand believed could be best avoided through legitimate government. Legitimacy did not emerge specifically from monarchy; rather,
it developed over time and was supported indirectly by the consent of
those ruled. Talleyrand explained:

> Authority, to be legitimate, must have existed for a long succes-
> sion of years; and, accordingly, we see that legitimate power …
> is the form of government least likely to expose the people to the
> perilous chances of revolution, and is, therefore, the form to which
> they are bound in their best interests to submit. (Pallain 1881: 241)

In this sense, Talleyrand followed Burke in regarding rule as being
legitimated not by principles but by custom. In the European context
this clearly gravitated towards monarchy.

Monarchy may have been central to the international order founded
at Vienna, but it could no longer be solely justified through history
and precedent, as these had been undermined first by the revolution
and then by 'the grand usurpation' of Napoleon (Metternich 1880:
278). Writing to his king at the conclusion of the Congress, Talleyrand
described the changed situation with great clarity when reflecting on
'what is legitimacy, whence it proceeds, and in what it consists':

> In the time when religious feelings were all-powerful and deeply
> engraved in hearts and minds of men, it was possible to believe
> that the sovereign power was an emanation from the Divinity.…
> But in these days, in which there remains scarcely a trace of these
> feelings … men will no longer allow the claim of legitimacy to this
> origin. In the present time the general opinion, one that it would
> be vain to attempt to weaken, is that Governments exist only for
> the sake of the people; a necessary corollary to this opinion is that

legitimate power is the form of government best calculated to secure the prosperity and tranquillity of the people. (Pallain 1881: 240–1)

Shorn of divine blessing and historical right, monarchy would have to be legitimated in a much more direct manner than in the past.

While Talleyrand may have been more attuned to the need to adjust to these changed circumstances, Metternich was much more aware of the limits of compromise possible with the revolution's principles. He determined that the only way of protecting society against revolution was, quite simply, 'by allowing no innovations' (quoted in Bertier de Sauvigny 1962: 62). As Carsten Holbraad explains, Metternich 'wanted to maintain all established governments and existing institutions because he believed that a defeat of authority in any state could lead to a collapse of order throughout the society of Europe' (Holbraad 1970: 33). Monarchy embodied and preserved the old social order; the destructive principles of the French Revolution continued to threaten it. Like other apologists, Metternich employed democracy as a counter-concept to monarchy:

It is true that I do not like democracies. Democracy is in every case a principle of dissolution, of decomposition. It tends to separate men, it loosens society. I am opposed to this because I am by nature and by habit constructive. That is why monarchy is the only government that suits my way of thinking. (Quoted in Bertier de Sauvigny 1962: 39)

A prototypical apologist of the existing order, Metternich remained resolutely opposed to the revolutionary doctrine of popular sovereignty:

The sovereignty of the people can only be a fictitious idea because, since the meaning of sovereignty is unquestionably that of supreme power, and since that power is incapable of being exercised by the people, it must be delegated by them to an authority *other than the sovereign*. (Quoted in Bertier de Sauvigny 1962: 41; original emphasis)

While innovators in the United States and France had tried to deal with this problem through the representative system, Metternich was sceptical, regarding it as a dangerous compromise: 'It binds the hands of those in power without untying those of the people' (quoted in Bertier de Sauvigny 1962: 43). Despite his influence and his concerted efforts at refuting and suppressing popular doctrines, Metternich's alternative of vainly denying change could never be workable in the long run.

The international order constructed at Vienna was fashioned on what had come before, but was unavoidably built with tools inherited from the revolutionaries. To re-establish the *ancien régime*, precedent 'had to be replaced by principle, or, failing that, violence' (Osiander 1994: 186). This gave rise to what Henry Kissinger describes as 'the conservative's dilemma':

> The conservative, when he organizes himself politically, becomes, in spite of himself, the symbol of a revolutionary period. His fundamental position involves a denial of the validity of the questions regarding the nature of authority; but the questions, by exacting a reply, have demonstrated a kind of validity. (Kissinger 1973: 193)

With custom and precedent destroyed, conservatives were forced to answer the revolutionary question of rightful authority, and to legitimate the order they were constructing by recourse to abstract principles. There was, however, a certain futility in trying to maintain and reinforce the position of monarchy through legitimacy. Once framed in these terms a crucial concession had been made. Carl Schmitt makes this point strongly: 'What was still historically vibrant in the monarchy's principle of form did not lie in legitimacy.... A monarchy that is nothing other than "legitimate" is already politically and historically dead' (Schmitt 2008: 245).

In establishing principles of legitimacy that promoted and protected monarchy, a more immediate outcome of the Vienna settlement was the creation of an international society more homogeneous than that which had preceded it. As Andreas Osiander observes, 'by 1815 the variegated pattern of pre-revolutionary constitutional forms had given way to a considerably more standardized international landscape, which was shaped to a much greater extent than before by abstract theorizing' (Osiander 1994: 233). This transition arose in part from a new-found awareness of how the domestic and the international spheres were intertwined, with principles of legitimacy in the two realms being deeply connected. Revolutionary France had powerfully demonstrated that changes to the constitution of one state could have drastic consequences for others. At Vienna, a new relationship between international society and its members was established, one that regarded a state's domestic makeup as something of concern for all. In this regard, Talleyrand argued that legitimacy 'can alone secure internal tranquillity in individual states, and at the same time protect them from being subject in their mutual relations to the influence of force only' (Pallain 1881: 222). Heterogeneity in Europe, especially among the great powers, had come to be identified as a threat. The loss of spontaneity and the weakening of customary rights reinforced the need for a greater degree of homogeneity, as the *ancien régime* was much more susceptible to challenge. It was this belief in the intertwined fate of states that drove Metternich's insistence that change must be prevented anywhere. Europe may have been a society of sovereign states, but the fates of its members were closely connected, which necessitated a level of conformity around the monarchical principle.

Embedding domestic legitimacy so directly within international society in turn opened space for the corollary of intervention (Clark 2005: 94). On this point, however, the British would diverge from the eastern powers. In short, the former was concerned about revolution in France, whereas the latter were concerned about revolution anywhere. This manifested itself in the creation of the Holy Alliance between Austria, Prussia and Russia, which became the mechanism through which the conservative powers sought to suppress popular uprisings and uphold the monarchical principle. These differences would become more pronounced at the Congress of Aix-la-Chapelle in 1818, the first meeting of its kind since Vienna. The emerging interventionary doctrine of the Holy Alliance was guided by Metternich, who regarded Europe as a whole body, and revolution as a dangerous disease that would easily spread (Holbraad 1970: 21, 29). In contrast, Britain's Lord Castlereagh doubted that revolution in one country was necessarily contagious, and was also acutely aware that British public opinion would not countenance a general reactionary alliance (Bobbitt 2002: 166).

These respective positions became clearer at Troppau in 1820 and Laibach in 1821, where the great powers sought to deal with unrest in Spain and Italy. The British argued against intervention, stating that the Quadruple Alliance had been meant to stop France from reappearing as a threat, not to prevent revolution in general. It was not, in Castlereagh's words, 'an union for the government of the world or for the superintendence of the internal affairs of other States' (Breunig 1977: 139). For the eastern powers, however, any internal changes were regarded as necessarily a challenge to an international order composed of states legitimated through custom and historical right. Russia proposed a protocol that asserted a general right to intervene 'to prevent the progress of the evil with which the body social is menaced, and to devise remedies where its ravages have begun or are anticipated' (quoted in Bobbitt 2002: 167). Castlereagh countered:

> It is impossible not to consider the right which the Monarchs claim to judge and to condemn the actions of other States as a precedent dangerous to the liberties of the world ... No man can see without a certain fear the lot of every nation submitted to the decisions and to the will of such a tribunal. (Quoted in Bobbitt 2002: 167)

The Russian suggestion was initially withdrawn after this protest, but in the subsequent Troppau Protocol the members of the Holy Alliance restated an 'undeniable right' to intervene where revolution occurred (Hertslet 1875), which Castlereagh contested in a strongly worded circular. The split between Britain and the eastern powers was confirmed at the Congress of Verona in 1822, where the former clearly advocated a doctrine of non-intervention: 'Our engagements have reference wholly to the state of territorial possession settled at the peace; to the state of affairs between nation and nation; not ... to the affairs of any nation within itself' (quoted in Holbraad 1970: 122–3). The incompatibility between the liberal aspects of Great Britain's constitution and the staunchly conservative nature of the eastern powers had been successfully papered over during the wars and at Vienna due to the common French threat, as well as the unique bridging role played by Castlereagh. With these two factors now gone, the powers diverged.

Multiple challenges to the conservative project soon appeared, reflecting the great difficulty of trying to supress the popular principles that had emerged from the American and French revolutions. With the Monroe doctrine, the youthful United States sought to protect its interests and the newly born Latin American republics from European interference. Meanwhile in Europe, Greece and Belgium both gained their independence, representing notable victories for popular sovereignty. Of more importance was the 1830 revolution in France, which signalled the end of Bourbon rule and further weakened the conservative attempt to re-establish the historical foundations of the monarchical order. Even if the revolution did not result in a dangerous France, the damage was done in the French crown now being granted by the people (Albrecht-Carrié 1958: 32; Schroeder 1994: 667). Metternich was particularly dismissive of a monarchy resting on the consent of the people, describing it as 'a monster lacking vitality, an abstraction which no amount of work by its authors and partisans will ever furnish with substance' (quoted in Bertier de Sauvigny 1962: 293). With Louis-Philippe not the King of France, but the King of the French, the doctrine of popular sovereignty became the foundation for another great power.

Despite these important developments, the conservative cause was far from lost. The Holy Alliance proved, for the most part, successful at maintaining the conservative domestic arrangements that had been reinstituted at Vienna through to 1848. This was a major achievement, given the significant socio-economic changes underway, as well as growing liberal and nationalist pressures. The Holy Alliance was not only worried about Europe, however. Metternich was also troubled by what was taking place in the Americas, noting that the European sovereigns had to maintain there, 'as far as possible, the monarchical principle against the advance of universal democracy' (quoted in Bertier de Sauvigny 1962: 255–6). He was right to be concerned.

## THE TRANSFORMATION OF DEMOCRACY IN THE UNITED STATES

While reaction was in full force across Europe, democracy was making notable progress on the other side of the Atlantic. Following on the heels of the dramatic upheavals in the United States and France, revolutions in Latin America resulted in the establishment of a series of independent republics based on popular sovereignty. Further north, in the United States changes continued apace as the country expanded across the continent. The gulf separating the United States, established on popular sovereignty, from the conservative sentiment prevailing in Europe was observed by Jeremy Bentham, one of the few radical enough to talk of democracy positively in the immediate aftermath of the French revolution. In the 1817 pamphlet 'Plan of Parliamentary

Reform' Bentham asked rhetorically: 'By this bugbear word *democracy*, are the people of this country to be frightened out of their senses?' (quoted in Christophersen 1966: 94). In a clear case of conceptual contestation, he directly tried to counter the efforts made by statesmen at Vienna to demonise democracy when seeking to establish the monarchic principle: 'In the language of legitimacy and tyranny, and of the venal slavery that crawls under them, *democracy* and *anarchy* are synonymous terms' (quoted in Christophersen 1966: 95). Bentham chastised this attempt to 'strike terror into weak minds', arguing that the falsity of the position was demonstrated by the United States, which was the true embodiment of democracy's meaning. 'Two words – *Democracy* and *Anarchy* – produced the disease: one other word – *America* – may take the lead in the cure,' he boldly proclaimed (quoted in Christophersen 1966: 95, 98).

The shift towards a positive understanding of democracy in the United States began in the opening decades of the nineteenth century and was largely complete by the 1840s. The magnitude and speed of this development was not lost on contemporaries. Samuel Goodrich observed that 'the word democracy … has essentially changed its signification'. The transformation was so great that

> we who are now familiar with democracy, can hardly comprehend the odium attached to it.… [People] not only regarded it as hostile to good government, but associated it with infidelity in religion, radicalism in government, and licentiousness in society. It was considered a sort of monster. (Quoted in Morantz 1971: 11)

The *North American Review* reached a similar judgement in response to an address by the attorney general in which he described the United States as a 'representative democracy':

> No man knows better than he [the attorney general], what would have been the horror of the framers of the Constitution, could they have been told, that in fifty years time, the government they were setting up with such carefully framed safeguards against what they called *democracy* would be itself called a democracy by one of its own highest officers. (Quoted in Morantz 1971: 12–13)

This conceptual transformation is even more remarkable given that it occurred without a corresponding change in the formal political institutions of the United States.

The founding fathers described what they established as a republic, which entailed a representative government supported by checks and balances and based on popular sovereignty. In the opening decades of the nineteenth century democracy would slowly shed its Athenian baggage, and increasingly became associated with this representative system. Republicanism – pessimistic about human nature, constantly stressing the need for virtue and somewhat backward looking – was increasingly ill suited to the realities of nineteenth-century America. In contrast, democracy 'was a vision for the future. Progress-orientated, it conveyed a buoyant optimism about human nature and the endless possibilities open to the American nation' (Morantz 1971: 230). Both republicanism and democracy were underpinned by a conception of popular sovereignty, but whereas the former emphasised restraints on the people, the latter suggested a greater faith in them. Democracy thus came to be associated with a fuller degree of popular power and egalitarianism than republicanism. The growing acceptance of democracy in the United States can be seen in this statement by Elias Smith, an early exemplar of the shift taking place:

> The government adopted here is a DEMOCRACY. It is well for us to understand this word, so much ridiculed by the international enemies of our beloved country. The word DEMOCRACY is formed of two Greek words, one signifies *the people*, and the other the *government* which is in the people … My Friends, let us never be ashamed of DEMOCRACY! (Quoted in Dupuis-Deri 2002: 242–3)

In similar fashion, in 1816 Thomas Jefferson would declare that 'we in America are self-consciously … democrats' (quoted in Dupuis-Deri 2002: 243). The United States was starting to adopt democracy as a label.

The increasingly positive connotations of democracy, and its suggestions of greater popular power, emerged from political battles taking place during the establishment of the American party system. The presidential election of 1828 was a notable moment in this shift, in which Andrew Jackson won by presenting himself as a 'plain democrat', using the term to appeal to ordinary voters through its strong egalitarian connotations. It was in the context of Jacksonian democracy, as a new form of mass politics was emerging, that Alexis de Tocqueville and Gustave de Beaumont made their fateful journey to the United States. The result was Tocqueville's monumental *Democracy in America*, the first part published in 1835, and the second following in 1840. His highly influential work would strengthen the association between the United States and democracy in the European and American psyches. Tocqueville may not have been as conscious of his role as an innovating ideologist as some other actors considered thus far, but his work had similar consequences in terms of shaping the way people understood democracy.

Tocqueville's purpose for studying the United States was to better understand democracy and how it would develop in the future. In Europe the conflict between popular sovereignty and monarchy meant that it was difficult to ascertain the 'true character' of democracy, but in America 'democracy follows its own inclinations' (Tocqueville 2003: 228). The United States could provide insight on this emergent form: 'I have looked there for an image of the essence of democracy, its inclinations, its personality, its passions; my wish has been to know it if only to realize at least what we have to fear or hope from it' (Tocqueville 2003: 24). Given his stated aims, and that his account was widely read and interpreted as definitive, it is of great significance how Tocqueville understood democracy. While Tocqueville's use of the concept remains somewhat confused, being employed in multiple ways across the two volumes, democracy is primarily understood in sociological terms. Tocqueville observed that, devoid of the hierarchical social structure that defined European polities, 'the social condition of the Americans is eminently democratic' (Tocqueville 2003: 59). This led him to suggest that democracy – understood to entail a degree of social equality – was inevitable in Europe. He explained:

> The gradual unfurling of equality in social conditions is, therefore, a providential fact which reflects its principal characteristics; it is universal, it is lasting and it constantly eludes human interference … Any desire to halt democracy would then appear a struggle against God himself. (Tocqueville 2003: 15)

Developments towards greater egalitarianism in society would, in turn, place pressure for more equality in the political sphere (Tocqueville 2003: 66). The implication was clear: political democracy was, to a certain extent, an unavoidable consequence of the levelling impulses of democracy in the social realm.

In prophesying the 'irresistible revolution' towards democracy (Tocqueville 2003: 15), Tocqueville was not necessarily offering normative support for this shift. His thought was marked by a deep sense of ambivalence towards democracy. Tocqueville was first and foremost a liberal. He made this point emphatically in a parliamentary speech in 1841: 'I passionately love liberty, the rule of law, and respect for rights, but not democracy' (quoted in Canfora 2006: 18–19). His great fear was that democracy would give rise to the 'tyranny of the majority', which would destroy the civil and political rights he valued so highly. This led to a distinctive interpretation of America: 'My main complaint against a democratic government as organized in the United States is not its weakness, as many Europeans claim, but rather its irresistible strength' (Tocqueville 2003: 294, 776). Tocqueville's voice was to prove particularly influential in how the American experiment was received. At one end of the political spectrum, John Stuart Mill's thinking was clearly shaped by the idea of the 'tyranny of the majority' (John Stuart Mill 1991: chs 6–7), at the other, when reflecting on democracy Metternich would observe that 'I have always been of de Tocqueville's opinion' (Bertier de Sauvigny 1962: 39).

Similar concerns to Tocqueville's were voiced by James Fenimore Cooper in *The American Democrat*, published in 1838. Cooper saw the tyranny of the majority manifesting itself most fully through the over-riding force of public opinion: 'No tyranny of one, nor any tyranny of the few, is worse than this' (Cooper 1838: 71). Echoing the fears previously voiced by conservatives such as Burke and Maistre, Cooper suggested that what made this form of tyranny so terrible was its totality:

> In a monarchy, adulation is paid to the prince; in a democracy to the people, or the publick. Neither hears the truth … and both suffer for the want of the corrective. The man who resists the tyranny of a monarch, is often sustained by the voices of those around him; but he who opposes the innovations of the publick in a democracy, not only finds himself struggling with power, but with his own neighbors. (Cooper 1838: 147)

Cooper and Tocqueville shared with fellow liberals Constant and Kant a fear that democracy was liable to fall into despotism, but the source of their concern differed. For the former, the problem was sociological: the levelling nature of democracy was the root cause. For the latter, it was institutional: as they still understood democracy as a direct form of rule, the potential for tyranny stemmed from a lack of representation and insufficient constitutional safeguards. But what united these thinkers was a grave concern that the advent of democracy threatened hard-won individual liberties. As can be seen, it was not only conservatives and reactionaries that feared the emergence of democracy. Liberals remained wary, instead emphasising constitutionalism and representation, which were still generally regarded as distinct from democracy.

## EMERGING ARGUMENTS FOR DEMOCRACY

Despite residual concerns held by both conservatives and liberals, the shift in American discourse whereby democracy became a valued and positive concept was effectively complete by the middle of the nineteenth century. As Calvin Colton judged in 1844, 'we are a Democracy and Democrats. These are national designations, not party titles' (Colton 1844: 9). This was identified as a sign of things to come:

> Democracy will prevail. And it will prevail under that *name*. It is too late in the age of the world, in history, and in the progress of human society, to give another name to this thing. That is the *common* symbol destined to be employed, throughout the world, to denote popular forms of government. (Colton 1844: 10–11; original emphasis)

The United States, as Tocqueville eloquently announced, was at the vanguard of experiments with popular sovereignty and democratic rule. The American experience was seen as a harbinger of Europe's future, where the futility of rebuilding a monarchical order based on custom and freedom was becoming increasingly evident.

As the nineteenth century progressed, a number of different arguments accounting for the perceived rise of democracy can be identified. They are interrelated and overlapping but can be distinguished into four main types: (1) sociological, (2) natural rights based, (3) utilitarian and (4) nationalist. The more central a concept is to political discourse, the greater is the likelihood that there will be multiple, ambiguous and even conflicting meanings coexisting. This is what started to happen to democracy during this period. In this regard, Luciano Canfora suggests that between 1815 and 1848 democracy 'covered many ways of thinking, from progressive liberalism (or ex-Jacobinism or crypto-Jacobinism) to socialism in its newer and more remote incarnations' (Canfora 2006: 69). In contrast to W. B. Gallie's widely cited claim that democracy is 'essentially' contested, it can be seen that it was only during the nineteenth century that contestation became a significant feature of democracy, as its normative value and political utility increased. As explored in the previous chapter, it was not until the French Revolution that democracy began to re-emerge as a fighting word.

The sociological argument offered a broader and more expansive notion of democracy in which it represented a more equal kind of society, rather than a specific form of state or government. Tocqueville, as was seen above, provided the most influential account of this understanding: 'democracy constitutes the social state' (quoted in Costopoulos and Rosanvallon 1995: 150). He viewed the movement towards social equality as inevitable, and these changes would in turn lead to demands for greater equality in the political sphere. From this perspective, reactionary policies aimed at suppressing democracy were futile and ultimately self-defeating. The best strategy was to recognise this transformation taking place and seek to control it, or at least adjust to it. The power of the people was the future, and it was through recognising and responding to this that it might be possible to avoid the tyranny of the majority, and transition to a form of popular rule that protected liberal rights.

Natural-rights arguments for popular rule had a long lineage, with John Locke's early intervention being particularly determinative. In the late eighteenth century this line of thinking could be found in the American Declaration of Independence and the French Declaration of the Rights of Man and Citizen, two documents of great historical importance considered in previous chapters. The argument remained simple and powerful: all individuals have basic, inalienable rights based on their humanity. Individuals contract together to secure and protect these rights, with the state and government they constitute ultimately being based on the consent of these individuals. The people are thus sovereign. In *Rights of Man*, Thomas Paine stated this clearly: 'Governments must have arisen, either *out* of the people or *over* the people' (Paine 1988: 220; original emphasis). In Paine's words, government was 'a necessary evil', required for protecting the basic rights of the individual. And if the state did not do so, the people retained a residual right to revolution. While social-contract theory did entail popular sovereignty, it did not necessarily have to result in democratic government. As noted, many liberals remained sceptical of democracy's ability to properly protect individual rights, also worrying that its levelling instincts were a threat to property. Over time, however, the positive evaluations of more radical liberals, such as Paine, William Godwin and Richard Price, became more accepted. Godwin argued that democracy offered the possibility for individuals to better realise their innate potential:

> Democracy restores to man a consciousness of his value, teaches him by the removal of authority and oppression to listen only to the dictates of reason, gives him confidence to treat all other men as his fellow beings, and induces him to regard them no longer as enemies against whom to be upon his guard, but as brethren whom it becomes him to assist. (Godwin 1793: ch. 14)

For liberals to have confidence that this could occur it was necessary that popular rule should be tempered and restrained so that these natural rights were protected and ensured. In this regard, in the version of liberal democracy that developed it was the liberal element that was clearly dominant (C. Hobson 2009).

Utilitarian thinkers were sceptical of natural-rights arguments, famously dismissed by Bentham as 'nonsense upon stilts'. Yet they found other reasons to support democracy. James Mill identified the representative system as the best method of government, but still conceived of democracy as a direct form of rule (James Mill 1820). As noted, Bentham was much more explicitly positive about it. In setting out the utilitarian position, where the primary concern was promoting the greatest happiness of the greatest number, he regarded representative democracy as the form of government most capable of achieving this end. Bentham stated this clearly:

> The only species of government which has or can have for its object and effect the greatest happiness of the greatest number, is, as has been a democracy ... The only species of democracy which can have place in a community numerous enough to defend itself against aggression at the hands of external adversaries, is a representative democracy. (Quoted in Christophersen 1966: 97)

In contrast to the fears held by apologists of the *ancien régime*, Bentham strongly asserted that democracy was best suited to providing the greatest happiness for the greatest number of people. The utilitarian emphasis on the individual would also play a role in supporting the extension of the franchise, and in *Resolutions on Parliamentary Reform* Bentham was well ahead of his time in calling for universal suffrage and the secret ballot. 'I have not that horror of the people … I do not see in them that savage monster which their detractors dream of,' he wrote (quoted in Graudbard 1973: 662).

The fourth major line of reasoning in support of democracy came from nationalists, with the Italian revolutionary Giuseppe Mazzini being the most prominent exponent. For Mazzini, 'the great democratic idea which guides the world' was closely connected to a specific form of universal nationalism, a cosmopolitan vision of separate republican nations collectively living together in harmony, separately contributing to a common good (Mazzini 2001: 8). 'Our principle of the People', Mazzini explained, 'is simply the application of the doctrine of humanity to every nation' (quoted in Christophersen 1966: 108). This differed from the cosmopolitanism of liberals: 'For us, the end is *humanity*; the fulcrum, or point of support, *country*. For Cosmopolites, then, I freely admit, is also humanity; the fulcrum or point of support, is man – the *individual*' (Mazzini 2001: 68; original emphasis). He argued that by purely focusing on liberty as an end in itself, and on the individual shorn from the nation, the emerging liberal conception of democracy was incomplete. Interestingly, there was also a strong spiritual dimension to Mazzini's thought, as he regarded the establishment of democracy in separate nations as part of God's plan:

> When the arms of Christ, even yet stretched out on the cross, shall be loosened to press the whole human race in one embrace – when there shall be no more pariahs nor Brahmins, nor servants nor masters, but only *men* – we shall adore the great name of God with much more love and faith than we do now. This is democracy in its essentials … (Mazzini 2001: 10; original emphasis)

Combating the position of apologists such as Louis de Bonald and Joseph de Maistre, who powerfully argued that democracy was against the will of God, Mazzini instead proposed that it was the form of government most capable of fulfilling God's plans for humanity. That democracy took on a messianic quality in Mazzini's thought is illustrative of its growing significance and acceptance.

While the international order founded at Vienna may have prevented war between the great powers, it was less successful at repressing popular doctrines. Ongoing nationalist struggles and domestic unrest would ultimately peak with the 1848 revolutions. The 'springtime of the peoples' was both a highpoint for contestation over democracy in the nineteenth century (Christophersen 1966: 323) and a defining moment in the trajectory of popular sovereignty.

## 1848: 'THE TURNING POINT AT WHICH MODERN HISTORY FAILED TO TURN'

The attempt to restore the *ancien régime* was looking increasingly shaky by the 1840s. France had become a constitutional monarchy, Austria was led by a handicapped emperor, nationalist sentiment continued to grow across the continent, while food shortages and poor harvests combined with pressures caused by significant socio-economic changes to place great stress on Europe's rulers. In November 1847, the Swiss civil war resulted in a victory for liberal forces following Prince Metternich's failed attempt to mobilise a reactionary coalition. The weakness of the *ancien régime* was readily apparent, as was the possibility for serious change. The revolutions of 1848 began in January in Sicily and soon extended to other parts of Italy. A crucial development was unrest spreading to France, 'the great factory of revolutions', as Metternich put it (quoted in Bertier de Sauvigny 1962: 262). The barricades appeared on 22 February, and it was not long before King Louis-Philippe abdicated, taking with him the last vestiges of the French monarchy. Within months revolution had swept across the continent, engulfing France and the German and Italian states, as well as most of the Habsburg Empire. The situation was unhappily observed by François Guizot, who had been the French prime minister until the revolutionary turmoil had arrived:

Chaos is now concealed under one word – Democracy. This is now the sovereign and universal word which all parties invoke ... Such is the power of the word Democracy, that no government or party dares to raise its head, or believes its own existence possible, if it does not bear that word inscribed on its banner ... (Guizot 1849: 2–3)

Democracy played a central part in the tellingly named 'springtime of the peoples'. Increasingly it came to embody the demand for greater social change, due to its classical connotations of equality and levelling. Retained were the associations of social rule, only now the majority were identified as the poor working class. For many, the revolution was seen as incomplete if it did not extend to address socio-economic relations. In this sense, democracy came to be understood as an 'economic ideal and expressed the idea that the 1848 Revolution had to be pushed further' (Dupuis-Deri 2002: 282). These incipient social demands linked to democracy meant that liberals remained very wary, if not outright opposed to it. Reflecting on the revolutionary events he witnessed and participated in, Alexander Herzen acutely identified the halfway position of liberals: 'They want freedom and even a republic provided that it is confined to their own cultivated circle. Beyond the limits of their moderate circle they become conservatives' (quoted in Ellis 2000: 49). Liberals soon allied themselves with conservatives, fearing that any further changes might threaten property.

The economic and social demands expressed through the concept of democracy meant it would be more closely linked with socialism and communism. Pierre-Joseph Proudhon explicitly stated that democracy and socialism were synonyms, while Friedrich Engels went even further in announcing that, 'nowadays, democracy means communism' (quoted in Christophersen 1966: 294). Indeed, some of the loudest calls for democracy emerged from those representing and supporting the proletariat. In the immediate period leading up to the outbreak of the 1848 revolutions, there was a movement of Chartist Internationalism (Weisser 1971), which was an important precursor to the Communist Internationals. Perhaps the most notable group were the London-based Fraternal Democrats, with which Karl Marx and Engels were associated. The aim announced in their manifesto was 'to advance the cause of DEMOCRACY and promote THE FRATERNITY OF NATIONS' (Mazzini 2001: 92). Writing in the Chartist newspaper the *Northern Star,* Engels recounted the speech of the 'ultra-democrat' leader Alexandre Ledru-Rollin at one of the republican banquets in Paris:

> There is at this moment a great movement going on in Europe amongst all the disinherited, who suffer by heart or by hunger. This is the moment to console them, to strengthen them, and to enter into communion with them.... Let us, then, hold a congress of Democrats of all nations, now, when the congress of kings has failed! (Engels 1848)

Engels's call for a 'congress of democrats' reflected the upsurge in socialist and communist movements across Europe, many of which actively adopted the label: the Société démocratique française, the Association démocratique in Belgium, the Democratic Committee for Poland's Regeneration, and another society in London, the Democratic Friends of All Nations. Marx and Engels also explicitly used the term in the *Manifesto of the Communist Party*, published in 1848. They announced that 'the first step in the revolution by the working class is to raise the proletariat to the position of ruling class to win the battle of democracy' (Marx and Engels 1848).

Recognising the growing centrality of the concept, and undoubtedly influenced by his experiences in America, Tocqueville was a notable exception in trying to challenge democracy's associations with these more radical doctrines. Speaking to the French Constitutive Assembly, he sought to wrestle back control of the concept: 'Democracy and socialism are linked only by a word, equality; but the difference must be noted: democracy wants equality in freedom, and socialism wants equality in poverty and slavery' (quoted in Dupuis-Deri 2002: 284–5). Rather than being synonyms, in his rendering socialism became a counter-concept for democracy. Appreciating the political power of the concept at that moment, Tocqueville was no longer hesitant about advocating for democracy. He proclaimed that he wanted a French republic 'entirely democratic without being socialist' (quoted in Dupuis-Deri 2002: 284–5). This contestation over the meaning of democracy was representative of the pivotal role it played in political discourse during the 1848 revolutions.

In 1848 France was not the same disruptive force it had been in 1789, but it was still at the revolutionary forefront, especially in regards to developments related to democracy. One of the most important decisions made by the provisional government on assuming power was granting the vote to all male French citizens over the age of twenty-one, which enlarged the electorate from approximately 246,000 to almost

10 million (Fortescue 2005: 99). This was the first time that universal male suffrage had been instituted in a major European state.[2] Historically it had been the system of lot that defined democracy; now increasingly it would be the ballot. This change can be witnessed in the words of Alphonse de Lamartine, the president of the provisional government: 'By what procedure do citizens all participate by entitlement in government and legislation? By universal suffrage. Universal suffrage is, then, democracy itself' (quoted in McManners 1966: 400). Notably, a wide range of influential commentators and politicians – Lamartine, Tocqueville, Guizot, Renan, Proudhon, Carlyle, Marx, Engels and John Stuart Mill – all identified France as becoming a democracy in 1848 (Christophersen 1966: 318). Reflecting this shift, the provisional government proclaimed that it was their job to secure 'the democratic government that France owes to herself' (quoted in Dupuis-Deri 2002: 285).

The provisional government's identification of France as a democracy extended to its dealings with other states. This can most clearly be seen in the Manifesto on Europe, issued on 4 March 1848 by Lamartine. The document announced that France sought peace, but that it would not tolerate any external interference and it was strongly opposed to attempts by foreign powers to suppress nationalist revolts elsewhere. The French republic was 'desirous of entering into the family of established governments, as a regular power, and not as a phenomenon destructive of European order' (Lamartine 1849). Lamartine refuted the Holy Alliance's claim that the internal makeup of states was a concern for all:

> France is a republic. The French republic does not require to be acknowledged in order to exist. It is based alike on natural and national law. It is the will of a great people, who demand the privilege only for themselves. (Lamartine 1849)

*Contra* Metternich, Lamartine argued for a reciprocal right of non-intervention: each state should be free to determine its own constitution reflective of its own identity and history, and should allow others to do likewise. In seeking to assuage fears that France might soon become a 'violent democracy', Lamartine stressed that popular rule did not pose the threat it had previously, observing that 'democracy at once spread terror among thrones, and shook the foundation of society. But now, on the contrary, both kings and people are accustomed to the name, to the forms' of popular rule (Lamartine 1850: 45). The provisional government identified France with the popular principles of the first French revolution, but did not regard this as problematic: 'It is determined never to veil liberty at home; and it is equally determined never to veil its democratic principle abroad' (Lamartine 1850: 45). The French manifesto was not particularly amenable to the conservative powers, but they soon had bigger problems to worry about as revolution spread further, with clashes in Vienna, Budapest, Venice, Cracow, Milan and Berlin.

Elections for the French Constituent Assembly were held on 23 April 1848, with the more radical republicans and socialists being roundly defeated. To the surprise of many, universal male suffrage had resulted in a clear victory for conservative and more moderate liberal forces, who successfully countered the threat of 'ultra-democrats' and others demanding more far-reaching social changes. This outcome was particularly significant, as it demonstrated that democracy in the form of universal suffrage was not as dangerous to established interests as had previously been assumed. This observation would be further reinforced by the experiences of the second and third Reform Bills in Great Britain. Reflecting on these changes in *Unforeseen Tendencies of Democracy*, Edwin Godkin later suggested that the extension of the franchise in a large state actually worked to dilute its impact, thereby reducing the risks of mass democracy (Godkin 1898: 60–1). In this sense, it was gradually becoming apparent that the more moderate American experience was a better guide for judging the consequences of democracy in modern times than the turmoil and strife of the first French revolution.

The limited nature of France's revolutionary experience of 1848 was echoed across the continent. Elsewhere there were new constitutions, changes of government and abdications of monarchs, but the ruling houses were not overthrown. The collective fate of the revolutions was sealed by stopping 'at the foot of the throne' (Sperber 1994: 115). It was not long before the tide began to turn, with conservative forces regaining the upper hand by 1849. In Austria a new emperor was in power and quashed nationalist uprisings; meanwhile the republican movement had failed in Italy, and the attempt to unite the German states fell short when the Prussian king refused 'a crown from the gutter'. With Louis-Napoleon's *coup d'état* in France on 2 December 1851 conservatives had reasserted control across Europe. Popular hopes raised by the 'springtime of the peoples' had been dashed. Proudhon lamented the missed opportunity: 'Yes, we have been beaten and humiliated. We have all been scattered, imprisoned, disarmed and gagged. The fate of European democracy has slipped from our hands – from the hands of the people – into those of the Praetorian Guard' (quoted in Ellis 2000: 45–6).

The 1848 revolutions were memorably described by G. M. Trevelyan as 'the turning point at which modern history failed to turn' (quoted in Rude 1972: 262). This observation seems particularly apt when considered in reference to international politics. Turmoil swept across the continent, but the general war that many feared would attend a revolutionary outbreak failed to eventuate. France did not go on the march and unaffected states chose not to try to take advantage of the general unrest. The overarching international framework constructed at Vienna may have held firm, but the events confirmed that the attempt to defend monarchy through rebuilding historical right and establishing principles of legitimacy could not succeed. Reflecting on the outcome of the revolutions, Thomas Carlyle observed that 'the world does believe it; that even Kings now as good as believe it, and know, or with just terror surmise, that they are but temporary phantasm Playactors, and that Democracy is the grand, alarming, imminent and indisputable Reality' (Carlyle 1850: 12). In the short term, the forces of reaction had won the day, but maintaining the *status quo* was clearly gone as a long-term option, especially as the political and social trends towards democracy continued to gather pace. The result was an uneasy truce between conservative and popular forces. And so, like Marx's old mole, popular sovereignty had yet to fully supplant monarchy, but its time was fast approaching.[3]


## DEALING WITH THE INEVITABLE: DEMOCRACY IN THE LATE NINETEENTH CENTURY

It was not long after the inconclusive 'springtime of the peoples' that conflict would again shape the trajectory of democracy, only this time in the United States. Given that America was regarded as the great litmus test for democracy, the civil war was a crucial moment: were the sceptics right? Would America's experiment prove to be a fatal and short-lived mistake? The breakdown of the union seemed to confirm suspicions that the United States was not so different from Europe, and that democracy remained an unsustainable and volatile form of rule. In this regard, the British reaction is instructive, given that it had the progressed the furthest towards democracy out of any major powers. The situation in the United States was taken as a strong argument against further altering the balance of the British constitution towards the people. Reflecting on the outbreak of the civil war in 1861, *The Times* suggested that 'it is not too much to say that the form of democracy which has taken for the last thirty years, or since the Presidency of Jackson, was likely to lead to such a result' (quoted in Roper 1989: 111–12). *Blackwood's* was more explicit in its conclusions: 'Every sensible man in this country now acknowledges … that we have already gone as far toward democracy as is safe to go' (quoted in E. D. Adams 1925: 393). This was echoed by the *Saturday Review*:

> In that reconstruction of political philosophy which the American calamities are likely to inaugurate, the value of the popular element will be reduced to its due proportions.… We may hope, at last, that the delusive confusion between freedom and democracy is finally banished from the minds of Englishmen. (Quoted in E. D. Adams 1925: 387–8)

Prominent liberals such as William Gladstone conceded that the turmoil in the United States was of grave consequence, writing as 1861 came to a close: 'This has without doubt been a deplorable year for poor "Democracy" and never has the old woman been at a heavier discount since 1793' (quoted in E. D. Adams 1925: 389). The Earl of Shrewsbury was less sanguine: 'I see in America the trial of Democracy and its failure' (quoted in E. D. Adams 1925: 389). *The Times* concurred: 'The theories attributing immeasurable superiority to Republican forms of government have all been falsified in the plainest and most striking manner' (quoted in Grant 2000: 40). Talk of democracy's demise in the United States would prove distinctly premature, however.

Just as the collapse of the United States into civil war was taken as a clear warning against further democratisation, the subsequent victory of the North would soon be taken as additional evidence that the advancement of democracy was 'inevitable'. This was not the first time, and certainly not the last, that the outcome of war would play a decisive role in the historical development of democracy. The survival of a democratic United States was important in at least two respects.[4]

First, as a result of the conflict becoming about the abolition of slavery, the North imbued democracy with moral purpose (Roper 1989: 86). In doing so, it continued the process identified above of democracy's meaning expanding, coming to represent not just a set of institutions but also a set of values and ideals. This was best conveyed by the great American poet of democracy, Walt Whitman: 'According to you, dear friend, democracy is achieved if there are elections, politics, various party slogans, and nothing else. As for myself, I believe that the present role of democracy begins only when she goes farther and farther' (quoted in Roper 1989: 95). The second significant consequence of the United States surviving, and subsequently thriving in the reconstruction era, was that it maintained its role as the vanguard of democracy. Illustrative of this is Abraham Lincoln's famed Gettysburg Address. Delivered when the nation was in the depths of the war, still today it is taken by many as providing the perfect encapsulation of democracy's essence: 'government of the people, by the people, for the people' (Lincoln 1863).

The continuation of America's great experiment with popular rule strengthened a growing perception in Europe that the rise of democracy – in one form or another – was inevitable. Matthew Arnold reflected that 'at the present time, almost everyone believes in the growth of democracy, almost everyone talks of it, almost everyone laments it' (quoted in Bell 2007: 31). Henry Sumner Maine would make a similar observation:

> Nine men out of ten, some hoping, some fearing, look upon the popular government which, ever widening its basis, has spread and is still spreading over the world, as destined to last for ever, or, if it changes its form, to change it in one single direction. The democratic principle has gone forth conquering and to conquer, and its gainsayers are few and feeble. (Maine 1886: 5)

Commenting on the Third Reform Act of 1884, which added another six million men to the British electorate, Sir Wilfrid Lawson proclaimed that 'the great tide of Democracy is rolling on, and no hand can stay its majestic course' (quoted in Maine 1886: 69). This growing sense of inevitability in democracy's rise represented an adoption and extension of Tocqueville's analysis: rapid socio-economic changes were driving moves towards democracy in the political sphere.

Many commentators may have been fixated on the rise of democracy, but in reality its ascent took place within confines set by the increasingly dominant doctrine of liberalism. Indeed, it was through attempting to reconcile this seemingly inevitable trend towards democracy with established interests that the liberal democratic form would ultimately crystallise (C. Hobson 2009). Liberals sought to protect the rights of the bourgeoisie from the unfettered powers of kings on one side and the increasing demands of the working classes on the other. Constitutions, parliaments and representation were not simply a way of restricting the powers of monarchs; they also worked to grant more power to the people while limiting the most dangerous dimensions of democracy. As previously noted, representation effectively answered the two main concerns that had long dogged democracy: that it was impossible, and that it was undesirable. Representation allowed for popular rule over a larger territory, while also enabling the people to participate in government and legitimate power, albeit in a more restricted and indirect manner than in ancient democracies. A pivotal figure in completing this conceptual shift was John Stuart Mill, who built on the innovations of Madison, Sieyès and Paine. Mill argued that 'a completely popular government is the only polity which can make out any claim' to being 'the best form of government' (John Stuart Mill 1991: 244). No longer was democracy distinguished by being direct or not, Mill instead identified a democracy as 'true' or 'false' by its kind of representation: whether it represented all the people or the majority only (John Stuart Mill 1991: ch. 7). This reflects a gradual, but significant, shift in which democracy became more politically acceptable and desirable through having its most challenging dimensions – extensive participation, greater social equality – removed or limited. Before Woodrow Wilson sought to make the world safe for democracy, there had been an earlier process of democracy being made safe for the world.

The second half of the nineteenth century represents a period of transition between monarchical and popular sovereignty. The rise of representative government was at the heart of a more general liberal constitutional movement, which operated to restrict both executive and legislative powers. As Gianfranco Poggi explains:

> The system of representative government which ... marked the distinctive nineteenth-century advance in the career of the modern state, deliberately fostered the anti-absolutist legacy of earlier

constitutionalism by laying explicit boundaries around the action of state organs, including elective legislatures. (Poggi 1990: 57)

The advancement of the liberal programme acted to further undermine monarchic sovereignty, in that the power of kings and queens was now limited by constitutions. Even if more monarchs now explicitly ruled by the grace of the people, wherever constitutions and parliaments had been instituted a fundamental concession had been made to popular sovereignty. Constitutionalism came to represent an important element of the classical 'standard of civilisation' that determined full membership in international society, whereby 'civilised' states were distinguished from 'semi-civilised' and 'uncivilised' outsiders that were denied full sovereignty (Gong 1984). As Ido Oren notes, before the First World War there was 'a select group of states – modern, constitutional, administrative, cohesive nation-states' that were seen as the most developed, and the difference between them 'and the rest of humanity was perceived as far greater than the differences among members of the group themselves' (Oren 1995: 155). Constitutionalism became an important marker of being 'civilised', which helped lay the foundations for the later conceptual transformation in which authoritarian rule was identified as illegitimate and 'uncivilised'.

## DEMOCRACY AND EMPIRE

Another important aspect of the standard of civilisation was the role it played in justifying imperial expansion and colonialism. In this regard, two of the most significant trends of the second half of the nineteenth century were first, the rise and consolidation of popular sovereignty in Europe, and second, the dividing up of the 'barbarian' world by 'civilised' great powers. While both phenomena have separately been examined in detail, much less attention has been given to the linkages between them. Writing in 1898, William Lecky was one of the few to openly consider them in tandem: 'It is, indeed, most curious to observe the passion with which nations that are accustomed to affirm the inalienable right of self-government in the most unqualified terms have thrown themselves into a career of forcible annexation in the barbarous world' (Lecky 1899: 480). In the late nineteenth and early twentieth centuries, democracy and empire were generally not considered a contradictory pairing, however. Colonised peoples were regarded as savages or barbarians, and hence not capable of self-determination. Quite simply, few Europeans entertained the possibility that popular sovereignty could, or should, apply to others. F. J. C. Hearnshaw argued that while that the British dominions had been given a 'unique opportunity for democratic development', this could not be extended to the empire's uncivilised dependencies: 'In countries where the people is still ignorant, primitive, divided and inarticulate … democracy is not a good form of government; it is not, indeed, a form of government at all, but merely a delusion' (Hearnshaw 1920: 151). James Bryce was equally dismissive of 'backward races' having democracy: 'it is as if one should set a child to drive a motor car' (Bryce 1921b: 549).

An interesting dynamic could be found in the British Empire, whereby different degrees of democratic government were identified as existing in various parts. One commentator observed that 'the main dividing line is between self-governing dominions and dependencies. The former are more democratic than the mother country; the latter, in outward appearance and institutions, know little or nothing of democracy' (Lucas 1916). The dominions were actually at the forefront in democratic experimentation, with New Zealand and Australia the first places to give women the right to vote and to stand for office. As with the United States, the relative blank slates they commenced with offered something of a testing ground for popular rule. Given the sense of inevitability in democracy's rise, the dominions were seen as undertaking valuable 'democratic experiments' that would help 'to solve the problems with which we know we must deal', as the author of *Our Colonial Empire* noted (quoted in Bell 2007: 23). In this sense, the British dominions played a similar role to that which Tocqueville had assigned to the United States. It was partly for such reasons that Franklin Henry Giddings in *Democracy and Empire* suggested a synergistic relationship existed between the two: 'Democracy and empire, paradoxical as such a relationship seems, are really only correlative aspects of the evolution of mankind' (Giddings 1900: v). This relationship was not as benign as Giddings suggested, however. It is necessary to emphasise that the supposed *terra nullius* that allowed for the founding and successful democratisation of these settler societies was ultimately premised on displacing indigenous communities and dispossessing them of their land (Mann 2005: ch. 3).

Not only did the dominions provide a testing ground for democracy, the British Empire offered a crucial safety valve for managing popular pressures at home. The material benefits that flowed back to the imperial core helped in reducing unrest among the growing working and poorer classes (Bell 2007: 2). Imperial conquest also provided a useful distraction and was a way of strengthening national identity and a sense of common purpose. Furthermore, in the domestic contest between conservatives and radicals over the extension of political rights, both sides drew on arguments related to the empire. Conservatives argued that the demands of maintaining the empire, so crucial to Britain's international standing, warned against greater popular participation. This reflected a belief that democratic control should not be extended to the realm of foreign policy. Conversely, 'British liberals and radicals consistently conceived the case for extending the franchise at home in terms of a contrast with colonial subjects whose incapacity for participation in political power they deemed self-evident' (Pitts 2005: 249). Emphasising the gap between British and colonised subjects was a way of minimising perceived differences between enfranchised and disenfranchised groups within Britain. In this way, the extension of the vote to the lower classes and women was assisted by comparison with colonial subjects. Understood in this manner, the simultaneous growth of democracy and empire appears less paradoxical, instead being related phenomena. The democratisation of Great Britain in the nineteenth century, often taken as a paradigmatic case (Zakaria 2007: 48–51), was underwritten by its empire.

## CONCLUSION

The history of political and state theory in the nineteenth century
could be summarized with a single phrase: the triumphal march
of democracy. No state in the Western European cultural world
withstood the extension of democratic ideas and institutions.
Carl Schmitt (1985: 22)

At the Congress of Vienna the new international order was constructed against the popular doctrine that had emerged from revolutionary France. Democracy was widely derided and stigmatised, with the damaging memories of Jacobin excesses compounding deep-seated fears inherited from the classics. Yet, as Eric Hobsbawm concludes, 'rarely has the incapacity of governments to hold up the course of history been more conclusively demonstrated than in the generation after 1815'

(Hobsbawm 1962: 109). While the international order constructed at Vienna was able to endure, conservative attempts to re-establish monarchy based on principles of legitimacy were ultimately unsuccessful. Like the proverbial genie in the bottle, once released the principle of popular sovereignty could not be fully contained. In this regard, the revolutions of 1848 paradoxically were both a high and a low point for democracy. It achieved a prominence not before seen in modern politics, to the extent that François Guizot complained of 'the empire of the word *Democracy*' (Guizot 1849: 6). Yet it was more like a wave that peaked and soon receded, as the revolutions failed to be definitive.

In the second half of the nineteenth century democracy continued to grow in prominence and significance. It took on a range of multiple, sometimes conflicting meanings; democracy was understood in political, economic, social and even messianic terms. For some, it was still a classical polity, for others it was a representative form of government. The political understanding increasingly centred on suffrage, and hence the representative system, which was underpinned by the doctrine of popular sovereignty. Meanwhile, many socialists regarded democracy's longstanding connotations of social equality as giving it significance for the proletariat's struggle. For others still, it even began to take on a more abstract, ideal quality. Writing in 1852, Louis Auguste Blanqui despairingly summarised the situation: 'So, tell me, please, what is a *democrat*? This is a vague word, banal, without any specific meaning, a rubber word.... Everyone claims to be a *democrat*' (quoted in Dupuis-Deri 2002: 286; original emphasis). That democracy was becoming a 'rubber word' reflected its growing centrality in political discourse. In this regard, Carl Schmitt suggests that democracy had been able to maintain a more fixed meaning when it was primarily a counter-concept directed against monarchy, but 'as its most important opponent, the monarchical principle, disappeared, democracy itself lost its substantial precision' (Schmitt 1985: 24). This is part of the story, but the process was more dynamic: with its growing significance, it also became more politically valuable and thus further contested.

In the late nineteenth century popular sovereignty slowly but surely supplanted its monarchical predecessor in Europe. Liberal constitutionalism worked to restrain the powers of the monarch while keeping the proletariat at bay. Democracy's seemingly inevitable rise was channelled through the representative system, being heavily shaped by liberalism, which worked to control many of its most threatening features.

An essential part of democracy's rise was precisely that it was revised in such a way that it was no longer a fundamental threat to the interests of the ruling classes. Another way that democratisation was managed was through imperial conquest and colonialism, but this also contributed to the heightening of tensions between great powers. Combined with massive socio-economic changes and the rise of nationalism, which was increasingly associated with a crude form of social Darwinism, the old international order was placed under great stress as the twentieth century commenced. When these long-term structural pressures interacted with the contingencies of history, the eventual result would be the Great War, a conflict that would be determinative in shaping the fate of democracy.

## Notes

1 This is paraphrasing Henry Kissinger: 'It is the dilemma of conservatism that it must fight revolution anonymously, by what it is, not by what it says' (Kissinger 1973: 3, 9).
2 The Jacobin constitution of 1793 contained similar provisions but was never instituted.
3 'But the revolution is thoroughgoing. It is still travelling through purgatory. It does its work methodically. By December 2, 1851, it had completed half of its preparatory work; now it is completing the other half … And when it has accomplished this second half of its preliminary work, Europe will leap from its seat and exult: Well burrowed, old mole!' (Marx 1995).
4 It may be the case that if the outcome of the civil war had been different, democracy would have continued in the North, and potentially even in the South, albeit in a heavily restricted and debased manner. Indeed, parallels were often drawn between the South and ancient Greece, in so far as both were democratic in part, but underpinned by a system of slavery.

*Chapter 6*

# THE WILSONIAN REVOLUTION: WORLD WAR ONE

Democracy is more vindictive than Cabinets. The wars of peoples
will be more terrible than those of kings.
Winston Churchill (1901) (quoted in Canfora 2006: 113)

The world must be made safe for democracy.
Woodrow Wilson (1917) (Fried 1965: 308)

## INTRODUCTION

The consequences of the Great War were felt long after the guns fell
silent on 11 November 1918. The course of the war and its outcome
would decisively shape democracy's emergence in international relations. When hostilities commenced there was certainly little thought
about the war being waged for democracy, or any other great idea
for that matter. The nature of the conflict would alter dramatically as
a result of two events in 1917: the Russian Revolution and the entry
of the United States into the war. The manner in which US President
Woodrow Wilson defined the war in reference to democracy, followed
by the defeat of the Central Powers, would prove pivotal in the normative and political rehabilitation of the concept. One of its most important outcomes was the completion of a process that had commenced
with the American Revolution, as popular sovereignty supplanted
monarchy as the dominant form of state legitimacy. This also confirmed democracy's remarkable ideational transformation into a normatively acceptable, and for many a desirable, method of government.
'After 1919 democratic values were increasingly accepted as a kind of
ideological equivalent to the coin of the realm,' James Mayall observes,
'even if circumstances prevented it from being minted in most parts of

the world' (Mayall 2000a: 64). Put differently, even if the descriptive component of democracy was heavily contested, and would remain so, the evaluative side of the concept had completed its remarkable shift from negative to positive.

The magnitude of the shift that had taken place in how democracy was perceived can be appreciated through comparing the Versailles peace conference with its predecessor, the Congress of Vienna. When international society was rebuilt in Vienna, it was explicitly constructed against the popular doctrines that had emerged from revolutionary France. Yet little more than a hundred years later, the statesmen in Versailles worked through the consequences of fighting and winning a war meant to make the world 'safe for democracy'. Carl Schmitt observed the significance of this shift: 'The development from 1815 until 1918 could be depicted as the development of a concept of legitimacy: from dynastic to democratic legitimacy. The democratic principle must today claim an importance analogous to that earlier possessed by the monarchical' (Schmitt 1985: 30). This chapter will explore the role of the First World War in completing and confirming that transition.

## THE OUTBREAK OF WAR

The advance of democracy has not been as pronounced as many people were inclined to suppose ... There has been a tendency ... to over-estimate the strength of democracy, or rather to under-estimate the power of the old forces that have held sway for so long.

Arthur Ponsonby (1915: 36)

The assassination of Archduke Franz Ferdinand of Austria in Sarajevo on 28 June 1914 proved to be the spark that would set Europe's smouldering tensions alight. Within a month Europe broke down into a state of general war. Given how central democracy became in framing the conflict, it is notable, though not necessarily surprising, that it was absent from considerations in 1914. The speed with which events unfolded meant that no parties were clear in declaring their war aims at the outset. Even if they had been, any goals would have likely been traditional in nature, as both sides sought to make territorial gains and establish a favourable balance of power. Alliances were determined by these considerations, not regime type. This was reflected in the Entente, composed of Britain and France, the most liberal and democratic powers in Europe, and Russia, the most despotic. This arrangement troubled many British, who felt they had much more in common with Germany. During the House of Commons debate over Britain's entry into the war, one MP succinctly conveyed these doubts: 'We must look upon this question as a whole, and remember that we are fighting for Russia when we are fighting against Germany, and that if Germany stands for tyrannical government, Russia stands for atrocious tyrannical government' (Hansard 1914). Russia's place in the Entente would remain a source of consternation and embarrassment for the British, effectively foreclosing any possibility of pursuing more liberal war aims. This reflects that when the conflict began it was one primarily *between* the so-called civilised powers, with their perceived similarities far outweighing their differences. Simply put, the war was not yet seen as a struggle between democracy and autocracy.

That democracy was not initially identified as a war aim may have also been related to popular control not having been extended to foreign affairs. In Great Britain, where democracy had advanced furthest, foreign policy was still removed from popular oversight. This reflected a longstanding belief that the people were too ignorant of the subtle intricacies of diplomacy, and further democratisation in this realm posed grave risks to state interests. In his influential study *Modern Democracies*, James Bryce summarises this influential argument:

> Statesmen, political philosophers, and historians have been wont to regard the conduct of foreign relations as the reproach of democratic government. The management of international relations needs – so they insist – knowledge, consistency, and secrecy, whereas democracies are ignorant and inconsistent, being moreover obliged, by the law of their being, to discuss in public matters unfit to be disclosed. (Bryce 1921b: 402)

These warnings were strongly contested in Great Britain by the Union of Democratic Control (UDC), which included notable figures such as Norman Angell, John Hobson, Arthur Ponsonby, Bertrand Russell and Charles Trevelyan. The UDC were confident that the people would 'rise to the occasion and prove themselves worthy of the charge entrusted to them', just as they had 'proved themselves in the successive stages of internal self-government' (Ponsonby 1915: 110). The UDC also believed that extending democratic control to foreign affairs would create the possibility for pacifying relations between states. While the UDC were somewhat marginalised because of their pacifism, they still helped to direct public opinion towards liberal war aims, and their arguments notably found a receptive audience in Woodrow Wilson.[1]

The UDC was not alone in recognising that the war would have significant consequences for democracy's fortunes. Writing in 1915, Albert Bushnell Hart, an American commentator, reflected on 'the war and democracy', observing that 'democracy was considered the ripest flower of the highest civilization.... Today ... democracy seems, for the time being, submerged' (Hart 1915: 1–2). Hart's concerns were twofold: first, whether the conflict signalled 'the end of European democracy', and second, anticipating Wilson's fears, whether America's democracy could survive in a world dominated by non-democratic states. Hart's conclusion was straightforward, but accurate: 'The future trend from or towards democracy will depend on who is the victor' (Hart 1915: 32). Speaking a month later, President Wilson was fully cognisant of the changes the war was bringing, but was less certain as to what they would mean:

> This is a struggle which will determine the history of the world, I dare say, for more than a century to come. The world will never be the same again after this war is over. The change may be for weal or it may be for woe, but it will be fundamental and tremendous. (Scott 1918: 164)

Wilson's words would ring true, and as the war progressed the president developed a clearer vision of what this new world should look like. Fundamental to his programme was the principle of 'government by the consent of the governed', whereby 'every people should be left free to determine its own polity' (Fried 1965: 287). Two momentous events in 1917 would result in the war soon being framed in these terms, increasingly conveyed in a single phrase: 'self-determination'.

## THE RUSSIAN AND WILSONIAN REVOLUTIONS

The year 1917 would prove to be a definitive one not only for the conflict, but for the whole century. The event for which it is best known is the Russian Revolution, but there was a second ideational development that was also of great significance. This could be called 'the Wilsonian revolution', a term that encapsulates the changes brought about through America entering the war in democracy's name. In this regard, communism was not the only doctrine that emerged in 1917; this was also the year when democracy fully stepped onto the international stage.

In Russia longstanding socio-economic and political problems combined with the strain of a failing and costly war effort to push the tsarist regime to collapse. Shortly after demonstrations broke out in Petrograd, Tsar Nicholas II abdicated on 15 March 1917, taking with him the 300-year-old Romanov dynasty. One immediate consequence for the war was that it meant the battle lines between the Entente allies and the Central Powers could be redrawn. Great Britain, and to a much lesser degree France, had been constrained in their ability to advocate liberal war aims due to their alliance with tsarist Russia. Fighting alongside one of the most despotic states in Europe prevented the conflict being presented as between democracy and autocracy. Tomáš Masaryk would later recall that it was not until the downfall of Nicholas II that he felt assured that the aims of the Entente were 'the liberation of small peoples and the strengthening of democracy' (quoted in Cobban 1945: 11). The Entente could now present itself as fighting for democracy and self-determination, terms that were much more favourable to progressive world opinion and more importantly, to the US president.

The overthrow of the Russian tsar by a putatively democratic revolution was also fortuitous for Wilson, who was feeling increasingly compelled to enter the war on the side of the Entente. Shortly after the abdication of Nicholas II news reached Washington that three US merchant ships had been destroyed by German U-boats. Secretary of State Robert Lansing, stressed to Wilson that 'to go to war solely because American ships had been sunk and Americans killed would cause debate ... the sounder basis was the duty of this and every other democratic nation to suppress autocratic governments like the German' (quoted in Mayer 1959: 167). Framing the conflict in this manner was necessary to win over a Congress and public that remained sceptical about the United States abandoning its isolationist policy. Lansing was clear in presenting the war as one between the opposed systems of democracy and autocracy: 'The Entente Allies represent the principle of Democracy, and the Central Powers, the principle of Autocracy, and ... it is for the welfare of mankind and for the establishment of peace in the world that Democracy should succeed' (quoted in Ambrosius 1987:

31). It was in these terms that Wilson would announce America's entry into the war two weeks later. Returning to the conceptual discussion in Chapter 2, here one can see how utilising the concept of democracy, which had become a politically valuable term in American political discourse, made a certain course of action – the United States entering the war – possible.

On 2 April 1917 President Wilson went before Congress to ask for a declaration of war against Germany. Unlike the other belligerents, Wilson was explicit about America's reasons for fighting. The president announced:

> Neutrality is no longer feasible or desirable where the peace of the world is involved and the freedom of its peoples, and the menace to that peace and freedom lies in the existence of autocratic governments backed by organized force which is controlled wholly by their will, not the will of their people. (Fried 1965: 305)

Strongly echoing Kant, Wilson identified autocracy as the source of war. The conflict was not the fault of the German nation, but their rulers, who still practised the old kind of politics in which the 'people were nowhere consulted … and wars were provoked and waged in the interest of dynasties or of ambitious men' (Fried 1965: 306). In contrast, public opinion prevented 'cunningly contrived plans of deception or aggression' emerging from 'self-governed nations' (Fried 1965: 306). For Wilson, the form of government determined whether a state could be trusted to pursue war or peace, with democracies following the latter path and autocracies the former. Signalling the need for a democratic league of nations, Wilson continued:

> A steadfast concert for peace can never be maintained except by a partnership of democratic nations. No autocratic government could be trusted to keep faith within it or observe its covenants. It must be a league of honor, a partnership of opinion … Only free peoples can hold their purpose and their honor steady to a common end and prefer the interests of mankind to any narrow interest of their own. (Fried 1965: 306)

Here Wilson explicitly set out the opposition between democracy and autocracy that would subsequently frame the war.

Wilson imbued democracy with great significance by explicitly linking it to the war aims of the United States and its allies. He was clear that as long as an autocratic Germany remained, 'there can be no assured security for the democratic Governments of the world' (Fried 1965: 308). Instead of democracies, it was now autocracies that were identified as behaviourally and ontologically threatening to international society. And the danger they represented provided the primary reason for America's entry into war. Wilson powerfully proclaimed that 'the world must be made safe for democracy' (Fried 1965: 308). These words have been so commonly repeated that much of their original force has been lost. Without too much exaggeration it can be said that in this speech, and specifically with these words, Wilson reshaped the very terms on which the Great War was fought. Only one month earlier the conflict remained a carryover of nineteenth-century balance-of-power politics, with no clear ideological distinction between the opposing sides. Moreover, the aims of the belligerents were certainly not to advance any high-minded ideals, as the disclosure of secret treaties by the Bolsheviks would soon reveal. Georges Clemenceau would later admit: 'One must have the courage to say it, but we did not enter the war with a liberation program' (quoted in Mayer 1959: 184). This was certainly not the case for the US president, however, who wanted to simultaneously liberate peoples from autocracy and the world from war. In Wilson's mind these two goals were deeply interconnected: if the world could be made safe for democracy, democracy would make the world safe.

In Wilson's speech the progressive traits of democracy were identified through their antithesis in autocracy, with the two working as counter-concepts. The former entailed 'the right of those who submit to authority to have a voice in their own Governments', whereas the latter 'did what it pleased and told its people nothing' (Fried 1965: 307, 309). Central to this conceptual opposition was a temporal comparison, whereby autocratic Germany was associated with the 'old, unhappy days' in contrast to progressive democracies, which pointed towards the future. This difference was reflected in the distinction drawn between 'old' and 'new' diplomacy. Wilson's programmatic 'Four Points' speech in 1918 offered a particularly clear demonstration of this temporal opposition:

On the one hand stand the peoples of the world … opposed to them … [are] governments clothed with the strange trappings and the primitive authority of an age that is altogether alien and hostile to our own. The Past and the Present are in deadly grapple. (Fried 1965: 329)

This conceptual pairing is an example of a 'temporal asymmetric opposition', whereby 'the ones who define themselves as living in the present justify their actions against the ones that are trapped in the past' (Feres 2006: 271). The counter-concepts of democracy and autocracy were also connected to the civilised–barbarian conceptual pair, with Germany's autocratic government leading to its reclassification as being beyond the bounds of civilisation (Salter 2002: 82–3). The war effort thus gained a certain civilising dimension: temporally advanced democracies would give birth to a more progressive international society by destroying the backward autocratic regimes responsible for the war.

The manner in which Wilson employed democracy in this consequential speech is a powerful example of ideological innovation. By defining the purpose of the Great War – a conflict by then recognised as epochal in nature – primarily in terms of democracy, Wilson placed in the concept a value and importance that was unprecedented in modern international politics. At the time of the war, democracy's position was far from assured, and proponents feared that the conflict would be a significant setback for its fortunes. With the US president stepping into the fray, democracy was no longer on the defensive. Wilson effectively transposed the positive evaluative dimension of democracy from the American domestic context into the international realm. Without qualification or hesitation, he announced popular sovereignty as a legitimate form of state and democracy as a desirable form of government. The US president effectively inverted the formula that held at Vienna: domestic principles of legitimacy remained of fundamental importance for international society, only now popular sovereignty and democracy were not a threat but necessary cornerstones for peace and stability.

When considering Wilson's legacy there is a tendency to focus on his unfulfilled hopes of a new liberal international order, which means the profound consequences of his decision to fight in democracy's name are overlooked. His bold pledge to make the world safe for democracy was heard across the globe, with the address being widely reported, printed and translated (Manela 2007: 36). Wilson's powerful defence and advocacy of democracy reinforced the normative shift that had occurred in the late nineteenth century and helped transfer it into the international realm. The manner in which the war was subsequently formulated in terms of the democracy–autocracy conceptual opposition reflected how successful he was as an ideological innovator. Quite simply, Wilson announced that democracy would henceforth be a pivotal concept in international society, one that would influence political discourse and shape standards of legitimacy.

## THE BOLSHEVIK CHALLENGE

In his address to Congress Wilson made explicit reference to 'the wonderful and heartening things' taking place in Russia (Fried 1965: 306). Developments did not proceed as he had hoped, however. The ineffectual provisional government unwisely chose to honour Russia's war commitments, and found itself increasingly challenged by the radical Bolshevik party, which mobilised around discontent over this matter. In November there was a second revolution, with the Bolshevik-dominated soviets overthrowing the provisional government. Considering that communism has been regularly portrayed as anti- or non-democratic, the role played by the concept of democracy in the Bolsheviks' original programme is striking. This partly reflected the fact that while liberalism and democracy had been largely reconciled, democracy's connotations of social equality meant it remained associated with socialism and communism. That Vladimir Lenin and the Bolsheviks framed their actions partly in reference to democracy indicates that Wilson was not the only major source of contestation and revision in the concept during the war. Indeed, it could be argued that Wilson's rhetoric was also a way of further laying claim to democracy, delimiting the concept in such a manner that it was clearly distinguished from these more radical doctrines.

One of the clearest examples of this counter-discourse of democracy was the Bolsheviks calling for a 'democratic peace'. Given the subsequent monopolisation of the term by liberals, and its common association with the post-war plans of Wilson, it is a valuable corrective to consider how this idea was employed by the Bolsheviks. An underappreciated dimension of the contest between Wilson and Lenin for leadership of the 'new diplomacy' programme included opposing visions of what 'democratic peace' entailed. The first of Lenin's 'April Theses', which recalled his theory of imperialism, stated that 'without over-throwing capital it is impossible to end the war by a truly democratic peace, a peace not imposed by violence' (Lenin 1917b). A month later, the All-Russian Conference of Bolsheviks declared that if they were to take power, they would 'immediately and openly' offer all peoples 'a democratic peace' (quoted in Mayer 1959: 81). This was reaffirmed by Lenin after the overthrow of the provisional government, with the Bolsheviks calling on 'all the belligerent peoples and their government to start immediate negotiations for a just, democratic peace'. Lenin explained that this meant 'an immediate peace without annexations … and without indemnities'. He contrasted this policy to 'the deception practised by governments which pay lip-service to peace and justice, but in fact wage annexationist and predatory wars' (Lenin 1917a). What can be seen is that the Bolsheviks employed 'democratic peace' differently to Wilson's conception and current liberal understandings, in which it entails the absence of war between liberal democratic states. For Lenin, 'democratic' was an epithet, describing the *kind* of peace, namely, a just, fair, equitable one based on self-determination of all peoples. As he explained in his April Theses, such a peace was not possible among capitalist states, regardless of whether they claimed to be democratic or not. Leon Trotsky was even more forthright during the Brest-Litovsk negations: 'The Allied Governments have in no way shown, and, in view of their class character, they could not show, their readiness to accept a really democratic peace' (Trotsky 1918). For the Bolsheviks, the key factor determining the possibility for peace was not democracy, but capitalism. *Contra* liberal arguments that capitalism promotes peace, for the Bolsheviks it was just the opposite.

For Lenin and the Bolsheviks capitalism not only prevented a 'democratic peace', it also inhibited democratic rule. Echoing Marx, Lenin regarded capitalist democracy as a necessary stage for society to pass through:

Democracy is of enormous importance to the working class in its struggle against the capitalists for its emancipation. But democracy is by no means a boundary not to be overstepped; it is only one of the stages on the road from feudalism to capitalism, and from capitalism to communism. (Lenin 1993)

As it stood, 'bourgeois democracy' was 'always hemmed in by the narrow limits set by capitalist exploitation' (Lenin 1993). The institutions of liberal democracy, notably the practice of elections, operated to 'conceal the truth', namely, that power relations remained unchanged, with the numerically superior working class continuing to be exploited at the hands of the much smaller group that held the means of production (Lenin 1919a). For the Bolsheviks the form of democracy for which Wilson sought to make the world safe was radically incomplete. They instead saw the events in Russia, and the larger war to which they were tied, as an opportunity to challenge and eventually overthrow the bourgeois order. The Great War had 'stripped bourgeois democracy of its camouflage' (Lenin 1919b), and the revolution in Russia offered hope that a new kind of democracy could emerge, one that would rule in the interests of the true majority, the proletariat. Recalling democracy's past, Lenin noted that in different stages of history it had taken on different forms, and this would happen again, with 'democracy for the rich [being replaced] by democracy for the poor'. The consequences of this would be 'a gigantic, world historic extension of democracy, its transformation from falsehood into truth' (Lenin 1919a). This process would eventually entail transcending democracy itself: 'The more complete the democracy, the nearer the moment when it becomes unnecessary' (Lenin 1993). From this perspective, democracy was not an end in and of itself, but a means towards the more fundamental goal of human emancipation.

It is important not to overstate the role of democracy in the thought and discourse of the Bolsheviks. Calls for a democratic peace were soon buried under the oppressive conditions imposed by the Germans at Brest-Litovsk, and while Lenin's stature would later grow, at that time it was dwarfed by the figure of Wilson (Manela 2007: 10). Of greater consequence was the introduction of the term 'self-determination' by Russia's provisional government at the behest of the Bolsheviks. A statement issued on 9 April 1917 declared 'that the purpose of free Russia [was] not domination over other peoples, nor spoliation of their national possessions, nor the violent occupation of foreign territories, but the establishment of a permanent peace on the basis of the self-determination of peoples' (quoted in Mayer 1959: 75). This was the first time self-determination was explicitly identified as a war aim by any of the major belligerents. While the programme of self-determination would soon become strongly identified with Wilson, it is important to recall that it first emerged from revolutionary Russia.[2] When employed by the Bolsheviks it carried a very specific meaning related to their revolutionary project of overthrowing capitalism (Armstrong 1993: 129–30; Manela 2007: 37, 42). As will be seen, the idea was wrestled away by Wilson, who emptied it of the Bolsheviks' radical intent. In this regard, a remarkable parallel exists with the French revolutionary attempt to overthrow international society, which boomeranged and ultimately reinforced the very anarchical order they sought to transcend. Self-determination was introduced by the Bolsheviks as part of their goal of destroying the capitalist international order, but was subsequently coopted and transformed in such a manner that again the anarchical nature of international politics was preserved, as was the capitalist system.

## THE ENDS OF WAR AND THE END OF WAR

The principle of self-determination was soon taken up by the Entente allies, becoming central to their programme in the final year of the war. First to adopt the term was not President Wilson, but the British prime minister, David Lloyd George, under increasing domestic pressure to announce progressive war aims. The rhetoric that emerged from the Brest-Litovsk negotiations pushed him towards a clear statement on the matter (Rothwell 1971: 145–53). On 5 January 1917 he set out the British war aims in a carefully drafted speech. While denying that war was being waged to change Germany's constitution, Lloyd George mirrored Wilson's understanding of the relationship between domestic regime type and international behaviour, identifying Germany's 'military, autocratic constitution [as] a dangerous anachronism in the twentieth century' (Lloyd George 1918). Lloyd George also employed the same democracy–autocracy asymmetrical conceptual pairing: 'The adoption of a really democratic constitution by Germany would be the most convincing evidence that in her the old spirit of military domination had indeed died in this war' (Lloyd George 1918). Democracy was associated with peaceful behaviour; in contrast, autocracy was militaristic, dangerous, and ill fitting to the modern world. To reinforce this dichotomous framing, the British prime minister emphasised that democracy was a common attribute joining the allies together (Lloyd George 1918). In concluding, one of the three conditions Lloyd George identified as necessary for a 'just and lasting peace' was that 'a territorial settlement must be secured, based on the right of self-determination or the consent of the governed' (Lloyd George 1918). Not for the first time in the speech Lloyd George equated 'self-determination' with 'consent of the governed'. Erez Manela describes this as a 'promiscuous rhetorical flourish', whereby the considerable differences between 'the radical anti-imperialist agenda suggested by the former and the liberal reformism implied in the latter' were papered over (Manela 2007: 39). When identifying self-determination as a central war aim of the allies, Lloyd George carefully redescribed it in a way to remove any traces of its socialist origins. The success of this ideological innovation was evidenced in Wilson's subsequent shift from talking of the 'consent of the governed' to using 'self-determination', an important change that became more pronounced through 1918 and 1919.

The Treaty of Brest-Litovsk was signed on 3 March 1918, allowing Soviet Russia to exit from the war, albeit at a very high cost as the Germans imposed especially punitive conditions. Kaiser Wilhelm II hailed the treaty as one of the 'great successes of world history', but for the US president it exposed the true nature of the German regime and made clear that peace could only be assured with its destruction (Link 1979: 85). Discussing the treaty, Wilson emphasised the fundamental incompatibility of Germany's aims with those of the allies: 'In such a program our ideals, the ideals of justice and humanity and liberty, the principle of the free self-determination of nations upon which all the modern world insists, can play no part' (Fried 1965: 325). In accepting what he saw as a basic contradiction between these two world-views, Wilson concluded that 'there is, therefore, but one response possible from us: Force, Force to the utmost, Force without stint or limit' (Fried 1965: 325). What had been implicit in Wilson's thinking was now brought to its logical conclusion: to make the world safe for democracy, 'the destruction of every arbitrary power' that threatened peace was necessary (Fried 1965: 329). It was at this time that Wilson's programme for a new international order began to crystallise, one that included the end of autocratic government. He summarised his vision as follows: 'What we seek is the reign of law, based upon the consent of the governed and sustained by the organized opinion of mankind' (Fried 1965: 330).

The conflict was increasingly defined in dichotomous terms: democracy and autocracy, pacificism and militarism, progressiveness and backwardness, self-determination and conquest. Jan Smuts, one of the most influential and eloquent members of the imperial war cabinet, strongly echoed Wilson's words:

> Now for the first time you have the great historical issue brought before you in the sharpest form. On the one hand you have the autocracies of Germany, Austria, and Turkey.... On the other hand, you have the free nations of the world. (Smuts 1917: 105)

Lars Oppenheim, the renowned international jurist, judged it an 'epoch making' conflict: 'Whatever may be the war aims of the belligerents, at bottom this World War is a fight between the ideal of democracy and constitutional government on the one hand, and autocratic government and militarism on the other' (Oppenheim 1919: 11). In the words of an American commentator, the war was 'a life-and-death struggle' between 'two antagonizing principles or philosophies of government, democracy and autocracy' (Luckey 1920: 111–12). Lloyd George concurred: 'The whole future of democracy ... all over the world is involved. It is a final test between military autocracy and political liberty' (Bryce 1917: 199). This is only a sample of the explosion of speeches, pamphlets and articles from 1917–18 that promoted the democracy–autocracy framing of the conflict.

Conceiving of the war as being between two opposed systems was by no means limited to the Allied powers. In an attempt to counteract Wilson's rhetoric, leading German thinkers presented a series of lectures to the Prussian Diet, which were soon printed under the title of *Die Deutsche Freiheit* ('The German Freedom'). Notably, they did not shy away from the dichotomous framing promoted by Wilson, with Germany's opponents being labelled as 'democracies' and collectively the 'democratic world', only they regarded such a designation as negative (Christophersen 1966: 222). This worldview was echoed by Kaiser Wilhelm II. In March 1918, he stated in belligerent fashion that 'if a British parliamentarian comes to sue for peace, he must first kneel before the imperial standard, for this is a victory of monarchy over democracy' (quoted in Fischer 1967: 618). Speaking at a banquet to celebrate thirty years ruling Germany in July 1918, Wilhelm's opinion would mirror that of his counterparts in America and Britain: 'This war is a struggle between two world philosophies' (quoted in Fischer 1967: 618). With the war being framed in such momentous terms by both sides, the subsequent defeat of Germany also took on the greater meaning of the victory of democracy over autocracy. Emblematic of this was Guglielmo Ferrero's announcement in 1919 that, 'the world war has now annihilated one of the principles of authority which ruled Europe, namely Divine Right … No other principle remains, therefore, but that of the Will of the People expressed by means of representative institutions' (Ferrero 1919: 270).

Central to Wilson's emerging vision of a new international order was that states should be based on the consent of the people. In 1918 he increasingly used the term 'self-determination' to express this long-held belief. Speaking at a joint session of Congress of 11 February 1918, the president proclaimed, 'Self-determination is not a mere phrase. It is an imperative of action, which statesmen will henceforth ignore at their own peril' (Scott 1918: 368). For Wilson self-determination entailed more than just popular sovereignty: it also naturally extended to democratic government. James Mayall expresses Wilson's thinking well: 'For what other purpose would a people claim the right to self-determination if not to rule themselves?' (Mayall 1990: 44). A strong confidence in the inherent superiority of democracy, combined with his faith in public opinion, led Wilson to the belief that self-determination would necessarily result in democratic government, as had happened in the United States. Indeed, for Wilson, 'self-government must be a *continuing* process and must therefore be synonymous with the *democratic* form of government' (quoted in Pomerance 1976: 17; original emphasis; see also Cobban 1945: 20). In Wilson's worldview, popular sovereignty and democratic government – *forma imperii* and *forma regiminis* – were effectively merged.

The way the principle of self-determination developed during the Great War meant it was not simply used as an equivalent to popular sovereignty; rather, it entailed a specific understanding and elaboration of it. Wilson firmly believed in the sentiment earlier expressed by John Stuart Mill: 'One hardly knows what any division of the human race should be free to do, if not to determine, with which of the various collective bodies of human beings they choose to associate themselves' (John Stuart Mill 1991: 428). It begged the question, though, of how the boundaries between these different groups would be determined. The answer given was the one that had emerged from the French Revolution: the nation. Thus, self-determination became *national* self-determination. Based on the American experience, Wilson mirrored the earlier thought of Abbé de Sieyès in understanding the nation in civic, political terms. Yet this thinking was a poor fit for comprehending the situation in Europe. As Michla Pomerance observes, 'the "self" in Wilson's "self-government" was not necessarily the "nation" of continental Europe' (Pomerance 1976: 17). This became increasingly apparent as Wilson's words were transposed into the complicated realities of eastern Europe, and the 'self' transmogrified from a civic to an ethic conception of community (Lynch 2002). It is in this sense that Alfred Cobban and Anthony Whelan talk of self-determination as the combination of democracy and nationalism, in which the latter defines the boundaries of the former (Cobban 1945; A. Whelan 1994).

Another important element of Wilson's vision for a new liberal order was the creation of some kind of international organisation to prevent a similar catastrophe from reoccurring. Wilson did not offer too much detail about what it would look like, but his emphasis on the pacifying effects of public opinion and the untrustworthy, militaristic nature of autocracies suggested that any such organisation should be composed of democratic states. This was apparent in the final of his Four Points, which called for 'the establishment of an organization of peace which shall make it certain that the combined power of free nations will check every invasion of right' (Fried 1965: 330). If this organisation was to promote and preserve peace, it could not 'rely upon the word of outlaws' (Fried 1965: 334). Many of the proposed plans for an international organisation were much more forthright in calling for exclusively democratic membership, as Wilson remained determined that its constitution should be determined as part of the peace settlement. The British League of Nations Union advocated a 'World League of Free Peoples for the securing of international justice, mutual defence, and permanent peace', while their French counterparts proposed that membership 'should be granted only to nations whose sincerity is guaranteed by democratic institutions' (Phelps 1919: 49, 51). For such an organisation to achieve its aims, it must be composed of nations

> able to enter into valid covenants, especially in matters of war and peace, a possibility conditioned on [their] possessing a modicum of democratic institutions which will make certain that the will of the people prevails and that the government is adequately controlled. (Phelps 1919: 53)

Meanwhile, H. G. Wells's prominent book *In the Fourth Year* called for a 'League of Free Nations', proposing that for it to 'signify anything more than a rhetorical flourish, then certain consequences follow' (Wells 1918: 27). He explained:

> If they [Germany] or any other peoples wish to take part in a permanent League of Free Nations it is only reasonable to insist that so far as their representatives on the council go they must be duly elected under conditions that are by the standards of the general league satisfactorily democratic. (Wells 1918: 28)

John Dewey went even further, arguing that it was not just members of the League that needed to be democratic. The conception of international legitimacy he proposed was far-reaching:

> The United States, at least, has been largely in the war precisely because it realized that the dividing line between domestic institutions and foreign policies has become wholly artificial. It was precisely the autocratic domestic institutions of Germany which drew us into … war … The logic of the situation demands such friendly oversight of the affairs of other states from which world-wide conflagration might spring … (Phelps 1919: 274–5)

Dewey's logic mirrored that of Prince Metternich and the Holy Alliance in arguing that the domestic constitution of states was directly of concern for all members of international society. The key difference is that the threat had been reversed: democracies were regarded as capable of maintaining peace, whereas autocracies were seen as inherently dangerous.

If this new organisation was to be restricted to democracies, there would need to be a way of identifying which states were eligible for membership. Viscount Grey was clear that the 'League of Nations must not be a sham … [and] that means that you must have every government in the League of Nations representing a free people' (Phelps 1919: 90). For this to occur it was necessary to be able to 'define democracy – real democracy, and not sham democracy' (Phelps 1919: 90). Grey's response to this dilemma was that people are capable of 'knowing a democracy when they see it' (Phelps 1919: 90). This position was hardly satisfying, though it reflected the increasing descriptive variability in the concept, an emergent characteristic identified in the previous chapter. As the positive normative connotations surrounding democracy became more widespread, its value for political actors increased, but with this increased usage what exactly democracy meant became more contested and unclear. This situation was unhappily observed in a book entitled *The Meaning of Democracy*, where its author complained that 'it really does not help us much to talk of "making the world safe for democracy," when what A calls democracy, B calls plutocracy, and what C calls democracy, D calls anarchy, Bolshevism, and the end of all things' (I. Brown 1920). The American edition of *The Economist* posed a similar question: 'And what is a "democratic peace," pray? Why democratic? Is this a democratic war, and therefore there must be democratic peace? Why not plain "peace"? … It is not a "democratic peace" but an "American peace" that we want' (Phelps 1919: 199). For Wilson these were the one and the same thing.

The US president would soon find out what kind of peace could be constructed. On 11 November 1918 the Central Powers offered their surrender on the basis of his Fourteen Points. Now the battles would move from the trenches to the Palace of Versailles, where statesmen would try to establish a new international order. Given that democracy had become so central to the conflict, it was now to be seen how significant a role it would play in the post-war settlement.

DEMOCRACY AT VERSAILLES:
VISION, REALITY, COMPROMISE

Contrary to the wishes of many in Europe and America, President Wilson was determined to go to France for the peace negotiations. Reflecting his Burkean sensibilities, Wilson wanted progressive and controlled change, rather than revolution (Ambrosius 1987: 1). Setting sail for Paris, he expressed this underappreciated pragmatic dimension to his idealism:

> The conservatives do not realize … what forces are loose in the world at the present time. Liberalism is the only thing that can save civilization from chaos – from a flood of ultra-radicalism that will swamp the world … Liberalism must be more liberal than ever before, it must even be radical, if civilization is to escape the typhoon. (Quoted in Gardner 1993: 264)

This suggests a more nuanced position than the naive optimism commonly associated with Wilson. The international order he envisaged would, as is well known, never come to fruition. This is not so surprising given how untenable the situation was. As Ian Clark suggests, 'this was not a settlement in which the peacemakers carelessly let the opportunity for consensus-building slip through their fingers: the basic problem of Versailles was that no such consensus could possibly be found' (Clark 2005: 109–10). There were multiple reasons for this, an important one being the changed conditions under which peacemakers were now operating. The options open to statesmen during the conference were curtailed by the increasingly prominent role played by public opinion. The framing of the war as one of just, righteous democracies fighting against barbaric, autocratic powers would now limit the possibilities for compromise, as publics called for the evil warmongers to be punished (Knock 1998: 117).

The focus here is primarily the drafting of the League of Nations covenant. Debates over the nature of this new organisation, specifically in regard to its membership, represent the most important reflections on democracy and international legitimacy at Versailles. They offer far more fertile soil to till than discussions among the Council of Four, which are light on principles and heavy on specificities. And given the previously widespread calls for an exclusively democratic league it is worthwhile exploring to what extent this hope was actualised.

### The League of Nations: Homogeneous or Heterogeneous?

> The old institutions on which militarism and autocracy flourished lie crumbled in the dust; a great wave of advanced democracy is sweeping blindly over Europe ... The psychological and moral conditions are ripe for a great change. The moment has come for one of the great creative acts of history.
>
> Jan Smuts (1918) (quoted in Miller 1928b: 47)

In preparation for the conference, interested parties made plans for the League of Nations, with the US and British drafts proving the most consequential. Wilson finally outlined his ideas in more detail, and in his first Paris draft he proposed the following article in regard to membership in the new organisation: 'Any power not a party to this Covenant, whose government is based upon the principle of popular self-government, may apply to the Body of Delegates for leave to become a party' (quoted in Miller 1928b: 85–6). In contrast, the British draft prepared by Lord Robert Cecil was much more cautious, suggesting that 'definitely untrustworthy and hostile States should be excluded. Otherwise, it is desirable not to be too rigid in scrutinising qualifications' (quoted in Miller 1928b: 61). This less rigorous approach reflected the British preference for a more inclusive organisation (Hinsley 1973: 121). As early as July 1918, Cecil expressed his concerns to Colonel Edward House:

> I do believe that we might devise an efficient sanction for the commands of a League of peace. One great danger, however, I see in its way: the French suggest that it should be confined to democratically governed nations – at least so I understand them. I cannot help feeling that this is a most dangerous path for us to travel … Prussian militarism is indeed a portentous evil, but if, misled by our fear of it, we try to impose on all the nations of the world a form of government which has been indeed admirably successful in America and this country, but it is not necessarily suited for all others, I am convinced that we shall plant the seeds of very serious international trouble. (Quoted in Schwarzenberger 1936: 28)

Cecil presented here a strong preference for a more pluralist international order. His misgivings were sufficient that in the later Cecil–Miller draft, a combination of British and American proposals, the reference to 'popular self-government' found in Wilson's text had been removed (Miller 1928b: 139–40). It remained, however, in all of Wilson's subsequent drafts, reflecting his strong attachment to the principle (Miller 1928b: 151).

The conference finally opened on 18 January 1919 and with the British pragmatically siding with Wilson's demand that the League be at the fore of issues dealt with, the Commission on the League of Nations was appointed at the second plenary session on 25 January. Wilson spoke of the centrality of the League to the new international order being founded, as well as the more democratic conditions under which they were now operating: 'I may say without straining the point that we are not representatives of governments, but representatives of peoples. It will not suffice to satisfy governmental circles anywhere. It is necessary that we should satisfy the opinion of mankind' (Miller 1928b:

155). Despite this need to 'satisfy the opinion of mankind' the drafting of the covenant was open only to Allied and Associated powers. The defeated Central Powers were excluded, and even neutral nations were not formally included; a problematic situation given the aspirations that the League would become the institutional representation of international society.

The Commission on the League of Nations was personally chaired by Wilson, who used his position to steer the discussion. Commencing with a working draft that had been tabled by the British and the Americans, a final version was produced with remarkable speed, taking just thirteen meetings across February and March. In these sessions the commission made their way through each article in the working draft. At the third meeting on 5 February 1919, the article that dealt with the League's membership was debated for the first time. As Wilson had decided to introduce the Hurst–Miller text rather than his own, no reference to self-government was initially included. This led Wilson to open the discussion by proposing that the article be amended along the lines of his own draft: 'Only self-governing States shall be admitted to membership in the League; Colonies enjoying self-government privileges may be admitted' (Miller 1928a: 164). After two years of loudly proclaiming this principle, Wilson and his fellow statesmen were now faced with the question of what exactly it meant. Cecil, representing the British, was the first to allude to the problem of limiting membership to self-governing states, observing that '"self-government" is a word which is hard to define, and it is hard to judge a country by this standard. For example, on paper the Reichstag was a democratic institution.' He concluded that 'the bare use of the word "self-governing" is therefore unfortunate', and would prefer a system whereby a majority of members could impose specific conditions on different states seeking admission (Miller 1928a: 164–5). To this Wilson immediately replied:

I have spent twenty years of my life lecturing on self-governing states, and trying all the time to define one. Now whereas I haven't been able to arrive at a definition, I have come to the point where I recognize one when I see it. For example, regardless of how it appeared on paper, no one would have looked at the German government before the war, and said that the nation was self-governing. (Miller 1928a: 165)

Given the centrality of democracy to Wilson's thought and political programme, this represents a truly remarkable admission.

Wilson's troubles with definitively defining democracy indicated that the great difficulty in seeking to delimit membership to democratic states was determining which states qualified. The growing contestation and variability in the concept of democracy made it highly problematic to apply in practice. Nonetheless, Wilson was resolute that it must be included, regardless of any potential difficulties that might arise in determining which states were democratic and thus eligible for membership. He explained:

> We have said that this war was carried on for a vindication of democracy. The statement did not create the impulse but it brought it to consciousness. So soon as it was stated that the war was being waged to make the world safe for democracy, a new spirit came into the world.... They knew that governments derived their just powers from the consent of the governed. I should like to point out that nowhere else in the draft is there any recognition of the principle of democracy. If we are ready to fight for this, we should be ready to write it into the covenant. (Miller 1928a: 165)

Wilson displayed here a keen awareness of the significance of fighting in the name of democracy. The way the conflict had been framed now placed limits on what the statesmen were able to do. This is an example of the theoretical point made in Chapter 2, whereby language can operate to both enable and restrict action. Having been proclaimed so loudly, the principle of democracy needed to be included – in one form or another – in the post-war settlement.

One of the French representatives, Léon Bourgeois, responded to Wilson: 'What of countries which do not enjoy full self-government? The definition is difficult.... Whether the form of the government is republican or monarchical makes no difference. The question ought to be, is this Government responsible to the people?' (Miller 1928a: 166). Vittorio Emanuele Orlando, the Italian representative, indicated similar concerns:

> This is an exceedingly hard matter to define. You can't say 'parliamentary' very well, because that is not the true test, and we may want some nations in the League whose government would

not come within this class. You can't say 'free government' ('*pays libres*') because that doesn't take into consideration its external relations. (Miller 1928a: 166)

Wilson remained unconvinced by these interventions, falling back on his previous argument: 'While "self-government" is not susceptible of definition, neither is "free". But we all know when a government is properly described by one of these phrases' (Miller 1928a: 167). The discussion was inconclusive, resulting in Wilson's proposal being provisionally accepted, with the exact wording to be decided later.

In the ninth meeting, held on 13 February, the commission began a second reading of the covenant draft, after it had been amended by the drafting committee. In regard to the article covering membership, there was a change in the wording, with 'free countries' replacing 'self-governing'. It now read that membership 'shall be limited to free countries, including Dominions and Colonies' (Miller 1928b: 309). This provoked a discussion arising from '*pays libres*' – the French translation of 'free countries' – carrying different, and more precise, connotations than in English. The French delegate Ferdinand Larnaude explained that '*pays libres*' 'was employed by writers on constitutional law to describe a State whose institutions were democratic or liberal', and that it 'was used in regard to the internal constitution of the State' (Miller 1928b: 303). This opinion was echoed by Orlando, who noted that in Italian law '*pays libres*' 'was used in the same sense – its meaning being clear, and understood to refer to the internal freedom of States' (Miller 1928b: 303). The French and Italian delegates did not share Wilson's habit of merging popular sovereignty and democratic government. Rather, they saw the two notions as distinct, and believed that only popular sovereignty should be considered in determining league membership. This complication resulted in the English text being changed to the awkward 'fully self-governing countries', which was provisionally translated into French as '*pays de self-government total*' (Miller 1928a: 228).

In the final version of the Covenant of the League of Nations the article dealing with membership was placed at the front of the document. The wording was: 'Any fully self-governing State, Dominion or Colony not named in the Annex may become a Member of the League', with the corresponding French reading: '*Tout État, Dominion ou Colonie qui se gouverne librement*' (Miller 1928b: 720–1). Wilson's interpretation of 'self-governing' pointed towards a League of Nations made up of democracies in both senses: *forma imperii* and *forma regiminis*, but the above discussion suggests this is not how his European counterparts understood 'fully self-governing' or states *'qui se gouverne librement'* (which translates directly as a state 'which governs itself freely'). In the discussion that led to *'pays libres'* being removed, the French and Italian representatives made it clear that this term was inappropriate because it was about the domestic form of government, which they regarded as beyond the remit of the league. There is no evidence from the minutes of the meetings that 'fully self-governing' was thought to specifically incorporate democratic government, with the implication being that it was understood in a more limited sense in reference to external sovereignty. As noted, it was contrasted *against* the French term *'pays libres'*.

The lack of clarity over what 'fully self-governing' actually meant (this was never finally determined) reflected a deeper ambiguity surrounding democracy's place in the covenant. While democratic government was not considered a *de jure* condition of membership, Wilson hoped that it would be a *de facto* requirement. His Burkean belief that the League would develop organically suggests that he may have expected 'fully self-governing' to take on a more extensive meaning over time. Furthermore, the emphasis placed on public opinion by both Wilson and Cecil, the two most influential proponents of the League, strongly implies that some degree of democratic government – understood in terms of representative institutions that mediated and responded to public opinion – was regarded as necessary for the new organisation to fulfil its peace-bringing function. Cecil conceded that 'what we rely upon is public opinion ... and if we are wrong about it, then the whole thing is wrong' (quoted in Sharp 1991: 62). In this sense, it is best to see democracy operating in the covenant as a regulating, but not binding, ideal. While falling short of the 'homogeneous universality' that Wilson favoured, the inclusion of 'freely self-governing' in defining membership indicated that the League would not be reconciled to a condition of 'heterogeneous universality', as it entailed something more than open membership.[3] In essence, the result was a diluted form of homogeneity. 'Fully self-governing' was, in a certain sense, a successor to the notion of 'civilised'. While the classical 'standard of civilisation' continued to operate following the end of the First World War, the distinction between a 'civilised' Europe and a 'barbaric' other had started to unravel (Salter 2002: 82–3). To be considered a full member of international society – indicated through membership in its institutional expression, the League of Nations – a state now needed to be 'fully self-governing'.

The lack of clarity regarding league membership reflected unresolvable tensions between contending visions for the post-war order. The covenant could never simply be a Wilsonian statement; it was unavoidably a product of diplomatic bargaining. In concluding this discussion, it is helpful to consider how Wilson justified the covenant and advocated for its ratification after returning to the United States, as it reinforces the suggestion that in Wilson's mind 'fully self-governing' did entail both popular sovereignty and democratic rule:

> Only the free peoples of the world can join the League of Nations. No nation is admitted to the League of Nations that cannot show that it has the institutions which we call free. No autocratic government can come into its membership, no government which is not controlled by the will and vote of its people. (Foley 1923: 64–5)

Wilson's interpretation went much further than the actual text suggested. Echoing the dichotomous logic of his speeches of 1917–18, there was a clear inference that for the League to fulfil its function of maintaining peace, autocratic governments must be excluded. According to Wilson, 'the League of Nations sends autocratic governments to Coventry' (Foley 1923: 128–9). Autocratic states were dangerous because of what they *did*, which was fundamentally a result of what they *were*. A League of Nations based on democratic states offered the best chance of safety against autocracies as well as a more peaceful international order. In this sense, for Wilson the League had both protective and developmental functions: 'it is not only a union of free peoples to guarantee civilization; it is something more than that. It is a League of Nations to advance civilization' (Foley 1923: 67).

There was a clear discrepancy between Wilson's understanding of the covenant and how it was interpreted by other signatories, who regarded the membership criteria as far less demanding, entailing popular sovereignty but not democratic government. Indeed, of the thirty original members, less than half were democracies, a figure which still represented a highpoint in the democratic makeup of the organisation (T. Smith 1994). Nonetheless, even if there was a certain ambiguity over whether the term 'fully self-governing' extended to democratic institutions, it clearly entailed popular sovereignty. In itself, this was a fundamental development in international society, representing the final step in it supplanting monarchical sovereignty. Wilson announced this in sensational terms: 'It is the most remarkable document, I venture to say, in human history, because in it is recorded a complete reversal of the processes of government which had gone on throughout practically the whole history of mankind' (Foley 1923: 52–3). Minus the hyperbole, his judgement was largely correct: popular sovereignty had arrived. It would take another world war and the collapse of the European empires to globalise this principle, but at Versailles popular sovereignty was firmly embedded within international society.

*Expectation and Reality: Self-determination and the Versailles Settlement*

The challenges of incorporating popular sovereignty and democracy into this new international order were also evident when statesmen had to reach an agreement on the territorial settlement. The strong emphasis placed on self-determination in the final stages of the war meant that it could not be easily avoided or forgotten about afterwards, as some parties might have preferred. The central place of self-determination in the war aims of the Allies, thrust there by Lloyd George and Wilson, created an 'imposing standard' against which the peace settlement would be judged (Bain 2003: 90). In attempting to include self-determination in the settlement they faced grave, perhaps insurmountable difficulties, which shaped the manner in which it was upheld.

The idea of self-determination may have seemed like an intuitively good one (at least to Wilson), but implementing this principle was incredibly difficult. As Sir Ivor Jennings famously observed, 'on the surface, it [the doctrine of self-determination] seemed reasonable: let the people decide. It was in fact ridiculous, because the people cannot decide until someone decides who are the people' (Jennings 1956: 55–6). Equally memorable were Robert Lansing's remarks, whose legalistic mind worried about the practical problems that came with this high-minded ideal:

When the President talks of 'self-determination' what unit has he in mind? Does he mean a race, a territorial area or a community? Without a definite unit which is practical, application of

> this principle is dangerous to peace and stability ... The phrase is simply loaded with dynamite. It will raise hopes which can never be realized. It will, I fear, cost thousands of lives ... What a calamity the phrase was ever uttered! What misery it will cause! (Quoted in Pomerance 1976: 10)

But the phrase had been uttered, repeatedly in fact, and therefore it needed to be dealt with as part of the settlement. Furthermore, Wilson remained committed to the principle, even if this was soon tempered by his discovery of the realities of eastern Europe. Indeed, his lack of knowledge of the area led to a number of mistakes that seriously undermined the application of the principle. As Wilson later admitted, 'when I gave utterance to those words [that all nations had a right to self-determination], I said them without a knowledge that nationalities existed, which are coming to us day after day' (quoted in Heater 1994: 8).

The difficulties with the principle were manifold: how the 'self' in 'self-determination' could be established, how competing claims between different 'selves' could be reconciled, and how this all could be done in a manner consonant with the interests of the great powers and international society more generally. In addition to these significant practical challenges, few of the key participants at Versailles were supportive of Wilson's agenda. In particular, France and Italy pursued traditional strategies in which self-determination was disregarded, except where it worked in their favour. Moreover, by the time he had reached France, Wilson's bargaining power had diminished considerably, thereby limiting his ability to make self-determination a deciding factor when resolving many of the awkward territorial issues the peacemakers had to deal with. While Wilson did stand firm in specific instances, in many cases he ceded ground, hoping that the League of Nations would be able to address these shortcomings in the future (Foley 1923: 60; Lynch 2002: 426). This was cold comfort for those nationalities that did not benefit from the implementation of the principle in 1919, however.

Self-determination was certainly honoured more in the breach at Versailles, but it is misleading to focus solely on instances where it was not implemented, or done so imperfectly. In itself, that self-determination was incorporated into the treaty at all was a significant, if not revolutionary, change. As Rodney Bruce Hall rightly observes, 'the post-First World War map of Europe was the most substantial institutionalization of the new, system-legitimating principle of national self-determination achievable at that time, and is a monument to the strength of the new principle' (R. B. Hall 1999: 250). The way it was incorporated at Versailles, self-determination entailed a specific reading of popular sovereignty: the people – the nation – were understood primarily in cultural, ethnic terms. Furthermore, it did not carry the double-barrelled meaning – popular sovereignty *and* democratic institutions – that Wilson ascribed to it. While democracy had emerged as a legitimate form of constitution, it was overshadowed by the prior and more widely accepted principle of popular sovereignty, activated in the form of national self-determination. The result was that after 1918, 'the dominant political form was the nation-state' (Mayall 1990: 45).

While self-determination was meant to be the guiding principle for shaping what would follow in the wake of the Austro-Hungarian and Ottoman empires, it was much less clear whether it should also apply beyond Europe. The manner in which the war had been framed, combined with Wilson's strongly held beliefs, worked against a policy of outright annexation, as much as this may have frustrated people like Australian prime minister Billy Hughes. The situation was finessed and resolved through the mandates system, a compromise solution first proposed in a highly influential paper by Jan Smuts. While believing that self-determination should be applied to eastern Europe, Smuts regarded it as completely inappropriate for dealing with Germany's colonies. He explained that 'the German colonies in the Pacific and Africa are inhabited by barbarians, who not only cannot possibly govern themselves, but to whom it would be impracticable to apply any idea of political self-determination in the European sense' (Miller 1928b: 28). The 'standard of civilisation' was extended to include the notion of self-determination, thereby continuing the practice of applying a different logic of behaviour for dealing with those beyond Europe not considered as civilised (Keene 2002: 128–9). Wilson regarded the right to self-determination to be universal, but he also was a strong believer in democracy being an evolutionary process, which manifested itself in a clear paternalistic streak in his thinking. As an academic, he commented that democracy was 'not created by aspirations ... it is built up by slow habit' and that 'immature peoples cannot have it' (quoted in Anthony 2008: 247). Given this dimension of Wilson's thought it is perhaps not surprising that he strongly agreed with Smuts's proposal.

The basic idea animating the mandate system was that the League of Nations would act as trustee for peoples not yet sufficiently 'mature' or 'civilised' to exercise self-determination. In reference to the former colonies of the defeated powers, Article 22 of the covenant stated that to those territories 'which are inhabited by peoples not yet able to stand by themselves under the strenuous conditions of the modern world, there should be applied the principle that the well-being and development of such peoples form a sacred trust of civilisation' (Miller 1928b: 737). Imperial powers experienced in dealing with 'backwards peoples' were entrusted with mandates, which were separated into classes A, B, and C. As Bain notes, 'self-determination implied granting powers of self-government and autonomy in proportion to the capacity of a people to make good use of them' (Bain 2003: 92). Class A mandates were regarded as most advanced in progressing towards being ready for self-determination, while those in class C were seen as the furthest away. In reality, the distance between class C mandates and outright annexation was very small, but it was a compromise reached between the annexationist desires of the British dominions and Wilson's refusal to allow the inclusion of something so contradictory to the principles on which the Great War had been waged.

Even if still largely understood in terms of the civilised–uncivilised distinction, and containing more than its fair share of hypocrisy, the significance of the mandate system should not be discounted. Self-determination was most certainly not seen to apply for the time being, but the possibility that peoples could mature to such a status was left open: it represented the guiding principle and end point of the mandate system, in theory at least. In this sense, as well as further weakening the distinction between a European order of toleration and a non-European one of civilisation, it further sowed the seeds for empire's end (Keene 2002: ch. 5; Manela 2007: xxi).

## CONCLUSION

Considering Woodrow Wilson's part in the Great War, Winston Churchill wrote:

It seems no exaggeration to pronounce that the action of the United States with its repercussions on the history of the world depended, during the awful period of Armageddon, upon the workings of this man's mind and spirit to the exclusion of almost every other factor, and that he played a part in the fate of nations incomparably more direct and personal than any other man. (Quoted in Link 1979: 20)

The argument of this chapter generally supports Churchill's assessment. The tendency to focus on the failure of Wilson's grand vision for a new international order obscures what he helped achieve. Reflecting with great disappointment over what he saw as the incomplete and haphazard institution of the principle of self-determination at Versailles, Harold Nicolson dismissed the outcome as 'patchwork Wilsonism' (Nicolson 1933: 70). *Contra* Nicolson's lament of its 'patchwork' nature, it was remarkable that the settlement was Wilsonian *at all*. Wilson's championing of popular sovereignty and democracy was in stark contrast to a historical legacy of thought and practice that had only recently begun to change. In this regard, the current normative dominance of democracy tends to inhibit our ability to fully comprehend the significance of Wilson's move in waging war in democracy's name. Without succumbing to the 'great man' account of history, it can be argued that the American president played a pivotal role as ideational innovator, acting as both a catalyst and a symbol of the emergence of democracy as a legitimate form of state in international society.

By entering the war under the banner of democracy the United States fundamentally challenged and changed the terms under which it was fought. The reframing of the conflict as one of democracy versus autocracy was facilitated by revolution in Russia, but it was Wilson's intervention that thrust democracy onto international society's agenda. As Tony Smith observes, 'Wilson's commitment to democracy made him decidedly more radical abroad than he was at home' (T. Smith 1994: 61). His consistent support for democracy forced it to centre stage, and with the Allied victory it secured a place in the founding of the new international order. The strong emphasis placed on democracy and popular sovereignty helped to shape the Versailles settlement: self-determination could not simply be ignored. Democracy was by no means the ruling ideology, and it had to compete with other principles and interests, but it did place certain constraints on what statesmen at Versailles were capable of doing. Simply carving up the world with no regard for the wishes of local inhabitants, as their predecessors had always done, was no longer possible.

In the context of this study, the great significance of the First World War is that it decisively completed what the 'Age of Revolutions' had started: the transition from monarchic to popular sovereignty. This sentiment was expressed by H. G. Wells in *In the Fourth Year*:

> The European dynastic system ... is dead to-day; it is freshly dead, but it is as dead as the rule of the Incas.... Beyond the unstable shapes of the present the political forms of the future rise now so clearly that they are the common talk of men.... The stars in their courses, the logic of circumstances, the everyday needs and everyday intelligence of men, all these things march irresistibly towards a permanent peace based on democratic republicanism. (Wells 1918: 89–90)

A year later, Robert Lansing was even more explicit in arguing that 'to insure to the world a continuing state of international peace, democracy should be made the standing policy of civilization ... Democracy can make the world what it ought to be' (Lansing 1919). Here one can identify an understanding of democracy that corresponds to contemporary times, one in which it is strongly associated with peaceful behaviour, and regarded as a legitimate form of statehood and government.

## Notes

1  Many of the core elements of Wilson's open diplomacy programme are recognisable in these earlier arguments of the UDC. A letter by the UDC executive committee in May 1917, signed by Charles Buxton, Frederick Jowett, Ramsay MacDonald, E. D. Morel, Angell, Hobson, Ponsonby and Trevelyan, eventually made it to Wilson, via Colonel House, who had written in the margins that it was 'interesting because of the signatures' (Mayer 1959: 336).
2  The term had been used by socialists since the turn of the century, who had borrowed it from German metaphysics (Pomerance 1976).
3  These categories are taken from Schwarzenberger (1936: ch. 3).

*Chapter 7*

# FROM THE BRINK TO 'TRIUMPH': THE TWENTIETH CENTURY

Either the world will be governed by the ideology of modern democracy ... or it will be ruled by the laws of force.
                    Adolf Hitler (1925) (Hitler 1939: 148)

The great dilemma which modern European democracy is facing today is: totalitarian fascist and national socialist authoritarianism on one side, and Marxist socialism and communism on the other side. How democracy will try to save its existence, accepting in this dilemma a new, modern shape – that is today its life-and-death question. This question is almost insoluble – and still, it can be resolved and it must be resolved.
                    Edvard Beneš (1939: 16)

## THE FOUNDATIONS OF DEMOCRACY IN INTERNATIONAL SOCIETY

In *The Foundations of Modern Political Thought*, Quentin Skinner suggests that 'the clearest sign that a society has entered into the self-conscious possession of a new concept is ... that a new vocabulary comes to be generated, in terms of which the concept is then articulated and discussed' (Skinner 1978: x). An equivalent process has been explored thus far, examining the way the concept of democracy came to be articulated in modern international society. With the peace settlement at Versailles, 'a new set of words, like democracy, freedom, and self-determination,' Martin Wight notes, 'acquired general currency, replacing the older set of words' (Wight 1972: 27). Popular sovereignty was embedded in international society, and democratic government had come to be recognised as a legitimate form of constitution. It is

171

for these reasons that the Versailles settlement is widely recognised as a foundational moment in the development of democracy in international politics (Armstrong 1993; Clark 2005; Clark 2009; Franck 1992; Hinsley 1982; Mayall 2000a; Mayall 2000b; Navari 2007; Wight 1972). Ian Clark accurately observes the significance of this moment: 'It is not possible fully to appreciate the Versailles architecture without a clear focus on this cardinal principle of democracy as a proper concern of international society' (Clark 2005: 116).

Democracy's position after Versailles was both central and ambiguous. James Mayall subtly conveys this point when noting that the settlement did not entrench 'democracy itself, but democratic values, as the standard of legitimacy within international society' (Mayall 2000b). The defeat of the Central Powers completed a process that was already well underway in the second half of the nineteenth century: popular sovereignty – democracy as *forma imperii* – supplanted monarchy as the foundation on which members of international society would be based. Popular sovereignty, a term used interchangeably with self-determination, was embedded within the new international order, but it was not yet universalised. This would occur over the rest of the twentieth century. As Erez Manela notes, the Great War and the subsequent settlement 'launched the transformation of the norms and standards of international relations that established the self-determining nation-state as the only legitimate political form throughout the globe' (Manela 2007: 5; Mayall 1990: 45–7). In time, the principle of popular sovereignty would be turned against the imperial powers in the same way that the French revolutionaries had used it against the hapless Louis XVI. It would not be until the processes of decolonisation that followed the Second World War that popular sovereignty would be extended around most of the globe (Crawford 2002; Fabry 2010; R. Jackson 1993; Mayall 1990; Philpott 2001). The basic framework itself, however, had been established in international society half a century earlier. As Mikulas Fabry observes, 'decolonization was the triumph of Wilson's conception of self-determination' (Fabry 2010: 149).

The standing of democratic government (*forma regiminis*) in the new international order was less clear cut. Democracy had emerged as a legitimate form of constitution, and was ideationally in the ascent after the victory of the Allies, but it would exist in a pluralist international society in which it would compete against other forms of rule. The successful waging of the Great War in democracy's name had completed the remarkable transformation in the evaluative dimension of the concept from negative to positive. The situation that had prevailed only 150 years earlier, where democracy was widely reviled or avoided, was firmly something of the past. Democracy assumed a normative standing and political legitimacy it has yet to lose. As we will explore later in this chapter, democracy's existence was under great threat during the late 1930s and early 1940s as it was repudiated by fascist movements and deserted by many fair-weather friends. Yet even during these dark days, its light was never extinguished: the core democratic countries remained committed to this form of rule, even if there was much more doubt of its virtue and strength. The conceptual battles surrounding democracy in the twentieth century were no longer with the *ancien régime*, but the modern doctrines of fascism and communism. Democracy was certainly still contested, but the nature and participants of that battle had changed.

This study has focused primarily on one part of democracy's larger history, namely, its appearance and rise in modern international politics. During this period from the American Revolution through to the end of the First World War the trajectories of popular sovereignty (*forma imperii*) and the revival of democracy as a form of domestic rule (*forma regiminis*) were closely intertwined. Following the Great War, these two dimensions would be separated and the dynamic of contestation would change considerably. With popular sovereignty confirmed, conflict would be exclusively over the different forms of government (*formae regiminis*) that had emerged: democracy, communism and fascism. As Clark notes, 'what was left unresolved [at Versailles] was the legitimacy of dominant domestic constitutional forms, and it was around this issue that the epochal war of the twentieth century was to rage until 1990' (Clark 2005: 110). Philip Bobbitt terms this the 'long war', an ideological battle that lasted for most of the twentieth century over which constitutional form would be hegemonic in international society (Bobbitt 2002). This has been explored in detail by a number of scholars (Bobbitt 2002; Clark 2005; Fukuyama 1992; Fukuyama 2014b; Gat 2009; Mann 2012a; Mann 2012b; Mazower 1998; Müller 2013). It is important to note that this contestation surrounding democracy – in which it competed with the modern ideologies of communism and fascism – differed significantly from that which attended its emergence in international society, whereby popular sovereignty supplanted monarchical sovereignty and democratic government was re-evaluated as a positive form of rule. It is the latter story that has been the main focus of this book. As such, the purpose of this chapter is to outline the most significant dimensions of the ideational conflict that democratic government was involved with during the twentieth century, while observing that much of the conceptual framework for its ascendance had already been constructed by the time the 'long war' began.


## THE INTERWAR YEARS

Democracy's place in the Versailles settlement was more equivocal than Wilson and other liberals may have hoped for, but it still was ideationally in the ascent in the immediate years after the Great War. In his 1921 classic, *Modern Democracies*, James Bryce judged that there was a 'universal acceptance of democracy as the normal and natural form of government' (Bryce 1921a: 4). Bryce's work is one of the best-known examples from a wealth of literature published on democracy at this time. Richard Roberts observed in *The Unfinished Programme of Democracy* that

> during the past few years, we have become familiar with the idea of a world made safe for democracy; and in the minds of many people democracy ... stands as a sort of ultimate good which it is impious to challenge or to criticise. (R. Roberts 1920: 10)

This normative strength gave it political value, which meant that a wide range of actors sought to attach their projects to it. In this regard, Ivor Brown caustically remarked: 'Everyone in these days, except a few honest unbending junkers in each country, makes at least a superficial claim to be the true supporter of Democracy' (I. Brown 1920: 18–19). He was pessimistic about the consequences of this expansion in democracy's meaning: 'The word [democracy] has come to mean nothing; or rather it means so much that it means nothing at all' (I. Brown 1920: v). A similar judgement was reached by J. S. Fulton and C. R. Morris, who noted that while the war had been fought in democracy's name, 'if the question had been pressed what precisely this "democracy" was or what it meant, it is doubtful whether a satisfactory answer would have been forthcoming' (Fulton and Morris 1935: 1). This illustrative sample of the enormous literature on democracy from the interwar years indicates how democracy's centrality in political discourse meant that it became much more debated, contested and actively employed by various political actors, a far cry from matters a century before when it had been studiously avoided except for labelling opponents.

The normative strength of democracy was further reflected in the considerable expansion of democratic institutions across Europe. Suffrage was extended in many of the older democracies, with women gaining the vote for the first time in some countries. Most of the successor states to the fallen Romanov, Habsburg and Hohenzollern empires sought to institute democratic government. This was the peak of what Samuel Huntington identified as democracy's 'first wave' (Huntington 1993: 16–17), as democratic institutions spread across eastern Europe. As Nancy Bermeo observes, 'the interwar years were a watershed for democracy and for democratic theory. Never before had so many citizens in so many nations been accorded so many formal rights.... In 1920, 26 out of 28 European states were parliamentary democracies' (Bermeo 2003: 21). This was a drastic change compared with a few decades earlier when only a handful of democracies had existed. In the words of Michael Mann, 'liberal democracy seemed the coming, modern ideal. The sole deviant case, the Soviet Union, actually claimed to be more genuinely democratic' (Mann 2004: 38).

The expansion of democracy after the First World War represented – at that point in time – the greatest singular extension of this form of rule, but the movement was broad, not deep. While democracy may have been the ruling ideology, this in itself did not create the political, economic and social conditions necessary to allow for successful democratisation. With the benefit of hindsight and findings from the comparative politics literature on the topic, it is clear that most of these countries lacked the preconditions that make democratisation a likely and sustainable prospect.

It is also important to appreciate the magnitude and intractability of the problems governments faced in the interwar years. The devastation wrought by the First World War, followed by the Great Depression and the heightened class conflict that ensued, created and exacerbated fundamental political, economic and social tensions. Even in countries that had the longest experiences with democracy its prospects were far from certain. And those that had recently adopted democratic institutions lacked the political experience and democratic culture that would enable them to manage when the economic situation worsened. Furthermore, the strongly cultural, nationalist understanding of self-determination that emerged from the war would prove much less compatible with democracy than had initially been assumed. As Mark Thompson observes, 'aside from the problem of nations not closely matching state boundaries, excessive emphasis on nation-building often encouraged the rise of extreme nationalism that was unfavourable for the development of democratic government, to put it mildly' (Thompson 2002: 21). Simply put, these were hardly auspicious conditions for inaugurating new democratic regimes. As the political and economic climate darkened during the 1920s, many countries abandoned their experiments with democracy. The result was what Huntington identified as the 'first reverse wave': 'only four of the seventeen countries that adopted democratic institutions between 1910 and 1931 maintained them throughout the 1920s and 1930s' (Huntington 1993: 17).

The key development in shaping democracy's fortunes during the interwar years was undoubtedly the Great Depression. The economic turmoil unleashed greatly exacerbated the political and social tensions that had been mostly kept at bay. Economic problems may have been the most important factor causing the tide to turn away from democracy and towards authoritarianism, but 'material constraints were neither absolute nor unambiguous' (Berman 1998: 205; see also Bermeo 2003: 22). While all of Europe suffered from the Great Depression, not all of it became authoritarian. A decisive factor was whether political elites – especially conservative ones – chose to abandon democracy in favour of more authoritarian solutions as the political and economic situation worsened (Bermeo 2003: 26–7; Mann 2004: 24–5). A fear of communism and social revolution would prove a powerful force in motivating elites to look for non-democratic alternatives. 'Right across one-half of Europe, the upper classes turned toward more repressive regimes, believing these could protect themselves against the twin threats of social disorder and the political left' (Mann 2004: 24–5). In this regard, one of the most significant consequences of the Russian Revolution was that it would provide a foil for rising right-wing extremist parties, and the fears of the left that it engendered would dilute opposition to this growing movement. Most failed to appreciate that fascism represented a far more immediate and substantial threat.

Zara Steiner identifies 1929–33 as the 'hinge years', the decisive period that connected 'the two decades of the inter-war period, the decade of reconstruction and the decade of disintegration' (Steiner 2007: part 2). This period was bookended on one side by the Wall Street

Crash of 1929, which triggered the Great Depression, and on the other by the ascendance of Adolf Hitler to the German chancellorship on 30 January 1933, which would ultimately put Europe and the world on the path to a war more dreadful than anyone could yet imagine. Following Hitler's rise to power, ideology would become a more prominent factor in politics, with fascism emerging as a major challenger to democracy. Many of the countries that abandoned democracy did not follow Italy and Germany all the way in adopting fascism, but the ideology still played a significant role in this broader shift. As Marco Tarchi notes, 'each time a parliamentary democracy collapsed, fascism was evoked by both followers and enemies: sometimes it was really present on the scene, sometimes it was the "silent guest" of the new authoritarian regime, and its phantom excited popular passions' (Tarchi 2002: 128). Fascism seemingly offered what democracy could not: a set of answers to the political, economic and social problems that beset these countries, combined with decisive leadership and protection from revolution on the left.

The end of the Weimar Republic in Germany, the spread of authoritarianism and fascism throughout eastern Europe, and the considerable difficulties that established democracies faced during the Great Depression, collectively led to a widespread questioning of democracy. Certainly people such as Carl Schmitt had already begun doing so in the 1920s, when he powerfully argued in *The Crisis of Parliamentary Democracy* that there were fatal weaknesses in the way liberalism had reconciled itself with democracy. By the mid-1930s, discussion about the crisis of democratic government was far more widespread, with an explosion of literature on the topic. Writing as Europe lurched towards war, William Rappard observed that 'today, "popular power", of which Lord Bryce wrote fifteen years ago that it was "welcomed, extolled, worshipped", has come to be cursed in some quarters, apologetically defended in others, but questioned and indeed qualified everywhere' (Rappard 1938: 506). Democracy found itself under attack from both the left and the right. Communists and socialists argued that democracy limited to the political sphere was insufficient, and that it needed to be extended to economic relations. This sentiment was shared by many New Deal liberals and social democrats. Emblematic was John MacMurray's conclusion that 'unless we democratize our economic system it will surely strangle our political democracy' (MacMurray 1943: 38–9). Meanwhile on the right, fascists powerfully argued that democracy was a weak, ineffectual form of rule, lacking in vitality and purpose. Notably, these were different to the criticisms that had traditionally plagued democracy. As one commentator at the time remarked, 'democracy has been acquitted of these charges and a new indictment framed' (Merriam 1939: 63–4). Alfred Zimmern concurred: 'The issue today is no longer between democracy and the old order. The *ancien regime* … has passed away beyond recall.… Democracy today has a new opposition to face' (Zimmern 1929: 316).

The unique challenge fascism posed could be seen through its relationship with democracy. Compared with conservative doctrines, fascism did not seek the overthrow of popular sovereignty; rather, it understood it in a thoroughly exclusionary manner. In his attack on parliamentary democracy, Schmitt was clear that fascism was 'certainly antiliberal but not necessarily antidemocratic' (Schmitt 1985: 16). In making this claim, he asserted that 'every actual democracy rests on the principle that not only are equals equal but unequals will not be treated equally. Democracy requires, therefore, first homogeneity and second – if the need arises – elimination or eradication of heterogeneity' (Schmitt 1985: 9). Fascism adopted an extreme and exclusionary version of nationalism. Through such logic, popular sovereignty was not abandoned but perverted and radicalised. This also illustrates that while fascism had backward-looking elements, it was a thoroughly modern doctrine. As Michael Mann notes, 'the combination of modern nationalism and statism was to turn democratic aspirations on their head, into authoritarian regimes seeking to "cleanse" minorities and opponents from the nation' (Mann 2004: 2).

Another way in which fascism refashioned popular elements was through its mobilisation of the people. Indeed, democratic mechanisms played an important role in fascists achieving power. Most infamously, the rapid electoral success of the Nazi party in Germany paved the way for Hitler's ascension to the chancellorship. In fascism, the people were not removed from politics, but controlled and channelled. They were sceptical of elections, believing that 'popular sovereignty must be expressed "intuitively" through the fascist party and its leader' (Passmore 2002: 29). Again, this was different from traditional dismissals of democracy, in which conservatives had wanted the people to play no part. Instead, fascism harnessed and mobilised the people for essentially non-democratic ends. Writing at the time, John Dewey observed the uniqueness of this phenomenon: 'For practically the first time in human history, totalitarian states exist claiming to rest upon the active consent of the governed' (Dewey 1939: 131–2). In this sense, while the fascists strongly challenged the Versailles settlement, the doctrine of popular sovereignty it enshrined was largely accepted, albeit reinterpreted in an extreme and exclusionary manner.

Ruefully remembering the optimism surrounding democracy after the First World War, John Hobson recalled that 'the tide of history seemed firmly set towards democracy, nor was there any reason to suspect that it would turn' (J. Hobson 1934: 4). Yet, as Hobson was well aware, the tide did turn. Merely decades after Wilsonian ideals appeared triumphant, democracy's future was in question. As Samuel Huntington noted, 'the war fought to make the world safe for democracy seemed instead to have … unleashed social movements from the Right and the Left intent on destroying it' (Huntington 1984: 196). Democracy went from being the harbinger of a more peaceful and prosperous world to being derided as a weak and feckless form of rule soon to be placed in the dustbin of history. The loss of faith in democracy was widespread, and the consequences would be profound. Reflecting on the way democracy was increasingly abandoned and fascism was embraced, Hans Kohn regretfully observed that 'never before had mankind been so ready to betray itself' (Kohn 1942: 242).

## WORLD WAR TWO: FROM THE FLAMES TO THE FUTURE

During the 1930s the international order was challenged by the increasingly aggressive foreign policies of Germany, Italy and Japan. The League of Nations was exposed as ineffectual and few countries seemed ready to defend the Versailles settlement. On a more basic level, there was a failure to recognise the kind of threat Hitler posed. Democratic statesmen presumed they were playing the same game, mistakenly thinking that all sides would prefer to avoid war (Steiner 2011: 1051). With the memories of the Great War still fresh in people's minds, there was little appetite in democracies for more conflict. Writing at the time, Emery Reves suggested that

> All the mistakes and blunders committed during the past two fatal decades by the democratic governments were justified by the argument that only by accepting such acts could the democratic peoples preserve their precious peace. We had no policy, no

ideals, no purpose, save one – to prevent shooting. We wanted nothing but peace. So the war came. (Reves 1943: 51)

While a strong popular desire to avoid another war was significant, another reason democracies were slow to appreciate the threat posed by Hitler was that their judgement was clouded by an overriding fear of communism (Mann 2012a: 433–6). At the time Ramsay Muir suggested that 'the racial fanaticism of the Germans, the Japanese, and (in a less degree) the Italians, is far more dangerous to the peace of the world than the doctrinaire fanaticism of the Russians', but this position was not commonly held (Muir 1939: 2). Much more representative was Neville Chamberlain's mistaken opinion: 'I cannot believe that she [Russia] has the same aims and objects that we have or any sympathy with democracy as such' (quoted in Mann 2012a: 435). While fears of communism did not lead the countries of western and northern Europe to abandon democratic government, as in eastern Europe, it did prevent them from reaching an alliance with the Soviet Union that might have forestalled or limited the conflict.

Hitler's dreams of war were finally fulfilled when Germany invaded Poland on 1 September 1939. France, the United Kingdom, Australia, Canada, New Zealand and South Africa responded by declaring war on Germany in the days that followed. While this was a grouping of democratic states, they were not acting in democracy's defence. The world had stood by at Munich and accepted Hitler's dismemberment of Czechoslovakia, one of the few countries in the region that had stayed democratic, before going to war over Poland, a country that had earlier succumbed to authoritarian rule. Meanwhile, the United States remained firmly wedded to its strict policy of isolation. If it had been primarily concerned about defending democracy and liberal values, 'World War II was a war that should have engaged the United States from its outbreak in Europe in 1939' (Hagan and Bickerton 2007: 118). Yet as Hitler went on the attack, few were ready to mount an adequate defence of the beleaguered form of democracy.

The remarkable speed and ease with which Germany conquered much of Europe only reinforced the image of democracy as feeble and ineffectual. This was especially the case with the stunning collapse of France, which surrendered to Germany on 22 June 1940. The narrative that emerged to explain this defeat – *la décadence* – pointed towards the general malaise the country had had fallen into under a divided, impotent political class who embodied all the perceived failings of democratic government. Peter Jackson summarises this account:

> A bankrupt regime, in which parliamentary politics and narrow self-interest took priority over community and a spirit of collective sacrifice for the national good, the Third Republic was unable to marshal the energies of the nation in preparation for the inevitable war with Hitler's Germany. (Peter Jackson 2006: 872)

The shocking capitulation of France marked an ignominious end to the much-derided democracy of the Third Republic. Given this remarkable contrast between the weakness of democracy and the strength of fascism, 'opinion in Europe at the end of the 1930s was by no means opposed to the idea of an authoritarian reconstruction of the continent under German leadership' (Mazower 1998). Most had yet to comprehend the true nature of the Nazi regime, and Hitler's energetic leadership looked much more impressive than the indecision of the democracies.

By the end of 1940 Germany dominated Europe, with the United Kingdom left as the last major line of defence, bruised and battered but not defeated after successfully holding off the Luftwaffe. The greatly weakened position of the remaining democratic countries combating Hitler was forcing the US president and his country to reconsider its strict policy of isolationism. In a radio broadcast on 29 December 1940, Franklin Roosevelt cautioned his fellow citizens about the growing threat they faced: 'The Axis not merely admits but proclaims that there can be no ultimate peace between their philosophy of government and our philosophy of government' (Roosevelt 1940). He argued that America's best chance to avoid war was to provide further military supplies to the British and others resisting, and famously announced that in 'democracy's fight against world conquest' the United States 'must be the great arsenal of democracy' (Roosevelt 1940). This broadcast was followed a few days later by Roosevelt's 1941 State of the Union address, the influential 'Four Freedoms' speech, in which he warned 'that the democratic way of life is at this moment being directly assailed in every part of the world' (Roosevelt 1941a). In response he would offer a particularly spirited defence of this form of government. In making the case for the United States to abandon its isolationism, Roosevelt recalled how the country came to enter the First World War only after 'the American people began to visualize what the downfall of democratic nations might mean to our own democracy' (Roosevelt 1941a). The president was clear that the United States now faced a similar situation, observing that 'the future and the safety of our country and of our democracy are overwhelmingly involved in events far beyond our borders' (Roosevelt 1940). In these addresses Roosevelt presented the war as a conflict between democracy and authoritarianism, and warned that by refusing to participate the United States was putting its own democracy – and the democratic movement as a whole – in grave danger.

Roosevelt argued that this battle against authoritarianism would not only be waged in Europe, and that the United States must continue to strengthen democracy at home. He announced in straightforward, but inspirational, language what a democracy must provide:

> There is nothing mysterious about the foundations of a healthy and strong democracy. The basic things expected by our people of their political and economic systems are simple. They are: equality of opportunity for youth and for others; jobs for those who can work; security for those who need it; the ending of special privilege for the few; the preservation of civil liberties for all; the enjoyment of the fruits of scientific progress in a wider and constantly rising standard of living. These are the simple, basic things that must never be lost sight of in the turmoil and unbelievable complexity of our modern world. (Roosevelt 1941a)

Here Roosevelt powerfully distilled the most basic liberties that give democracy value and made it worth defending. The president went on to outline in further detail the 'four essential human freedoms' – freedom of speech, freedom of worship, freedom from want and freedom from fear – which should form the basis for a world that 'is the very antithesis of the so-called new order of tyranny which the dictators seek to create' (Roosevelt 1941a). It is worth noting that in offering this impressive defence of democracy Roosevelt was very conscious of critiques from the left about the need to democratise socio-economic relations, and presented an expansive programme that went beyond negative liberties.

At a time when democracy was on the retreat everywhere, and the Axis countries were reaching the apex of their powers, Roosevelt's

'Four Freedoms' speech offered a robust, visionary defence of democratic government. He recognised the social and economic tensions that countries were struggling with, but his response was not to question democracy further. Instead he presented a clear restatement of what democracy should be, and reaffirmed the belief that it is the form of government most capable of providing the fundamental freedoms desired by all humans. Responding to Hitler's apocalyptic plans for a world ordered by race and brute force, Roosevelt offered democracy, which represented 'the greater conception – the moral order' and the ultimate line of defence against the Nazis' dystopia (Roosevelt 1941a). This strong defence of democracy also distinguished him from Winston Churchill, who spoke little of it, instead emphasising the unity of the British Empire under the monarchy. While Churchill's moving oratory is justly celebrated, it is the words of his American counterpart that were more impressive when it came to democracy. Unlike Wilson, whose pledge in the First World War to make 'the world safe for democracy' would reframe how the conflict was understood, Roosevelt was hardly innovating in observing that Hitler and the Axis powers were attacking 'the whole pattern of democratic life' (Roosevelt 1941a). What made Roosevelt's intervention significant is that he provided a spirited, but ultimately humble and visionary, defence of democracy during its darkest days.

One of the most fateful developments in determining the outcome of the war occurred on 22 June 1941, when Germany commenced Operation Barbarossa and invaded the USSR. The Soviets would ultimately bear the heaviest costs of the conflict, with total war deaths estimated between 23.9 million and 25.8 million (Harrison 2003). It was their ability to withstand and repel the Germans that would prove decisive in defeating the Axis powers. On hearing the news of the German invasion, Churchill immediately pledged British support to the Soviets. He was conscious that this made for an odd ideological alliance, stating that 'no one has been a more consistent opponent of Communism than I have for the last twenty-five years.... But all this fades away before the spectacle which is now unfolding' (Churchill 1941). The British prime minister made clear that this would not alter the resolve of the democratic powers:

If Hitler imagines that his attack on Soviet Russia will cause the slightest division of aims or slackening of effort in the great democracies who are resolved upon his doom, he is woefully mistaken. On the contrary, we shall be fortified and encouraged in our efforts to rescue mankind from his tyranny. (Churchill 1941)

In a radio broadcast on 3 July 1941, Joseph Stalin thanked Churchill for his offer of assistance. Like his British counterpart, the Soviet leader put aside ideological differences in the face of a common danger:

> In this war of liberation we shall not be alone.... Our war for the freedom of our country will merge with the struggle of the peoples of Europe and America for their independence, for democratic liberties. It will be a united front of the peoples standing for freedom and against enslavement and threats of enslavement by Hitler's fascist armies. (Stalin 1941)

It is notable that Stalin explicitly declared that the Soviets were fighting to protect 'democratic liberties' and were 'standing for freedom'. This proved true: fundamental to democracy's survival during the Second World War was its alliance with its other great ideological rival, communism.

These developments were not enough for the United States to abandon its isolationist policy, although it deepened its support of those resisting the Axis powers. Reflecting this increased involvement, on 14 August 1941 the Americans and the British jointly issued the Atlantic Charter, which set out their aims for the post-war international order. Despite being agreed upon by the two leading democratic powers, the document offered rather tepid support for democracy. Notably, it did not mention the term, the third point instead stating that the countries 'respect the right of all peoples to choose the form of government under which they will live; and they wish to see sovereign rights and self government restored to those who have been forcibly deprived of them' (Roosevelt and Churchill 1941). This was not a defence of democratic government, but of the principle of popular sovereignty that had been enshrined at Versailles. Indeed, Churchill was not even happy about this limited reference to self-determination, emphasising that it did not apply to the British Empire and later trying to propose that the charter was an 'interim and partial statement of war aims designed to reassure all countries of our righteous purpose and not the complete structure which we should build after the victory' (quoted in Prazmowska 1995:

23). Yet the Atlantic Charter would become an important basis for Allied war aims, gaining support from the Inter-Allied Council a month later. In acknowledging its agreement, the USSR offered a clear defence of the understanding of self-determination that Churchill had been so loath to include:

> The Soviet Union defends the right of every nation to the independence and territorial integrity of its country and its right to establish such a social order and to choose such a form of government as it deems opportune and necessary for the better promotion of its economic and cultural prosperity. (Inter-Allied Council 1941)

While the Atlantic Charter failed to offer an explicit defence of democratic government, it was still understood as an agreement forged by two leading democracies against their non-democratic foes. This is how Roosevelt presented it to Congress, explaining that it was part of US policy to provide assistance 'to the democracies which East and West are waging war against dictatorships' (Roosevelt 1941c).

The United States was finally forced out of isolation following the surprise Japanese attack on Pearl Harbor, and the subsequent declaration of war by Germany. In responding to these events and declaring war on Japan on 8 December 1941, Roosevelt made no promises about 'making the world safe for democracy', as his predecessor once did. He instead emphasised the gravity of the threat the Allies faced:

> Never before has there been a greater challenge to life, liberty, and civilization…. Rapid and united effort by all the peoples of the world who are determined to remain free will insure a world victory of the forces of justice and of righteousness over the forces of savagery and of barbarism. (Roosevelt 1941b)

The Axis powers now faced the combined economic and military might of the United States, the Soviet Union and the British Empire. While the outcome of the conflict was still far from inevitable, this certainly created a material imbalance that greatly favoured the alliance of democratic and communist powers.

Democracy would emerge more clearly as a war aim at the Casablanca conference held in early 1943, which was attended by Roosevelt and

Churchill. In calling for the unconditional surrender of the Axis powers, the Allies – which now referred to themselves as the United Nations – explicitly identified their cause with democracy:

> In the years of the American and French revolutions the funda-mental principle guiding our democracies was established. The cornerstone of our whole democratic edifice was the principle that from the people and the people alone flows the authority of government. It is one of our war aims, as expressed in the Atlantic Charter, that the conquered populations of today be again the masters of their destiny. (United Nations 1943)

Roosevelt and Churchill met again at the end of the year in Tehran, together with Stalin. Once more, democracy was identified as a central part of their war platform, and they announced that they would win and establish an 'enduring peace', which would be constructed and maintained by 'a world family of Democratic Nations' (Churchill *et al.* 1943). While these declarations explicitly referenced democracy, what was meant was democracy as *forma imperii*: popular sovereignty or self-determination. This was primarily a war for the independence of states, rather than to advance a specific form of government.

Democracy would again assume a prominent place in the war aims announced at the Yalta conference in February 1945, where Roosevelt, Churchill and Stalin discussed plans for the post-war order as the defeat of the Nazis grew closer. The declaration stated that liberated peoples should be free 'to create democratic institutions of their own choice' (Churchill *et al.* 1945). This was taken to mean popular sovereignty, not democratic government, directly referencing the conservative Atlantic Charter: 'the right of all people to choose the form of government under which they will live' (Churchill *et al.* 1945). While the declaration pledged to assist liberated and former Axis states with 'the earliest pos-sible establishment through free elections of Governments responsive to the will of the people' (Churchill *et al.* 1945), the Soviets ensured that the language of the declaration was sufficiently vague that it need not entail liberal democratic government. Stalin was clear in his demand for a sphere of influence in the East, which was already being established as the Red Army moved across eastern Europe towards Berlin. Likewise at the Potsdam conference in July–August 1945, democracy was iden-tified as being a central part of post-war plans for Germany, with the aim being 'to prepare for the eventual reconstruction of German political life on a democratic basis and for eventual peaceful cooperation in international life by Germany', and with the end of war with Japan in sight they sought 'the revival and strengthening of democratic tendencies among the Japanese people' (Three Heads of Government 1945).

Ultimately this was not a war *for* democracy, but one *against* fascism. This was reflected in the grand alliance between the democratic powers and the Soviet Union, which together stood opposed to fascism and the German attempt to radically reorder Europe on the basis of racial hierarchy. The Nazi vision for Europe 'promised life to the Germans, an uncertain and precarious existence to most Europeans and extermination to the Jews' (Mazower 1998). What Japan offered Asia was little better. Certain human rights, and the need for greater economic and social equality, emerged as important themes that the United Nations claimed to be defending, but it was difficult to square these with the realities of an American democracy that remained racially segregated, European powers that were unwilling to abandon their empires, and the totalitarian nature of Stalin's USSR. The moral rectitude of the Allied cause was further sullied by doing little to try to stop the 'final solution', the pitiless wartime policies of Stalin and the extreme brutality of the conflict in the Pacific, which ended with the use of nuclear weapons against Japan. The victory of the Allied powers may have laid the foundation for the development of a liberal international order that would advance democracy and human rights, but the immediate virtue of their cause lay in the much worse fate they prevented.

Allied forces moved across Italy and Germany in April 1945. Mussolini was killed on 28 April, Hitler committed suicide on 30 April, and Germany surrendered unconditionally on 8 May 1945, bringing the war in Europe to a close. The conflict in the Pacific would continue until August. Following the Soviet declaration of war against Japan and the dropping of atomic bombs on Hiroshima and Nagasaki, the Second World War finally came to an end with the Japanese formally surrendering on 2 September 1945. This concluded a conflict that caused death and destruction on a scale the world had never witnessed, with an estimated 50–80 million deaths. Europe lay in ruins, the status of its empires was unclear following Japan's rampage through Asia, and the international order constructed at Versailles had been thoroughly destroyed. The Axis powers were decisively beaten, and with that defeat, Europe's terrible experiment with fascism reached an end. The

United States and the Soviet Union, embodying the opposed ideologies of democracy and communism, emerged from the fighting as the most powerful countries still standing.

The final outcome of the Second World War was not determined by any special properties of the United States or its democratic allies, but by the force of numbers on their side and the self-destructiveness of the fascists. As Michael Mann notes, 'fascism's enemies did not win because they were more virtuous, or because civilization inevitably defeats barbarism, but because there were more of them, and they were better armed' (Mann 2012a: 345). Germany and Japan were medium-sized countries with limited resources, which meant they simply did not have the same margin for error or capacity to mobilise as the countries aligned against them (Gat 2009: 4–8). And the hierarchical, exclusionary nationalist worldview of the fascists greatly restricted the possibility for forging the alliances that would have been necessary to overcome this material imbalance. It is also necessary to emphasise that the defeat of fascism was made possible through the massive sacrifices of the Soviets, who bore the heaviest losses in the conflict. Communism ensured fascism's defeat and democracy's survival. Now contestation would continue between these two remaining ideologies.

## THE 'LONG WAR' CONTINUES

The optimism that defined the periods after the end of the First World War and the Cold War stands in stark contrast to the sombre tone that followed the Second World War. The immense scale of death and destruction, the brutality of the fighting on all sides, the horrific reality of the Nazis' 'final solution', and the increasing ideological tension between the erstwhile democratic and communist allies, meant that this was hardly a time for celebrating victory. Rather, as Hannah Arendt wrote in 1950,

> two world wars in one generation, separated by an uninterrupted chain of local wars and revolutions, followed by no peace treaty for the vanquished and no respite for the victor, have ended in the anticipation of a third World War between the two remaining world powers. This moment of anticipation is like the calm that settles after all hopes have died. (Arendt 1973: vii)

There was a keen awareness of how close civilisation had come to complete collapse and in democracy's complicity in this. The challenge was twofold: to build an international order more durable than the shaky structure assembled at Versailles, and to find a way of strengthening democratic government so that it could manage the massive political, economic and social dislocation caused by the war. Utopian dreams had been replaced by a chastened worldview, deeply aware of the failings of the previous decades and the danger posed by the standoff between the democratic and communist powers.

Democracy had barely survived two world wars; there was limited faith it could survive a third. In comparison to assumptions about popular rule being a natural condition that flourishes simply through the removal of restraints and the protection of negative liberties, there was a strong appreciation of the constructedness of democracy. The recognition of the central role economic and social problems had played in the decline of interwar democracy, combined with the onset of the Cold War and renewed fears of communism, provided strong impetus to reform and strengthen democratic government.

The lesson taken from Great Depression was the need to revise the relationship between the political and economic spheres. Sheri Berman explains that after the war

> people began to perceive states as the guardian of society, and economic imperatives were often forced to take a back seat to social ones. The result was the reconciliation of things long viewed as incompatible: a well-functioning capitalist system, democracy, and social stability. (Berman 2006: 17)

This manifested itself in the development of the social welfare state, with governments playing a much more active role in limiting the destructive tendencies of capitalism and providing basic socio-economic goods for their citizens. The success of these innovations ensured that democracy survived and subsequently thrived.

There was a similar awareness that the mistakes of the interwar years could not be repeated when it came to rebuilding international society. In his stinging rebuke of liberal internationalism, E. H. Carr powerfully argued that 'the utopia of 1919 was hollow and without substance', as it had mistakenly believed that 'the unruly flow of international politics could be canalized into a set of logically impregnable abstract formulae inspired by the doctrines of nineteenth-century liberal democracy' (Carr 2001: 31, 207). Carr overstated his case: the failure of the Versailles settlement was not simply a result of misguided utopianism; it also reflected the intractability of the political, economic and social problems that the First World War had let loose. In comparison, the conditions in 1945 were more amenable to compromise and developing a stable order (Clark 2005: 149–50). Reflecting this, liberal ideas were not completely abandoned, but refashioned, qualified and updated. A new international organisation was built out of the failed League of Nations, the principles of popular sovereignty and non-intervention were reaffirmed, while the development of 'embedded liberalism' reflected an awareness of the need to alter the relationship between the political and economic spheres, based on the belief that 'multilateralism and the quest for domestic stability were coupled and even conditioned by one another' (Ruggie 1982: 398).

The ideological tensions between the democratic and communist countries meant the international society founded would be strongly pluralist, built more on common purpose than shared values. In this regard, G. John Ikenberry has argued that there were essentially two international orders that developed. One was a global settlement based on the balance of power between East and West, and 'the other was aimed at creating an open, stable, and managed order among the Western democracies' (Ikenberry 2011: 139). Within this context, the relevance of democratic government to the post-war settlement was strongly tempered by the realities of the emerging bipolar system. As Tony Smith explains, 'America's most basic political demand for the postwar world was that it be composed of independent (that is self-governing or self-determining) states; that these governments should be democratic was an important, but second-order, concern' (T. Smith 1994: 118). While there was little space for advancing democratic government within the wider global settlement, in the West a more solidarist order developed in which democracy would play an important role. This was a more complex vision that went beyond simply equating democratic government with peaceful behaviour. Rather, this Western settlement 'sought to calibrate the requirements of international order with the domestic political and socio-economic arrangements deemed necessary to support it' (Clark 2005: 131). In this regard, the Marshall Plan and specifically the democratisation of Germany and Japan offered sustained examples of the extent to which the American-led Western order was concerned with democratic stability among its members. It was based on the recognition that the source of the conflict had been the domestic makeup of the Axis powers, and thus 'international order depended on the ability of national political orders to produce democracy' (Rasmussen 2003: 91).

At the heart of the new international order founded was the United Nations, the successor to the discredited League of Nations. Democracy was noticeably absent from its foundational treaty, the UN Charter. In this regard, Edward Newman and Roland Rich offer the reminder that despite the UN's recent 'penchant for democracy', 'it is not one of the stated purposes of the United Nations to foster democracy, to initiate the process of democratization, or to legitimize other actors' efforts in this field' (Newman and Rich 2004: 5). This absence can be partly explained by increasing ideological tensions; it was largely under Soviet pressure that democracy was not mentioned in any of the founding documents (Archibugi 1995: 245). The Soviets were hardly alone on this point, however. The drafters of the UN Charter envisaged an organisation with universal membership, thereby overcoming one of the most serious flaws of the League, which had suffered from key states not participating. Ensuring universality meant avoiding stringent membership criteria. There was little support for France's proposal that states should demonstrate their peace-loving nature through the nature of their domestic constitutions, or Chile's suggestion that members should 'love the democratic system'. The British proposal was instead adopted, which became Article 4(1) of the UN Charter, and determined that membership would be open to all 'peace-loving states' (United Nations 1945). This allowed for 'maximum flexibility' while still establishing 'some, however superfluous, conditions for membership' (Haack 2011: 42).

The UN Charter may not have made reference to democracy, but it did notably commence with the phrase 'we the peoples of the United Nations'. This was inserted at the insistence of the United States, who consciously sought for it to echo their own constitution and meant it to convey popular sovereignty (Haack 2011: 43). This built on the minimalist understanding of popular sovereignty as self-determination that had been instituted at Versailles. Article 1(2) clearly identified that one of the core purposes of the new organisation was 'to develop friendly relations among nations based on respect for the principle of equal rights and self-determination of peoples'(United Nations 1945). The UN Charter reinforced the much more limited conception of self-determination that had developed during the First World War. Self-determination came to essentially mean little more than independence or external sovereignty, with its stronger connections to popular power lost. Through this process, it 'moved further away from its original philosophical meaning and became a concrete legal concept applicable in a specific context' (Haack 2011: 49). The UN Charter enshrined the principles of sovereign equality and non-intervention as the foundations of a pluralist international society, Article 2(1) establishing the organisation as 'based on the principle of the sovereign equality of all of its members' (United Nations 1945). What this meant was conveyed in Article 2(4) – 'all Members shall refrain in their international relations from the threat or use of force against the territorial integrity or political independence of any state' – and Article 2(7), which pledged that 'nothing contained in the present Charter shall authorize the United Nations to intervene in matters which are essentially within the domestic jurisdiction of any state' (United Nations 1945). This effectively confirmed the break that had occurred between democracy as *forma imperii*, popular sovereignty, and *forma regiminis*, democratic government. Popular sovereignty understood as self-determination entailed non-intervention, with separate peoples having the sole right to determine what form of government they would live under, democratic or otherwise. While there was now a hegemonic understanding of sovereignty (*forma imperii*), contestation would continue over which was the best form of domestic constitution (*forma regiminis*).

Democracy would play an important role in the ideological contest between East and West. The political potency of the concept meant that both sides tried to lay claim to it. Writing at the time, Ithiel de Sola Pool observed: 'Now, when there is a world-wide two-party struggle going on, it is clearly impossible for either party to yield the highly valued symbol of "democracy" to the other' (UNESCO 1951: 330). In this regard, the communists were unwilling to cede control of this important concept and contested democracy being associated exclusively with the West. In 1947 Stalin talked proudly of building a 'new, Soviet democracy, which rejects all, direct or indirect, inequality of citizens, sexes, races and nations, and ensures the right to work and the right to equal pay for equal work' (Stalin 1947). In the same year, Andrei Zhdanov, chairman of the Soviet of the Union, described the emerging Cold War in the following terms:

> The international arena [is split] into two major camps: the imperialist and anti-democratic camp, on the one hand, and the anti-imperialist and democratic camp, on the other. The principal driving force of the imperialist camp is the USA. Allied with it are Great Britain and France … The second camp is based on the USSR and the new democracies. (Quoted in Graebner 1963: x–xi)

The USSR presented its regime as a 'people's democracy' against the liberal-democratic model championed by the United States and its allies. The Soviet version represented the 'highest' or 'perfect' type of democracy, while its satellites in eastern Europe were 'democracy of a special type' that were transitioning towards the people's democracy of the USSR (Guins 1950). In this regard, N. S. Timasheff would observe that 'among the weapons used by the foe there is perhaps none more irritating to the Americans than the assertion that the Soviets enjoy real democracy while American democracy is but a ridiculous fake' (Timasheff 1950: 506). Yet for some it was more than simply an annoyance. Hans Kelsen, the influential jurist, warned that 'a more dangerous adversary than fascism and national socialism is Soviet communism, which is fighting the democratic idea under the disguise of a democratic terminology' (Kelsen 1955: 1–5).

Certainly Soviet claims to the mantle of democracy may have been a source of frustration or concern, but they were not without substance. In this regard, C. B. Macpherson suggested that both sides had legitimate claims based on democracy understood as a popular sovereignty, in which the indirect consent of the people gave the state a popular basis (Macpherson 1966). Bernard Crick agreed:

> How often has one heard: 'Well, at least the Communists claim to be democratic'? But the real trouble is, of course, that they do not pretend to be democratic. They are democratic. They are democratic in the sound historical sense of a majority actively willing to be ruled in some other way. (Crick 1964: 56)

Furthermore, as noted in previous chapters, historically democracy had been much more closely associated with socialism and communism. Reflecting this heritage, Lenin and the Soviets explicitly drew upon the language of democracy and self-determination during the Russian Revolution. Echoing his predecessor, Stalin did not reject democracy, but made a clear distinction between 'capitalist democracy, the democracy of the exploiting minority, based on the restriction of the rights of the exploited majority and directed against this majority' and 'proletarian democracy, the democracy of the exploited majority, based on the restriction of the rights of the exploiting minority and directed against this minority' (Stalin 1953: ch. 4). Whereas the Western understanding of democracy was primarily based on the political sphere, the Soviet interpretation emphasised control of the economic realm for determining the possibility of 'true' democracy. Timasheff explained this logic: 'In communist society, economic power belongs to the people; ergo, political power belongs to the people; ergo, a communist society is democratic by its very nature' (Timasheff 1950: 509).

Conceptual contestation over democracy was one facet of the more fundamental division between East and West that defined international relations after the Second World War. While this bipolar contest continued, principles of international legitimacy were minimalist, with an emphasis on sovereign independence and equality (Reus-Smit 2005b). This was reinforced through decolonisation, which globalised the understanding of self-determination that had emerged at Versailles. The Declaration on the Granting of Independence to Colonial Countries and Peoples, adopted by the UN General Assembly in December 1960, announced that 'all peoples have the right to self-determination; by virtue of that right they freely determine their political status' and reaffirmed the pluralist principles of 'equality, non-interference in the internal affairs of all States, and respect for the sovereign rights of all peoples' (United Nations 1960). While decolonisation was a significant development for the advancement of popular sovereignty, its immediate impact on the spread of democratic government was much less salutary. As Samuel Huntington notes, 'the decolonization of Africa led to the largest multiplication of independent authoritarian governments in history' (Huntington 1993: 21). This provided clear empirical proof that Woodrow Wilson's assumption that the expansion of popular sovereignty would lead to an expansion of democratic government was mistaken.

Cold War tensions, combined with decolonised states reacting to years of European interference, ensured that international legitimacy was defined in terms of the external characteristics of states, rather than their internal makeup. In sum, 'it is possible to see the period 1945–1989 as one marked by a rejection of standards of civilisation, culture and democracy as criteria for membership of the international community' (Simpson 2004: 272). While this observation is accurate on a global scale, during this same timeframe democratic government was confirmed as a defining characteristic of the Western order. Attempts by the Eastern bloc to present their regimes as 'true' democracies appeared increasingly strained and implausible. This meant that when the Cold War came to an end, the 'American-led open-democratic political order … was extended to the larger global system' (Ikenberry 2011: 161). The model of democracy that had developed in the West would emerge as the international standard.

## THE POST-COLD WAR WORLD

With the fall of the Berlin Wall on 9 November 1989 the 'long war' finally came to an end. The great communist experiment disintegrated under the weight of its internal contradictions, which had been amplified by the increasingly evident gap in living standards with the democratic West. The ideological contestation that had defined so much of the twentieth century had reached a conclusion, replaced by a remarkable consensus around liberal democracy. President George H. W. Bush confidently announced the change taking place: 'The eclipse of communism is only one half of the story of our time. The other is the ascendency of the democratic idea' (G. H. W. Bush 2009: 53). The academic version of this argument was presented most forcefully by Francis Fukuyama:

> What we may be witnessing is not just the end of the Cold War, or the passing of a particular period of postwar history, but the end of history as such: that is, the end point of mankind's ideological evolution and the universalization of Western liberal democracy as the final form of human government. (Fukuyama 1989: 3)

His confidence may have been excessive, but it was representative of the widespread optimism at the time. With communism following fascism into the dustbin of history, the ideational conflict that had defined much of the twentieth century was over. The answer to how states should govern themselves had seemingly been answered.

Only weeks after the fall of the Berlin Wall, Bush and Mikhail Gorbachev would meet in Malta and declare an end to the Cold War.

The Soviet leader made it clear that the USSR would now allow the countries of eastern Europe to freely decide by themselves what political system to adopt, and he openly recognised that they were moving in a democratic direction. Gorbachev effectively raised the ideological white flag, stating that it was right to let the 'people decide for themselves which God, figuratively speaking, to worship' (Archive of the Gorbachev Foundation 1989: 32). Yet he strongly cautioned against presenting these dramatic changes as the victory of 'Western values'. In the ensuing discussion the US secretary of state, James Baker, identified self-determination and free elections as 'Western values', leading his Russian counterpart to respond: 'Why are democracy, openness, [the free] market "Western values?"' Bush answered by suggesting that 'today it is really much clearer than it was, say, 20 years ago that we share these values with you'. Both sides concurred that the phrase 'Western values' would risk reigniting ideological confrontation and instead agreed that it was more appropriate to describe the political changes taking place as being based on shared 'democratic values' (Archive of the Gorbachev Foundation 1989: 30–3). The sharp ideological differences that had once separated the former adversaries melted away, with consensus around democracy as the political model people sought.

Democracy was a central component of the 'new world order' that was emerging from the ruins of the Cold War. In June 1990 the Conference on Security and Co-operation in Europe's 'Copenhagen Document', described by Thomas Buergenthal as 'a democratic manifesto' (Buergenthal 1990), announced that 'the development of societies based on pluralistic democracy and the rule of law' is a prerequisite 'for progress in setting up the lasting order of peace, security, justice and co-operation' (OSCE 1990b: 2). This laid the foundations for the CSCE summit held in Paris in November 1990. Philip Bobbitt and Ian Clark identify this meeting as a pivotal moment, effectively establishing legitimacy principles for the post-Cold War international order (Bobbitt 2002; Clark 2005). Democracy was at the heart of the Charter of Paris for a New Europe, which sought to confirm a 'new era of democracy, peace and unity'. The signatories declared that they would seek to 'build and strengthen democracy as the only system of government of our nations' (OSCE 1990a: 3). Democracy was understood in a very specific manner, with the charter providing the following definition: 'democracy, with its representative and pluralist character, entails accountability to the electorate, the obligation of public authorities to comply with the law and justice administered impartially' (OSCE 1990a: 3). Here the emphasis was on democracy as *forma regiminis*, explicitly identifying a certain form of domestic constitution – the Western liberal democratic model – as a marker of legitimate statehood.

The extensive legitimacy principles of the Paris charter were in stark contrast to the pluralist ethos of the original UN Charter, which strongly emphasised sovereign independence and non-intervention. The post-1945 international order confirmed popular sovereignty in the form of self-determination meaning external independence, but it was consciously agnostic about domestic constitutions. It could not have been otherwise during the ideological standoff between East and West. Now that the Cold War was over, legitimacy principles were extended to domestic regime type, with democracy become the defining feature of 'what a state should look like and how it should act' (Paris 2002: 654). Put simply, after 1989 the ballot box became the symbol of legitimate statehood. According to Clark, 'the evidence for the promulgation of a more pronounced set of domestic legitimacy tests since the end of the cold war is overwhelming', and these tests are primarily 'couched in terms of conformity to democratic standards of good governance' (Clark 2005: 174). A particularly clear example of this is arguments proposed by Thomas Franck and other jurists that a 'right' to democracy was 'becoming a requirement of international law, applicable to all and implemented through global standards, with the help of regional and international organizations' (Franck 1992). The idea that sovereignty may be conditional based on whether the state is democratic or not represents a significant break with the UN Charter and the pluralist order it instituted.

A key assumption shaping the development of post-Cold War legitimacy principles is that the domestic constitution of states plays a fundamental role in determining their international behaviour. Specifically, whether they are democratic is considered of great relevance to international society due to the increasingly widespread belief that there is a 'symbiotic linkage among democracy, human rights and peace' and that democracy contributes to the advancement of the international community's 'most important norm: the right to peace' (Franck 1992). This thinking could be found in *An Agenda for Peace*, an influential report written by then UN secretary general Boutros Boutros-Ghali: 'There is an obvious connection between democratic practices … and the achievement of true peace and security in any new and stable political order' (Boutros-Ghali 1992: 16). In the 1994 State of the Union address, President Bill Clinton proposed that 'the best strategy to ensure our security and to build a durable peace is to support the advance of democracy elsewhere. Democracies don't attack each other' (Clinton 1994). Underwriting such claims was a growing wave of liberal theorising inspired by Immanuel Kant's *Perpetual Peace* that identified the extension of liberal democracy as the key to creating a more progressive and peaceful international order. Piki Ish-Shalom observes that 'democracy as a cure for international violence was not an exclusive American belief … It swept the democratized world in a process that was initiated in the early 1990s' (Ish-Shalom 2013: 83). This scholarship was made by, and for, the liberal *zeitgeist*, reinforcing the belief that democratic states are 'different' and 'better'. And regardless of the validity of these claims, a distilled and simplified version of the thesis became a social fact: many political actors in the United States, and the West more generally, came to talk of democratic peace as if it exists. Adopting this perspective suggests that domestic regime type is of concern for international society as a whole, in that whether states are democratic or not may influence the likelihood of peace and cooperation.

The flipside to the emphasis on democratic government as a standard of legitimacy has been the increasing identification of non-democracies as a threat. Non-democracies have become both behaviourally and ontologically threatening, in so far as what these states are (not democratic) is seen as the source of their problematic behaviour. Thus, democratic India acquiring nuclear weapons has been grudgingly accepted, whereas the risk of Saddam Hussein developing WMD was sufficient to justify war. Indeed, it is hardly a coincidence that the 'rogue state' classification has emerged in the post-Cold War order, as it reflects the emergence of more extensive legitimacy principles based on domestic regime type. A 'sin' that has united rogue and pariah states is their undemocratic nature (Geldenhuys 2004: 31–3). Such thinking could be seen with great clarity in the 2002 State of the Union address by President George W. Bush, where a common feature shared by the 'axis of evil' was their non-democratic status (G. W. Bush 2002b). In the post-Cold War order 'democracy' and 'rogue regime' effectively operate as asymmetrical counter-concepts, with the laudable traits of the former mirrored by the problematic nature of the latter. Democracy has taken on the conceptual characteristics of 'civilisation', associated with notions of progress, development, modernisation and a host of other desirable features, whereas 'rogue regimes' are presented as dangerous, unstable, backward and violent. Reflecting the asymmetrical nature of this opposition, the features that mark democracies as different and more legitimate also can also justify intervention against non-democratic others (Geis 2013). This increasing push towards a far greater level of socio-political uniformity among states marked 'the reinvention of a restrictive international society', with democratic government coming to play a central role in defining standards of international legitimacy (Clark 2005; Clark 2009; C. Hobson 2008a).

This greater concern with the domestic makeup of states in post-Cold War international society has been further reflected in the rise of a much more expansive and assertive democracy promotion agenda. Underlying this shift is a belief in the superiority and greater legitimacy of democracy compared with other regime types. Democracy is seen to offer a host of domestic and international goods: it provides government that is more accountable and less corrupt; there is considerably less likelihood of genocide, extreme violence, famine or economic disaster; human rights and individual freedom are better protected (McFaul 2010: 34–7). Thus, democracy promotion is justified in both moral and instrumental terms, while qualms about the impact of such practices on state sovereignty have been largely discounted. With democracy promotion taken to be a 'norm' (McFaul 2004), states that oppose attempts by outsiders to influence the shape of domestic governance structures towards democracy are at best tolerated, but increasingly identified as delinquent. Indeed, that there is now frustration over a 'backlash' against democracy promotion – which essentially means resistance against the external interference in the domestic affairs of a state – is illustrative of how widespread and institutionalised these practices have become.

The terrorist attacks of 11 September 2001 reinforced and extended this concern with the domestic makeup of states. A consensus quickly emerged that the lack of democratic government in the Middle East was a root cause for the Islamic extremism that now threatened the United States and its allies (C. Hobson 2005). The promotion of democracy came to be seen as a strategic necessity, with liberal arguments being extended to suggest that democratic states are unlikely to breed terrorists or spread WMD. The expansion of democracy to the

Middle East emerged at the heart of the Bush doctrine and the 'War on Terror', with the 2002 National Security Strategy announcing the intention of the United States to 'create a balance of power that favors human freedom' and that it 'will defend the peace by fighting terrorists and tyrants' (G. W. Bush 2002a: i). The Bush doctrine revised and extended the Wilsonian tradition by 'making democracy the guarantee of a country's good conduct in world affairs, promising peace as a result of regime change, and linking American security internationally to these developments abroad' (T. Smith 2007). This thinking was most explicitly put into action with the coercive democratisation of Iraq, with the hope that it would trigger a new wave of democratisation across the Middle East. From this perspective, the spread of democracy was desired for defensive, as well as more progressive, reasons.

If the Bush doctrine represented one logical extreme of a concern with the domestic makeup of states, its overwhelming failure has been an important factor in the lessening emphasis on democracy in international society in recent years. The optimism of the 1990s following the 'victory' of the West, followed by the increasing pessimism of the 2000s as a result of America's self-destructive policies, illustrates the extent to which the trajectory of democracy has been shaped – for better or worse – by the United States. While liberals tended to downplay the importance of US power in underwriting the centrality of democracy to the post-Cold War order, this element is now becoming more apparent as the unipolar moment comes to an end. In this regard, Robert Kagan has recently argued that democracy's fortunes have been closely tied to geopolitics: 'It should be clear that the prospects for democracy have been much better under the protection of a liberal world order, supported and defended by a democratic superpower or by a collection of democratic great powers' (Kagan 2015: 30).

The full consequences of China's remarkable economic development still remain to be seen, but it may entail a shift back towards a more pluralist international order. China has consistently supported strict understandings of state sovereignty and non-intervention, and this is unlikely to change soon. Furthermore, the shift from a unipolar to a bipolar or multipolar balance of power could have an ideational component. Attending China's ascent has been mounting interest in its politico-economic form, which mixes a liberalised economy with a closed political system that allows for no meaningful political opposition to the ruling Communist Party of China. Committed liberals remain deeply sceptical about the sustainability of combining economic liberalisation with political closure (Deudney and Ikenberry 2009; Diamond 2014), but there is potential that China may have discovered a more stable balance. Regardless, the remarkable economic development of China is having important demonstration effects. This model of authoritarian capitalism it embodies presents itself as 'an alternate route to modern development: growth without democracy and progress without freedom' (Ignatieff 2014). The successes of China's authoritarian capitalist model, when combined with the problems associated with democracy following America's failed 'freedom agenda' and the 2008 financial crisis, collectively suggest that the overriding concern with domestic regime type in post-Cold War international society will be increasingly diluted.

Given that the considerable expansion of democracy promotion practices in the 1990s was partly predicated on a material and ideational balance of power in favour of liberal democracy, it is unsurprising that this agenda has been increasingly contested as part of the global power realignment now underway. Notable challenges include Hungary under the present rule of prime minister Viktor Orbán, who has been moving his country away from liberal democracy. In 2014 he announced something 'considered to be a sacrilege in the liberal world order', namely 'that a democracy is not necessarily liberal' and that there are alternate political-economic routes to success, as countries like China and Singapore demonstrated (Orbán 2014). And as relations have worsened between Russia and the West, Vladimir Putin has gone from talking of 'sovereign democracy' to questioning whether the United States can call itself democratic given its complex electoral college system: 'The President can be elected by a minority of voters. Is this democracy? What is democracy? It is power of the people. Where is people's power here? There is none. Meanwhile, you are trying to convince us that we don't have it' (Putin 2014). Putin's attacks have been supported by members of his United Russia Party, who recently proposed that '"democracy and democratic values" have "become the justification for the most odious actions of the West against Russia" and consequently Russia must drop any reference to democracy' (Goble 2014). That democracy is increasingly being explicitly challenged, and in some cases repudiated, is certainly significant, but the fact that these incidents are exceptional indicates how strong democracy's ideational hegemony remains. The confidence and belief that surrounded democracy in the early 1990s might have faded, but it is still the most widely accepted form of rule in contemporary politics. There may, however, be a shift occurring back towards a more pluralist international society, with less emphasis placed on democratic government as a marker of state legitimacy.


## CONCLUSION

This chapter has charted the trajectory of democracy following the end of the First World War, when popular sovereignty supplanted monarchic right, and democratic government emerged as a legitimate constitutional form. Until this point the fates of popular sovereignty (*forma imperii*) and democracy as a form of domestic rule (*forma regiminis*) had been closely connected, but then they diverged. Popular sovereignty was embedded within international society, and contestation would revolve around different constitutional forms (*formae regiminis*): democracy, communism and fascism. In this regard, the 'long war' of the twentieth century between competing modern ideologies was a different and distinct stage in democracy's development, compared with the period from the American Revolution through to the end of the First World War, in which it had battled and ultimately succeeded the *ancien régime*.

Immediately following the Great War, there was remarkable confidence in democracy. Emblematic was James Bryce's assessment that there was a 'universal acceptance of democracy as the normal and natural form of government' (Bryce 1921a: 4). Yet in a short space of time democracy went from being widely lauded and praised to being dismissed as a weak, ineffectual thing of the past. Democracy reached its lowest ebb at the middle of the Second World War, when a mere handful of democratic states remained. Fascism was defeated only through the communist and democratic powers joining forces, with the monumental sacrifices of the Soviets playing a pivotal role in the war's outcome. With the common fascist enemy defeated, 'the long war now continued because it had not truly been ended' (Bobbitt 2002: 45). At the heart of the Cold War was a contest between rival political-economic forms. This was ultimately resolved with the fall of the Berlin Wall, marking an end to the communist experiment and the 'long war' that had shaped much of the twentieth century. The basic geopolitical realignment caused by the collapse of the Soviet Union gave added impetus to the third wave of democratisation that swept across the globe. Surveying these changes, Samuel Huntington was not exaggerating in concluding that 'this dramatic growth of democracy in such a short time is, without doubt, one of the most spectacular and important political changes in human history' (Huntington 1997: 4).

The 'unabashed victory of economic and political liberalism', as Francis Fukuyama described it at the time (Fukuyama 1989: 3), strongly shaped the way democracy was understood and embedded in post-Cold War international society. The result was a shift away from the pluralist post-1945 international order that emphasised sovereign equality and independence. Rather, legitimacy principles were extended to incorporate the domestic makeup of states. 'Rogue regimes' were identified as threatening not simply because of their behaviour, but because this was seen to stem from their non-democratic nature. Democracy, usually thought of as being demanded from 'below', was increasingly something demanded from 'above', as it came to be taken as a marker of state legitimacy. The remarkably strong emphasis on democratic government present in the immediate post-Cold War order now appears to be diluting, however, as the ideational and material balance of power shifts away from the United States. With the end of the liberal interregnum, it is an open question what role democracy will play in the international order that is now taking shape.

*Chapter 8*

# CONCLUSION: DEMOCRACY AND HUMILITY

## INTRODUCTION

We obstinately hold to the language of democratic and liberal
principles in order to preserve these principles – I believe that we
are sincere – but it seems to me also that we speak this language
in order to preserve the ideological shadow of our fraying
dominance.

Pierre Manent (2014: 140–1)

The start – and end – for this study is the somewhat contradictory
position democracy finds itself in early in the twenty-first century. A
quarter-century after the collapse of communism, which signalled the
end of the 'long war', democracy still remains without peer. Yet the rise
of China, combined with Russia's bullish behaviour and the problems
of established democracies following the 2008 financial crisis, all point
towards the weakening of the West's ideational hegemony. If indeed
the post-Cold War era is coming to an end, as some have suggested
(Haas 2014), one sign of this might be democracy increasingly playing
a less central role as a marker of state legitimacy. The latest Freedom
House report ominously warns that 'acceptance of democracy as
the world's dominant form of government – and of an international
system built on democratic ideals – is under greater threat than at any
point in the last 25 years' (Freedom House 2015: 1). The liberal interregnum following the end of the Cold War may have come to an end,
and the geopolitical environment has certainly become less hospitable
for democracy, but this in itself does not portend crisis. On this point,
Philippe Schmitter cautions against inflated claims about democracy's
decline, suggesting that 'there is simply no plausible alternative in

204

sight, save for a few models (for example, Chinese meritocracy, Russian neo-Czarism, Arab monarchy, or Islamic theocracy) that are unlikely to appeal far beyond their borders' (Schmitter 2015: 32). Democracy's standing in the international order has undoubtedly weakened, but it still remains without a clear rival or alternative.

The greater danger to democracy might instead be one of default dominance slowly leading to death by a thousand cuts. One does not need to look very hard to identify serious political, economic and social problems that democracies, new and old, are struggling with. Reflecting on these trends, *The Economist* recently published an essay entitled 'What's gone wrong with democracy' (note the lack of question mark) (Economist 2014b). Another clear example of this change of mood is the shift in Francis Fukuyama's thinking: instead of celebrating the 'end of history', his latest work is focusing on political decay with a keen eye on the increasingly dysfunctional democracy of the United States (Fukuyama 2014b). From this perspective, democracy is less likely to suffer from a sudden implosion, but remains at risk of being steadily eroded and hollowed out, until one day what is left bears little resemblance to what we once understood 'democracy' to mean. In this regard, Thomas Meaney and Yascha Mounk warn that 'the death of "democracy" will not be announced', as politicians 'will invoke the aura of democracy long after whatever substance it once contained has been lost' (Meaney and Mounk 2014).

In this somewhat uncertain context, one of the assumptions underlying this book has been that gaining a more nuanced understanding of democracy's historical development is necessary to better comprehend its current standing and future trajectory. Rather than summarise the preceding study, this final chapter will instead build on it to offer a normative defence of democracy. Before doing so, it is valuable to highlight four important conclusions that have emerged, which all indicate notable limitations or qualifications to democracy's current ascendance. First, much of the conceptual and institutional architecture of contemporary democracy developed primarily in reaction to the *ancien régime*. Modern democracy was forged in response to a different set of political and social dilemmas to the ones we face today (Ankersmit 2002; Manin 1996; Urbinati 2006). As such, it is hardly surprising that a regime constructed from the late eighteenth to the mid-twentieth century is now struggling to deal with the complex realities of globalisation.

Second, democracy is a much more recent and contingent

achievement than we might care to remember. The outcomes of both world wars were far from preordained, and with less fortune, the twentieth century could have been one that reaffirmed the longstanding criticisms of democracy as a dangerous, unstable and weak form of rule (Gat 2009: 7). It was only after the Second World War that stable democracies were finally established across continental Europe, and it was not until the 1960s that full civil rights were granted to all citizens in the United States and Australia. As Jeffrey Isaac reminds us,

> it is a sobering thought that mature, functioning Western liberal democracy is of fairly recent vintage.... It is not so long ago that Europe lay in shambles, and the world was reeling from the experience of world war, Holocaust and totalitarian ascendancy. (Isaac 1998: 22–3)

Third, popular sovereignty and democracy developed in tandem with, and reinforced, the anarchical nature of international politics. Some of the revolutionaries who advocated popular doctrines sought to transcend a world of separate sovereign states, but ultimately the opposite happened, as the corollary of democratic self-determination has been state sovereignty and non-intervention. This was observed by Hans Morgenthau, who described it as a 'tragic contradiction of Shakespearean dimensions', in so far as the triumph of democracy 'strengthened immensely the sovereignty of the state and with it the anarchical tendencies in international society' (Morgenthau 1947: 63). This suggests that contemporary democracy is much more closely intertwined with the international realm than is sometimes appreciated.

Fourth, there has been a longstanding tension between, on the one hand, principles of sovereign equality grounded in self-determination, and on the other, standards of international legitimacy that tend to exert a homogenising influence. As Martin Wight remarks, there is a 'dislike for the variety and complexity of international society' (Wight 1972: 27), which means legitimacy principles gravitate toward certain forms of state. This has been reflected in the post-Cold War international order being one uniquely predisposed towards fostering democracy.

Collectively what these findings suggest is that democracy's fortunes are closely tied to its past, and that the international sphere has played a central role in shaping its development. In this sense, adopting a historically sensitive position encourages a more pluralist appreciation of contemporary democracy and its possibilities. This entails recognising both its empirical and its normative strengths, especially the manner in which it has offered a comparatively convincing answer to how different peoples should rule themselves in a world divided into separate states. While it may be fracturing and blurring, an anarchical society of states will most likely continue to survive for quite some time, in which case democracy – with all its flaws and limitations – remains very relevant. And by recognising that the agreement on democracy as something possible and desirable has been relatively brief historically, both humility and caution are promoted, in contrast to the overly optimistic and confident attitude that prevailed after 1989.

The account of democracy outlined here aims to chart a middle way between two unproductive extremes. On the one hand, excessive faith or overconfidence in democracy is unwarranted and potentially counterproductive. On the other hand, danger also lies in the increasing pessimism about democracy, as it risks misunderstanding the value and resilience of this form of rule. The approach taken here builds on Pierre Rosanvallon's observation that it 'is not simply a matter of saying democracy *has* a history. More radically, one must see that democracy *is* a history. It has been a work irreducibly involving exploration and experimentation, in its attempt to understand and elaborate itself' (Rosanvallon 2006: 38; original emphasis). Recognising this can, in turn, facilitate agency by helping to make actors more cognisant that the current order, and democracy's present place within it, is neither natural nor inevitable, but one that has been constructed over time. And as Friedrich Kratochwil explains, 'precisely because we know that things could have been different, the more we deepen our understanding of the past, we begin to sense the opportunities forgone and thereby become aware of our own potential as agents' (Kratochwil 2006: 8). This encourages an awareness of the possibility for challenging and changing existing power relationships and societal structures, which can have significant democratic consequences (Keane 2009: 875–80). In this regard, returning to democracy's past is a way of demystifying it, a way of avoiding simplistic platitudes about its virtues or shallow scepticism bred by its shortcomings. This process generates a sense of humility founded in the incomplete and fragile nature of these achievements, and a recognition of democracy's simple merits that make it worth fighting for and defending.

## HUMBLE DEMOCRACY

Between the idea
And the reality
Between the motion
And the act
Falls the Shadow
  T. S. Eliot (1925)

The historical and contemporary achievements of democracy certainly reflect the strength and value of this form of rule, but there has also been a huge amount of luck and fortune involved. The failure of its great historical rivals – fascism and communism – should not be equated with democracy's triumph. The end of the Cold War was closer to a technical knockout than a clear-cut victory, as communism ultimately collapsed under the weight of its internal contradictions. While the communist alternative lasted much longer, it has been suggested that fascism posed a greater challenge, in so far as it was able to develop a much more efficient and effective political-economic system (Gat 2009: 2–8; Mazower 1998: xiii). As Michael Mann observes, 'the simple explanation of fascism's demise is that Hitler killed it.... Without Hitler's Germany, fascism would have lasted much longer, and so would other European and Asian rightist despots' (Mann 2012a: 344–5). This is not to deny the considerable strengths of democracy, but simply to make the necessary point that there has been nothing inevitable or natural about its recent ascendance.

While recognising the failings of democracy's major ideological rivals and the historical contingency of its current positioning, it is important not to downplay the significant achievements of modern democracy. To date, democracy has offered the best answer to the question of how people should rule themselves. Combining pragmatic and principled reasons, Robert Dahl, one of the most influential democratic theorists of the twentieth century, summarises ten major desirable consequences of this form of rule: '(1) avoiding tyranny; (2) essential rights; (3) general freedom; (4) self-determination; (5) moral autonomy; (6) human development; (7) protecting essential personal interests; (8) political equality; (9) peace-seeking; (10) prosperity' (Dahl 1998: 45). Certainly the extent to which really existing democracies provide these values differs drastically (Fukuyama 2014b; Fukuyama 2015). Nonetheless, on the whole, democracy has provided a greater degree of freedom, equality, accountability and prosperity than its historical alternatives. In this regard, Mann completes his four-volume *magnum opus* by observing that ultimately democracy is 'validated by its intrinsic political merits, for it creates more freedom, considerably more than state socialism or fascism', which 'were born in wars and … always bore the marks of violence' (Mann 2012b: 418). A further feature that has distinguished democracy from its historical rivals has been its remarkable flexibility and ability for self-correction. This leads David Runciman to suggest that one of democracy's great virtues has been its ability to muddle its way through, slowly but surely finding solutions to the different crises it has faced (Runciman 2013; Fukuyama 2014b). Democracies may regularly fail to live up the lofty ideals they are meant to embody, but on the whole, this regime type has proven capable of providing key political goods that people value.

These empirical and normative strengths lead Larry Diamond to caution against concluding 'that the historical moment for democracy has passed' (Diamond 2014: 11). It is remarkable that he must even assert this: in a relatively short space of time unbounding optimism has been replaced by an increasingly widespread pessimism. Certainly this is partly a corrective to the exuberance of the late 1980s and early 1990s. As Steven Levitsky and Lucan Way rightly note, 'the global regime landscape looks darkened today because observers viewed the events of the initial post-Cold War period through rose-tinted glasses' (Levitsky and Way 2015: 48). Yet it also connects to the way democracy has been understood and studied. In this regard, Jeffrey Isaac identifies a further reason for this growing disillusionment:

> Much of the political science literature on democracy remains trapped in a discourse that is broadly positivistic and functionalist … Ironically, however, in its instrumentalism and its faith in the possibility of deploying political science to stabilize the instability of our political world by 'engineering' official responses to it, this literature tends to be rather overoptimistic, even naïve, about the possibility of … creating an orderly world of orderly liberal demo-cratic states. (Isaac 1998: 5)

Excessive confidence can, in turn, create the conditions for disappoint-ment and pessimism. This is arguably what can be witnessed now.

Certainly democracy has important features in theory, and often in practice, that give it value as a form of rule, and may recommend it over many other regime types. Yet these normative and empirical strengths can only partly account for democracy's rise and widespread acceptance. Its current position is as much – if not more – thanks to *fortuna* than any unique virtues it possesses. To take one important example: in making the First World War for democracy, President Wilson put all his chips in and luckily the gamble paid off. Had the United States and the Entente Powers lost the war – which remained a realistic possibility at the start of 1918 – democracy's role in the twentieth century would have likely looked drastically different. Likewise, by 1941 there were only a handful of democracies left in the world, as authoritarianism and totalitarianism appeared to represent the future. That democracy survived was due in large part to the remarkable resilience of the Soviets, which combined with the overwhelming material resources of the United States and the self-destructiveness of the Nazis to ensure the outcome of the Second World War. This leads Azar Gat to observe that

> a more context-sensitive understanding of the past ought to inspire ... a sense of awe, not only at the underlying trends of the historical drama, but also at its frailty and unfulfilled potentials, at the tremendous arbitrary forces and elements of chance that affect it. (Gat 2009: 181)

In this sense, returning to democracy's past allows an appreciation of the fragility and the unlikely nature of its rise. And being more attuned to this uneven, contested and fraught history can cultivate a sense of humility about democracy's current positioning and value.

Advocating humility is certainly meant as a corrective to the misplaced confidence, sometimes hubris, which has often prevailed when considering democracy in the post-Cold War world. It is more than this, however. It is a way of appreciating the resilience and value of democracy, while acknowledging how its fortunes have been shaped by the vicissitudes of history. Indeed, John Keane goes further in advocating the centrality of humility to democratic rule:

> Humility is the cardinal democratic virtue ... In a world of arrogance tinged with violence, humility emboldens. Unyielding, it gives individuals inner strength to act upon the world. It dislikes

hubris. It anticipates a more equal and tolerant – and less violent – world. (Keane 2009: 856)

What Keane is suggesting is that humility is a source not of weakness, but of strength. It represents a grounded awareness of the very real and significant achievements of democracy, while also acknowledging its failings and weaknesses. It is in this sense that Patrick Deneen reflects: 'Democracy is not an undertaking for the faint of heart: it calls for limitless reservoirs of hope against the retreat into easy optimism or the temptation to a kind of democratic cynicism or despair' (Deneen 2009: 12). This leads him to call for a form of 'democratic realism', which defends 'democracy not in the name of human potential for "perfectibility" but rather on opposite grounds, namely, based on fundamental and inescapable human imperfection, insufficiency, and frailty' (Deneen 2009: 191).

The most robust statement of the centrality of humility to democracy comes from the great theologian Reinhold Niebuhr in *The Children of Light and the Children of Darkness*, tellingly subtitled 'a vindication of democracy and a critique of its traditional defense'. Writing during the Second World War, the lowest ebb in democracy's modern history, Niebuhr offered a particularly compelling account of democracy. In the preface, he outlined a basic but powerful rationale for this form of rule: 'man's capacity for justice makes democracy possible; but man's inclination to injustice makes democracy necessary' (Niebuhr 2011: xxxii). In contrast to the rigidity of totalitarian doctrines, democracy must ultimately be supported by a spirit of toleration and openness. Niebuhr's understanding of this was grounded in his faith, and is worth quoting at length:

> Democracy therefore requires something more than a religious devotion to moral ideals. It requires religious humility. Every absolute devotion to relative political ends (and all political ends are relative) is a threat to communal peace.... Democratic life requires a spirit of tolerant cooperation between individuals and groups which can be achieved neither by moral cynics, who know no law beyond their own interest, nor by moral idealists, who acknowledge such a law but are unconscious of the corruption which insinuates itself into the statement of it by even the most disinterested idealists. (Niebuhr 2011: 151–2)

While humility is a virtue that has strong connections to Christian thought, I would differ with Niebuhr's belief that it must be grounded in religious faith. It is possible to extract his more general observation about the role humility plays in charting a path between the Scylla of excessive optimism and the Charybdis of corrosive pessimism.

It might seem inappropriate to be calling for humility at a time when democracy is facing a growing array of serious challenges, and doubts about it are voiced with increasing regularity and tenacity. Some might suggest that instead its virtues should be loudly extolled. While the achievements of democracy are significant and should not be easily discounted, the strength of democracy ultimately – albeit perhaps paradoxically – comes from what it lacks: its inevitable imperfectibility, its constant incompleteness. This reflects democracy's dual existence as a set of governing institutions and as an ideal, a vision of a society in which freedom and equality coexist. Put differently, democracy is both a means and an end, but it is an end that is never fully reached. In this regard, the leading democratisation scholar Guillermo O'Donnell reflects that 'what is best and most distinctive about democracy' is its 'intrinsic mix of hope and dissatisfaction, its highlighting of a lack that will never be filled' (O'Donnell 2007: 10–11). The gaps that define democracy – between the ideal and reality, the people and their representatives, power and accountability – will never be closed, but democracy is precisely about the ongoing attempts to reconcile these tensions and minimise such shortcomings.

In Jacques Derrida's words, democracy is 'always to come', it 'must have the structure of a promise' (Derrida 2005: 85–6). This thought can be traced back to Jean-Jacques Rousseau, who observed: 'If we take the term in the strict sense, there never has been a real democracy, and there never will be' (Rousseau 1923: ch. 6). Yet democracy is not for the gods, rather it is a thoroughly human method of rule. Appreciating the humanity of democracy – with all its inadequacies and contradictions – is necessary to better understand its strengths and weaknesses. The flaws and limitations of democracy accurately reflect the flaws and limitations of people, but they also reveal their vision and belief, both as individuals and as members of a collective. The lure of fascism and communism may have partly been in their promises of overcoming the frustrations and failings of democracy, but such plans for perfection cannot be squared with the flawed reality of humans. This is what democracy, in all its ugly beauty, represents and conveys.

Adam Michnik, the former Polish dissident, explains that democracy 'is a world of clashing viewpoints, fragmentary and conflicting interests where the overriding colour is grey. It's an endless search for compromise, eternal imperfection ... Democracy does not claim infallibility' (quoted in Demenet 2001: 48). Since re-emerging in the eighteenth century democracy has been founded on an idea that has been revolutionary but also reflects a simple truth of human existence: it is a form of rule that is created by people and for people. God, providence, monarchs or history do not give this community its ultimate meaning or justification; the people do that themselves.

## A DIFFERENT FORM OF DEMOCRACY SUPPORT

So what would adopting a humble approach to democracy actually entail, especially when understood in the context of international relations? For starters, it means actively engaging with its normative dimensions. On one level, this might seem like a rather obvious, even unnecessary, injunction. Yet the ideational dominance of democracy in the post-Cold War world has, in a strange way, actually resulted in a weakening of its normative defences. As Patrick Deneen avers, underpinning much contemporary work on democracy is an unacknowledged, transcendental belief in its value and virtue. He suggests that 'accompanying the ascendancy of democracy in the present age is an increasing inability to recognize, much less examine, presuppositions that undergird democratic faith precisely *because* it is rarely recognized as a form of faith' (Deneen 2009: 5–6; original emphasis). Given that democracy's hegemony is becoming more brittle, it is necessary to explicitly reconsider its value and restate why it should be defended. For, as Jeffrey Isaac notes, 'however much it remains an aspiration not yet achieved in many parts of the world, it also increasingly rings hollow as a repository of utopian impulses or as a meaningful vehicle of self-government' (Isaac 1998: 11). With that in mind, this section briefly sketches out a different form of democracy support.

Humility is necessary when viewing attempts at democratisation, appreciating what an incredibly difficult and fraught process political change unavoidably is. The frustration and impatience with the uneven and incomplete nature of the third wave of democratisation, as well as disappointment with the inconclusive direction of the Arab Spring, is based on a superficial reading of how democracy successfully developed elsewhere. As Samuel Huntington observes, each wave of democratisation has been followed by a reverse wave in which some countries revert to non-democratic rule (Huntington 1993: 13–26). Failed attempts at democratisation and the return of authoritarian regimes are hardly new phenomena, and should not be unexpected. Adopting a longer-term perspective, one more attuned to the vicissitudes of political change, is especially important for considering the Arab Spring. What is remarkable is that despite that movement being named in reference to Europe's 'springtime of the peoples', many seem to forget that the immediate consequences of the 1848 revolutions were thoroughly disappointing from the perspective of democracy. The revolutions, as we saw in Chapter 5, failed in the short term, but in the longer term they were a crucial step towards popular rule. For many of the countries involved, however, it was not until a century later – following two great wars – that stable democracies were finally established. In the case of Germany, it went through the failure of Weimar democracy and the horrible experiment with fascism before stable democratic government finally emerged.

Thus, when considering the uneven manner in which the Arab Spring has unfolded, it is important to recognise that these political transitions will almost certainly be slow, uncertain and not unidirectional. As Sheri Berman notes, those criticising the course of events in the region 'set absurdly high benchmarks for success, ones that lack any historical perspective', failing to appreciate that 'stable liberal democracy usually emerges only at the end of long, often violent struggles, with many twists, turns, false starts, and detours' (Berman 2013: 66). As noted, a distinguishing feature of the history of the eighteenth, nineteenth and twentieth centuries was the gradual, incomplete and frequently violent transitions towards popular rule. Given that it took the West hundreds of years – and considerable bloodletting – to successfully establish stable liberal democracies, it is unrealistic to expect these same processes to happen in a smooth and speedy manner elsewhere.

Appreciating the difficult, uneven nature of democratisation and the challenges involved with maintaining democracy is very relevant when thinking about democracy promotion. This was observed by Václav Havel, who noted 'the limited ability of today's democratic world to step beyond its own shadow'. In this regard, a defining feature of democracy promotion practice has been the unquestioned assumption that liberal democracy should be the end point of political change (C. Hobson and Kurki 2011). Havel further explained that

> as a consequence, democracy is seen less and less as an open system that is best able to respond to people's basic needs – that is, as a set of possibilities that continually must be sought, redefined, and brought into being. Instead, democracy is seen as something given, finished, and complete as is, something that can be exported like cars or television sets, something that the more enlightened purchase and the less enlightened do not. (Havel 1995: 7)

The fallacy of regarding democracy as simply a set of institutions that can be transferred and installed was especially evident in the failed attempts to bring it to Afghanistan and Iraq.

Reflecting the ideational strength of democracy since the end of the Cold War, democracy promotion has been premised on a belief in the superiority of liberal democracy, and that target states desire this form of government. In this regard, there is a danger of generalising from the 'velvet revolutions', which were defined by their 'anti-utopian, or at the very least non-utopian' nature (Garton Ash 2009). After half a century of collective experimentation with real-world communism, there was little appetite for further social engineering. There was widespread consensus over the desirability of the liberal democratic model of the West, which was associated with individual freedom and prosperity. As Ivan Krastev observes, following the Cold War 'the politics of "normalization" replaced deliberation with imitation' (Krastev 2010: 117). Yet the experience of the velvet revolutions is closer to the exception than the rule. One cannot assume that political change will naturally be directed towards liberal democracy. As Steven Levitsky and Lucan Way note, 'although the collapse of a dictatorship creates opportunities for democratization, there are no theoretical or empirical bases for assuming such an outcome. Yet that is exactly what many observers did in the 1990s' (Levitsky and Way 2015: 48–9). Furthermore, the strong performance of China, combined with the troubles the United States and Europe have been experiencing, means the ideological climate today is much less favourable to democracy compared with the early 1990s. On this point, Thomas Carothers recently stated:

Some Western aid practitioners ... seem startlingly unaware of just how damaged Western models have become in the eyes of others and how much democracy aid needs to be built on far more modest assumptions about the relative appeal of Western democracy. (Carothers 2015: 72)

In this sense, a more humble approach would be one that starts from the assumption that political change does not necessarily mean democratisation, but when it does occur, a desire for democracy does not necessarily mean a preference for the specific liberal democratic model found in the West.

Another notable feature of democracy promotion practice has been its remarkably undemocratic flavour: it has tended to proceed in a hierarchical, unidirectional manner. Adopting a more humble approach, one that views democracy as an ongoing process, suggests a more dialogic, two-way approach to democracy promotion, centred on mutual learning and exploration between the actors involved, as opposed to a hierarchical relationship between donor and recipient (C. Hobson and Kurki 2011). In this regard, there have been notable innovations that have emerged from democratising countries which established democracies could learn from. Madeline Albright famously described democracy promotion as not only 'the right thing to do. It is also the smart thing' (Albright 1998). This is representative of the typical liberal argument that promoting democracy is in the interests of the United States because it will lead to greater interstate peace, cooperation, protection of individual rights and so on. Yet these arguments – mistakenly grounded in an excessive confidence in American democracy – miss a much more fundamental way in which democracy promotion can serve US interests. A more open, dialogic approach would not only help the cause of democracy abroad, it could also help strengthen it at home. This could be especially relevant if US democracy is indeed in 'crisis' or 'decaying', as prominent commentators such as Fareed Zakaria and Francis Fukuyama have recently suggested (Fukuyama 2014b; Zakaria 2013). From this perspective, reshaping democracy promotion practices goes hand in hand with strengthening democracy at home.

Humility is also needed in the way we study democracy. This suggests a drastically different ethos from the one that has underpinned much liberal scholarship in the post-Cold War period. Flush with confidence in their finding that the 'absence of war between democracies

[is] as close as anything we have to an empirical law in international relations' (Levy 1988: 662), democratic peace proponents spent much of the 1990s pronouncing the relevance and importance of their conclusions for foreign policy. Yet as Anna Geis and Harald Müller point out, 'studies on the separate democratic peace abound and have been celebrated as a rare example of a progressive research programme in International Relations, whereas complementary research on the external use of force by democracies has remained comparatively scarce' (Geis and Müller 2013: 5–6). Not only was much less time spent on the darker side of democratic peace, little effort was expended on seriously considering what would happen to their ideas if taken up by political actors. And so when the Bush administration and the neo-conservatives adopted and politicised the core findings of democratic peace research, its proponents lacked the political and normative resources to challenge this politicisation (C. Hobson 2011; Ish-Shalom 2013). Certainly these scholars are not completely responsible for the way their probabilistic and cautious claims were transmogrified into a motivation and justification for US adventurism in the Middle East (C. Hobson *et al.* 2011). Nonetheless, given that these findings were reached by *political* scientists, they should have been much more cognisant of how their scholarship might be appropriated for other ends.

Treating the significance of democratic peace research findings with caution is warranted given that it represents a limited, incomplete and only partly explainable phenomenon. While appreciating the strong correlation that has existed between stable, liberal democracies and interstate peace since the Second World War, proponents have still failed to convincingly demonstrate that it is democracy which *causes* this outcome (Levy 2011; Rosato 2003). In pointing to a wide range of additional factors that have contributed to the increasing pacification of democracies, Azar Gat suggests that 'a far more complex causal process has been at work than a simple relationship between an independent variable, liberal democracy, and a dependent one, democratic peace' (Gat 2009: 111). Even if it is possible through using rigorous social scientific methods to separate these different factors and isolate democracy as the sole cause, it does not promise that the situation will continue in the future. In this regard, the methods adopted actually restrict exploring how democracy may undergo more complex changes than simply becoming more or less democratic according to the Polity scale.

These methodological choices mean that mainstream democratic peace scholarship may show a detailed awareness of how democracy's institutions operate, while lacking a deeper awareness of what gives democracy meaning and vitality in the first place. The resulting outcome is rather odd: this considerable body of work related to democracy actually has very little to say about its substance or ethical value. As Mikkel Vedby Rasmussen notes, 'though democratic peace theorists discuss endlessly the democratic nature of different societies (for example Wilhelmine Germany), they rarely discuss how democracy itself could be better and how making democracy better could make the world more cosmopolitan and more peaceful' (Rasmussen 2003: 185–6). Related to this point, while this scholarship is aware of threats to the zone of peace from outsiders, there is little consideration of internal threats that also exist.

An unsaid assumption underlying most scholarship is that while there might be some backsliding at the edges, the key states that constitute the democratic zone of peace will remain at peace and remain democratic. Not only does such a linear conception of history clash with democracy's much more uneven past, it fails to account for the possibility that democracy may disappear, be undermined or undergo great change. By avoiding normative and historical reflection, mainstream democratic peace scholarship lacks the resources to be able to properly assess such issues. This should both encourage a broadening of the research agenda and counsel caution in the claims being made: a humble appreciation not only of democracy, but also of our ability to understand it.


## CONCLUSION

The future of democracy and its flourishing will depend decisively
on our capacity to imagine a more capacious rather than
constricted view of its possibilities and also of its fragilities.
                                    Dilip Parameshwar Gaonkar (2007: 2)


Shortly after the First World War, another moment when democracy was in the ascent, James Bryce reflected on whether democracy represents the 'final form' of human government, concluding that, 'whatever else history teaches, it gives no ground for expecting finality in any human institutions' (Bryce 1921b: 656). These words hold true:

democracy is an incomplete and imperfect system that humans have devised for ruling themselves. History suggests there is little inevitable about the present importance attached to democracy or the manner in which it is practised. Nonetheless, while democratic government might regularly fail to live up to the high ideals associated with it, on the whole it has proven capable of providing a greater degree of freedom, safety and prosperity to people than its historical alternatives. In this regard, John Dunn observes in depreciating fashion that 'no one could readily mistake it [democracy] for a solution to the Riddle of History. But, in its simple unpretentious way, it has by now established a clear claim to meet a global need better than any of its competitors' (Dunn 2005: 183). That democracy now finds itself without peer competitors owes much to the internal contradictions and failings of its great rivals – communism and fascism – but separate from this, it is important to appreciate that democracy has positively demonstrated its value through providing important political, economic and social goods.

As this study has shown, the fate of democracy has been closely intertwined with the development of the modern states system. Revolution and war have been vital in determining democracy's fortunes. By focusing almost exclusively on the relationship between democracy and peace, liberal scholarship overlooks the extent to which war has shaped the rise of modern democracy, creating the conditions that have made a democratic peace possible. Furthermore, the limited concern with understanding the way democracy and war interrelate has left most democratic peace scholarship with little to say about the consequences of the belligerence of the United States and its democratic allies in recent years. In tackling this issue democratic peace scholars would be well advised to return to the concerns of America's founding fathers that 'no nation could preserve its freedom in the midst of continual warfare' (Madison 1795). In this regard, the understanding of democracy presented in this book might jar with much contemporary IR scholarship; this is quite intentional. The topic of democracy has effectively been monopolised by liberal scholars to the detriment of our understanding. On this point, this book has been inspired by Reinhold Niebuhr's observation that 'the consistent optimism of our liberal culture has prevented modern democratic societies both from gauging the perils of freedom accurately and from appreciating democracy fully as the only alternative to injustice and oppression' (Niebuhr 2011: xxxiii). This study has consciously sought to develop an alternative way of understanding democracy and international relations, and in doing so, offer a substantive contribution to the emerging body of critical democratic peace scholarship.

Democracy's current meaning and shape bear the scars of a long, varied and tumultuous history. Its ascent from obscurity and ignominy to becoming a key marker of international legitimacy is both remarkable and humbling. The present form and future possibilities of democracy are partly structured, but not determined, by this past. And by being more attuned to democracy's uneven, contested and fraught trajectory, one can cultivate a sense of humility and cautious appreciation of its strengths. As Frank Ankersmit notes, history suggests that 'democracy is a far more subtle, sophisticated, and therefore also a far more vulnerable political system than we tend to believe' (Ankersmit 2002: 230–1). While past and present successes may provide a degree of hope, the antinomies, limits and complexities that mark democracy suggest humility, counselling an awareness of the contingency and potential impermanence of its present normative and political ascendancy. By foregrounding the fact that democracy's meaning and the value now attached to it are neither determined nor fixed, an alternative vision is forged, one explicitly more open and political. It reminds us that democracy is inevitably incomplete: the tensions, contradictions and inadequacies can sometimes be resolved, narrowed or managed, but they can never be fully overcome. Indeed, if democracy is always still 'to come', if it exists in an inevitably incomplete form, strictly speaking it is more appropriate to talk of democratisation than democracy. This is what leads Adam Michnik to recall the Greek myth of Sisyphus when explaining democracy: an endless struggle towards an unreachable end (Demenet 2001). There will always be a gap between democracy as an ideal and democracy as a reality. In turn, this should create motivation for further developing and expanding democracy, while also generating a profound sense of humility in pursuing this challenging task. Ultimately if we value democracy, and there are important reasons for doing so, we should not take it as fixed or a given but constantly seek to explore, confront and renovate what it means.

# BIBLIOGRAPHY

Adams, Ephraim Douglass (1925). *Great Britain and the American Civil War*. New York: Plain Label.

Adams, W. Paul (1970). 'Republicanism in Political Rhetoric before 1776'. *Political Science Quarterly* 85(3): 397–421.

Albrecht-Carrié, René (1958). *A Diplomatic History of Europe since the Congress of Vienna*. London: Methuen.

Albright, Madeleine (1998). 'Remarks at 1998 Asia Society Dinner', New York, 17 June. US Department of State Archive, http://www.state.gov/1997-2001-NOPDFS/statements/1998/980617a.html (accessed 24 February 2015).

Alderson, Kai and Andrew Hurrell, eds (2000). *Hedley Bull on International Society*. Basingstoke: Macmillan.

Ambrosius, Lloyd (1987). *Woodrow Wilson and the American Diplomatic Tradition: The Treaty Fight in Perspective*. Cambridge: Cambridge University Press.

Ankersmit, F. R. (2002). *Political Representation*. Stanford, CA: Stanford University Press.

Anthony, Constance G. (2008). 'American Democratic Interventionism: Romancing the Iconic Woodrow Wilson'. *International Studies Perspectives* 9(3): 239–53.

Archibugi, Daniele (1995). 'Democracy at the United Nations'. In Takashi Inoguchi, Edward Newman and John Keane (eds), *The Changing Nature of Democracy*. Tokyo and New York: United Nations University Press.

Archibugi, Daniele and David Held (2011). 'Cosmopolitan Democracy: Paths and Agents'. *Ethics and International Affairs* 25(4): 433–61.

Archibugi, Daniele, Mathias Koenig-Archibugi and Raffaele Marchetti, eds (2011). *Global Democracy: Normative and Empirical Perspectives*. Cambridge: Cambridge University Press.

Archive of the Gorbachev Foundation (1989). 'Soviet Transcript of the Malta Summit'. Available at http://www2.gwu.edu/~nsarchiv/NSAEBB/NSAEBB298/Document%2010.pdf (accessed 23 February 2015).

Arendt, Hannah (1973). *The Origins of Totalitarianism*, new ed. New York: Harcourt, Brace, Jovanovich.

Aristotle (2006). *Politics*. Fairford, Gloucestershire: Echo Library.

Armitage, David (2007). *The Declaration of Independence: A Global History*. Cambridge, MA: Harvard University Press.

Armstrong, David (1993). *Revolution and World Order: The Revolutionary State in International Society*. Oxford: Clarendon Press.

Aron, Raymond (1966). *Peace and War*, tr. Richard Howard and Annette Baker Fox. London: Weidenfeld & Nicolson.

Babst, Dean (1972). 'A Force for Peace'. *Industrial Research* 14(4).

Bagby, Laurie M. Johnson (1994). 'The Use and Abuse of Thucydides in International Relations'. *International Organization* 48(1): 131–53.

Bagehot, Walter ([1867] 2001). *The English Constitution*. Cambridge: Cambridge University Press.

Bailyn, Bernard (1967). *The Ideological Origins of the American Revolution*. Cambridge, MA: Belknap Press.

Bain, William (2003). *Between Anarchy and Society: Trusteeship and the Obligations of Power*. Oxford: Oxford University Press.

Baker, Keith Michael (1989). 'Sovereignty'. In François Furet and Mona Ozouf (eds), *A Critical Dictionary of the French Revolution*, tr. Arthur Goldhammer. Cambridge, MA: Harvard University Press.

Baker, Keith Michael (2001). 'Transformations of Classical Republicanism in Eighteenth-century France'. *Journal of Modern History* 73(1): 32–53.

Ball, Terence (1988). *Transforming Political Discourse: Political Theory and Critical Conceptual History*. Oxford: Basil Blackwell.

Ban Ki-moon (2009). *Guidance Note of the Secretary-General on Democracy*. United Nations, http://www.un.org/democracyfund/sites/www.un.org.democracyfund/files/file_attach/UNSG%20Guidance%20Note%20on%20Democracy-EN.pdf (accessed 13 February 2015).

Barkawi, Tarak and Mark Laffey (1999). 'The Imperial Peace: Democracy, Force and Globalization'. *European Journal of International Relations* 5(4): 403–34.

Barkawi, Tarak and Mark Laffey, eds (2001). *Democracy, Liberalism, and War*. Boulder, CO: Lynne Rienner.

Bartelson, Jens (1995). *A Genealogy of Sovereignty*. Cambridge: Cambridge University Press.

Bedford, David and Thom Workman (2001). 'The Tragic Reading of the Thucydidean Tragedy'. *Review of International Studies* 27(1): 51–67.

Bell, Duncan (2007). *The Idea of Greater Britain: Empire and the Future of World Order, 1860–1900*. Princeton, NJ: Princeton University Press.

Beneš, Edvard (1939). *Democracy Today and Tomorrow*. New York: Macmillan.

Berman, Sheri (1998). *The Social Democratic Moment: Ideas and Politics in the Making of Interwar Europe*. Cambridge, MA: Harvard University Press.

Berman, Sheri (2006). *The Primacy of Politics: Social Democracy and the Making of Europe's Twentieth Century*. New York: Cambridge University Press.

Berman, Sheri (2013). 'The Promise of the Arab Spring: In Political Development, no Gain without Pain'. *Foreign Affairs*, January–February: 64–74.

Bermeo, Nancy (2003). *Ordinary People in Extraordinary Times: The Citizenry and the Breakdown of Democracy*. Princeton, NJ: Princeton University Press.

Bertier de Sauvigny, G. de (1962). *Metternich and His Times*, tr. Peter Ryde. London: Darton, Longman & Todd.

Biersteker, Thomas and Cynthia Weber, eds (1996). *State Sovereignty as a Social Construct*. Cambridge: Cambridge University Press.

Black, Jeremy (1999). *Eighteenth-century Europe, 1700–1789*, 2nd ed. Basingstoke: Macmillan.

Blanning, T. C. W. (1986). *The Origins of the French Revolutionary Wars*. London: Longman.

Bobbitt, Philip (2002). *The Shield of Achilles: War, Peace and the Course of History*. London: Allen Lane.

Boutros-Ghali, Boutros (1992). 'An Agenda for Peace', 17 June. Available at http://www.unrol.org/files/A_47_277.pdf (accessed 24 February 2015).

Breunig, Charles (1977). *The Age of Revolution and Reaction, 1789–1850*, 2nd ed. New York: W. W. Norton.

Brown, Ivor J. C. (1920). *The Meaning of Democracy*. London: Richard Cobden-Sanderson.

Brown, Michael E., Sean M. Lynn-Jones and Steven E. Miller, eds (1996). *Debating the Democratic Peace*. Cambridge, MA: MIT Press.

Bryce, James, ed. (1917). *The War of Democracy: The Allies' Statement*. Garden City, NY: Doubleday, Page.

Bryce, James (1921a). *Modern Democracies*, vol. 1. London: Macmillan.

Bryce, James (1921b). *Modern Democracies*, vol. 2. London: Macmillan.

Bueno de Mesquita, Bruce (2002). 'Domestic Politics and International Relations'. *International Studies Quarterly* 46(1).

Buergenthal, Thomas (1990). 'Copenhagen: A Democratic Manifesto'. *World Affairs* 153(1): 5–8.

Bukovansky, Mlada (1999). 'The Altered State and the State of Nature: The French Revolution and International Politics'. *Review of International Studies* 25(2): 197–216.

Bukovansky, Mlada (2002). *Legitimacy and Power Politics: The American and French Revolutions in International Political Culture*. Princeton, NJ: Princeton University Press.

Bull, Hedley (2002). *The Anarchical Society: A Study of Order in World Politics*, 3rd ed. Basingstoke: Palgrave.

Burke, Edmund (1999). *Select Works of Edmund Burke*, vol. 2. Indianapolis: Liberty Fund.

Burley, Peter (1989). *Witness to the Revolution: American and British Commentators in France, 1788–94*. London: Weidenfeld & Nicolson.

Bush, George H. W. (2009). *Speaking of Freedom: The Collected Speeches*. New York: Scribner.

Bush, George W. (2002a). *The National Security Strategy of the United States of America*, September. Available at http://nssarchive.us/NSSR/2002.pdf (accessed 24 February 2015).

Bush, George W. (2002b). 'President Delivers State of the Union Address', 29 January. White House Archives website, http://georgewbush-whitehouse.archives.gov/news/releases/2002/01/20020129-11.html (accessed 24 February 2015).

Butterfield, Herbert (1950). *The Whig Interpretation of History*. London: G. Bell.

Buzan, Barry (2004). *From International to World Society? English School Theory and the Social Structure of Globalization*. Cambridge: Cambridge University Press.

Canfora, Luciano (2006). *Democracy in Europe: A History of an Ideology*, tr. Simon Jones. Malden, MA: Blackwell.

Canovan, Margaret (2005). *The People*. Cambridge: Polity.

Carey, George and James McClellan, eds (2001). *The Federalist*. Indianapolis: Liberty Fund.

Carlyle, Thomas (1850). *Latter-day Pamphlets*. London: Chapman & Hall.

Carothers, Thomas (2015). 'Democracy Aid at 25: Time to Choose'. *Journal of Democracy* 26(1): 59–73.

Carothers, Thomas and Saskia Brechenmacher (2014). *Closing Space: Democracy and Human Rights Support under Fire*. Washington, DC: Carnegie Endowment for International Peace, http://carnegieendowment.org/files/closing_space.pdf (accessed 24 February 2015).

Carpenter, William Seal (1928). 'The Separation of Powers in the Eighteenth Century'. *American Political Science Review* 22(1): 32–44.

Carr, E. H. (2001). *The Twenty Years' Crisis, 1919–1939: An Introduction to the Study of International Relations*, new ed. Basingstoke: Palgrave Macmillan.

Cavallar, Georg (2001). 'Kantian Perspectives on Democratic Peace: Alternatives to Doyle'. *Review of International Studies* 27(2): 229–48.

Chan, Steve (1997). 'In Search of Democratic Peace: Problems and Promise'. *Mershon International Studies Review* 41(1): 59–91.

Chernoff, Fred (2004). 'The Study of Democratic Peace and Progress in International Relations'. *International Studies Review* 6(1): 49–78.

Christophersen, Jens A. (1966). *The Meaning of 'Democracy' as Used in European Ideologies from the French to the Russian Revolution: An Historical Study in Political Language*. Oslo: Universitetsforlaget.

Churchill, Winston (1941). 'Alliance with Russia', 22 June. Churchill Centre website, http://www.winstonchurchill.org/learn/speeches/speeches-of-winston-churchill /1941-1945-war-leader/809-the-fourth-climacteric (accessed 24 February 2015).

Churchill, Winston, Franklin D. Roosevelt and Joseph Stalin (1943). 'The Tehran Conference', 1 December. Avalon Project website, http://avalon.law.yale.edu/wwii/ tehran.asp (accessed 24 February 2015).

Churchill, Winston, Franklin D. Roosevelt and Joseph Stalin (1945). 'The Yalta Conference', 24 March. Avalon Project website, http://avalon.law.yale.edu/wwii/ yalta.asp (accessed 24 February 2015).

Clapham, J. H. (1899). *The Cause of the War of 1792*. Cambridge: C. J. Clay.

Clark, Ian (1999). *Globalization and International Relations Theory*. Oxford: Oxford University Press.

Clark, Ian (2005). *Legitimacy in International Society*. Oxford: Oxford University Press.

Clark, Ian (2009). 'Democracy in International Society: Promotion or Exclusion?' *Millennium: Journal of International Studies* 37(3): 563–81.

Clinton, Bill (1994). '1994 State of the Union address', 25 January. Washington Post website, http://www.washingtonpost.com/wp-srv/politics/special/states/docs/ sou94.htm (accessed 24 February 2015).

Cobban, Alfred (1945). *National Self-determination*. London: Oxford University Press.

Cobban, Alfred (1960). *In Search of Humanity: The Role of Enlightenment in Modern History*. London: Jonathan Cape.

Coggan, Philip (2013). *The Last Vote: The Threats to Western Democracy*. London: Allen Lane.

Colton, Calvin (1844). *The Junius Tracts*. New York: Greeley & McElrath.

Constant, Benjamin (1988). *Political Writings*, ed. and tr. Biancamaria Fontana. Cambridge: Cambridge University Press.

Continental Congress (2007). 'A Declaration by the Representatives of the United States of America, in General Congress Assembled'. In David Armitage (ed.), *The Declaration of Independence: A Global History*. Cambridge, MA: Harvard University Press.

Cooper, James Fenimore (1838). *The American Democrat*. Cooperstown, NY: H. & E. Phinney.

Corwin, Edward (1925). 'The Progress of Constitutional Theory between the Declaration of Independence and the Meeting of the Philadelphia Convention'. *American Historical Review* 30(3): 511–36.

Costopoulos, Philip J. and Pierre Rosanvallon (1995). 'The History of the Word "Democracy" in France'. *Journal of Democracy* 6(4): 140–54.

Coupland, R. (1940). 'Introduction'. In William Pitt, *The War Speeches of William Pitt the Younger*, ed. R. Coupland, 3rd ed. Oxford: Clarendon Press.

Cox, Michael, G. John Ikenberry and Takashi Inoguchi, eds (2000). *American Democracy Promotion: Impulses, Strategies, and Impacts*. Oxford: Oxford University Press.

Crawford, Neta C. (2002). *Argument and Change in World Politics: Ethics, Decolonization, and Humanitarian Intervention*. Cambridge: Cambridge University Press.

Crick, Bernard (1964). *In Defence of Politics*. Harmondsworth: Pelican.

Dafoe, Allan, John R. Oneal and Bruce Russett (2013). 'The Democratic Peace: Weighing the Evidence and Cautious Inference'. *International Studies Quarterly* 57(1): 201–14.

Dahl, Robert A. (1971). *Polyarchy: Participation and Opposition*. New Haven, CT: Yale University Press.

Dahl, Robert A. (1998). *On Democracy*. New Haven, CT: Yale University Press.

Demenet, Philippe (2001). 'Adam Michnik: The Sisyphus of Democracy'. *UNESCO Courier*, September.

Deneen, Patrick (2009). *Democratic Faith*. Princeton, NJ: Princeton University Press.

Der Derian, James (1987). *On Diplomacy: A Genealogy of Western Estrangement*. Oxford: Basil Blackwell.

Derrida, Jacques (2005). *Rogues: Two Essays on Reason*, tr. Pascale-Anne Brault and Michael Naas. Stanford, CA: Stanford University Press.

Desch, Michael C. (2007). 'America's Liberal Illiberalism: The Ideological Origins of Overreaction in US Foreign Policy'. *International Security* 32(3): 7–43.

Deudney, Daniel H. (2007). *Bounding Power: Republican Security Theory from the Polis to the Global Village*. Princeton, NJ: Princeton University Press.

Deudney, Daniel and G. John Ikenberry (2009). 'The Myth of the Autocratic Revival: Why Liberal Democracy Will Prevail'. *Foreign Affairs*, January–February.

Dewey, John (1939). *Freedom and Culture*. New York: G. P. Putnam's Sons.

Diamond, Larry (2014). 'The Next Democratic Century'. *Current History*, January: 8–11.

Donnelly, Jack (2006). 'Sovereign Inequalities and Hierarchy in Anarchy: American Power and International Society'. *European Journal of International Relations* 12(2): 139–70.

Doyle, Michael (1983a). 'Kant, Liberal Legacies and Foreign Affairs'. *Philosophy and Public Affairs* 12(3): 205–35.

Doyle, Michael (1983b). 'Kant, Liberal Legacies and Foreign Affairs, Part 2'. *Philosophy and Public Affairs* 12(4): 323–53.

Dunn, John (2005). *Setting the People Free: The Story of Democracy*. London: Atlantic.

Dunn, John (2013). *Breaking Democracy's Spell*. New Haven, CT: Yale University Press.

Dunne, Tim (2001). 'Sociological Investigations: Instrumental, Legitimist and Coercive Interpretations of International Society'. *Millennium* 30(1): 67–91.

Dupuis-Deri, Francis (2002). 'The Political Power of Words: "Democracy" and Political Strategies in the United States and France (1776–1871)'. PhD dissertation, University of British Columbia.

Duvall, Raymond and Jutta Weldes (2001). 'The International Relations of Democracy, Liberalism, and War: Directions for Future Research'. In Tarak Barkawi and Mark Laffey (eds), *Democracy, Liberalism, and War*. Boulder, CO: Lynne Rienner.

Echeverria, Durand (1957). *Mirage in the West: A History of the French Image of American Society to 1815*. Princeton, NJ: Princeton University Press.

Economist (2014a). 'What China Means by "Democracy"'. *The Economist*, 25 November.

Economist (2014b). 'What's Gone Wrong with Democracy'. *The Economist* website, http://www.economist.com/news/essays/21596796-democracy-was-most-successful-political-idea-20th-century-why-has-it-run-trouble-and-what-can-be-do (accessed 24 February 2015).

Eliot, T. S. (1925). 'The Hollow Men'. In *Poems 1909–1925*. London: Faber & Gwyer.

Ellis, Geoffrey (2000). 'The Revolution of 1848–1849 in France'. In R. J. W. Evans and Hartmut Pogge von Strandmann (eds), *The Revolutions in Europe 1848–1849: From Reform to Reaction*. Oxford: Oxford University Press.

Engels, Frederick (1848). 'The "Satisfied" Majority'. *Northern Star*, 8 January. Available at https://marxists.anu.edu.au/archive/marx/works/1848/01/08.htm (accessed 19 February 2015).

Everdell, William R. (1983). *The End of Kings: A History of Republics and Republicans*. New York: Free Press.

Evrigenis, Ioannis D. (2006). 'Hobbes's Thucydides'. *Journal of Military Ethics* 5(4): 303–16.

Fabry, Mikulas (2010). *Recognizing States: International Society and the Establishment of New States since 1776*. Oxford: Oxford University Press.

Farr, James (1989). 'Understanding Conceptual Change Politically'. In Terence Ball, James Farr and Russell L. Hanson (eds), *Political Innovation and Conceptual Change*. Cambridge: Cambridge University Press.

Feres, João Jr (2003). 'The History of Counterconcepts: "Latin America" as an Example'. *History of Concepts Newsletter* 6: 14–19.

Feres, João Jr (2006). 'Building a Typology of Forms of Misrecognition: Beyond the Republican-Hegelian Paradigm'. *Contemporary Political Theory* 5(3): 259–77.

Ferrero, Guglielmo (1919). *Problems of Peace: From the Holy Alliance to the League of Nations*. New York: G. P. Putnam's Sons.

Ferrero, Guglielmo (1941). *The Reconstruction of Europe: Talleyrand and the Congress of Vienna 1814–1815*, tr. Theodore R. Jaeckel. New York: G. P. Putnam's Sons.

Fischer, Fritz (1967). *Germany's Aims in the First World War*. London: Chatto & Windus.

Foley, Hamilton, ed. (1923). *Woodrow Wilson's Case for the League of Nations*. Princeton, NJ: Princeton University Press.

Forsyth, Murray (1981). 'Thomas Hobbes and the Constituent Power of the People'. *Political Studies* 29(2): 191–203.

Forsyth, Murray (1987). *Reason and Revolution: The Political Thought of the Abbé Sieyès*. Leicester: Leicester University Press.

Fortescue, William (2005). *France and 1848: The End of Monarchy*. Abingdon: Routledge.

Franck, Thomas M. (1990). *The Power of Legitimacy among Nations*. New York: Oxford University Press.

Franck, Thomas M. (1992). 'The Emerging Right to Democratic Governance'. *American Journal of International Law* 86(1): 46–91.

Freedom House (2015). *Freedom in the World 2015*. Washington, DC: Freedom House, https://www.freedomhouse.org/sites/default/files/01152015_FIW_2015_final.pdf (accessed 13 February 2015).

Frey, Linda and Marsha Frey (1993). '"The Reign of the Charlatans Is Over": The French Revolutionary Attack on Diplomatic Practice'. *Journal of Modern History* 65(4): 742–3.

Fried, Albert, ed. (1965). *A Day of Dedication: The Essential Writings and Speeches of Woodrow Wilson*. New York: Macmillan.

Fukuyama, Francis (1989). 'The End of History?' *National Interest*, Summer: 3–18.

Fukuyama, Francis (1992). *The End of History and the Last Man*. New York: Free Press.

Fukuyama, Francis (2012). 'The Future of History: Can Liberal Democracy Survive the Decline of the Middle Class?' *Foreign Affairs*, January–February: 53–61.

Fukuyama, Francis (2014a). 'At the "End of History" Still Stands Democracy'. *Wall Street Journal*, 6 June.

Fukuyama, Francis (2014b). *Political Order and Political Decay: From the Industrial Revolution to the Globalization of Democracy*. New York: Farrar, Straus & Giroux.

Fukuyama, Francis (2015). 'Why Is Democracy Performing So Poorly?' *Journal of Democracy* 26(1): 11–20.

Fulton, J. S. and C. R. Morris (1935). *In Defence of Democracy*. London: Methuen.

Furet, François (1981). *Interpreting the French Revolution*, tr. Elborg Forster. Cambridge: Cambridge University Press.

Furet, François (1992). *Revolutionary France 1770–1880*, tr. Antonia Nevill. Oxford: Blackwell.

Gallie, W. B. (1964). *Philosophy and the Historical Understanding*. London: Chatto & Windus.

Gaonkar, Dilip Parameshwar (2007). 'On Cultures of Democracy'. *Public Culture* 19(1): 1–22.

Gardner, Lloyd C. (1993). 'The United States, the German Peril and a Revolutionary World'. In Hans-Jürgen Schröder (ed.), *Confrontation and Cooperation: Germany and the United States in the Era of World War I 1900–1924*. Providence, RI: Berg.

Garton Ash, Timothy (2009). 'Velvet Revolution: The Prospects'. *New York Review of Books*, 3 December.

Gartzke, Erik and Alex Weisiger (2013). 'Permanent Friends? Dynamic Difference and the Democratic Peace'. *International Studies Quarterly* 57(1): 171–85.

Gat, Azar (2007). 'The Return of Authoritarian Great Powers'. *Foreign Affairs*, July–August.

Gat, Azar (2009). *Victorious and Vulnerable: Why Democracy Won in the 20th Century and How It Is Still Imperiled*. Lanham, MD: Rowman & Littlefield.

Geis, Anna (2013). 'The "Concert of Democracies": Why Some States Are More Equal than Others'. *International Politics* 50(2): 257–77.

Geis, Anna and Harald Müller (2013). 'Investigating "Democratic Wars" as the Flipside of Democratic Peace'. In Anna Geis, Harald Müller and Niklas Schörnig (eds), *The Militant Face of Democracy: Liberal Forces for Good*. Cambridge: Cambridge University Press.

Geis, Anna and Wolfgang Wagner (2011). 'How Far Is It from Königsberg to Kandahar? Democratic Peace and Democratic Violence in International Relations'. *Review of International Studies* 37(4): 1555–77.

Geis, Anna, Lothar Brock and Harald Müller, eds (2006). *Democratic Wars: Looking at the Dark Side of Democratic Peace*. Basingstoke: Palgrave Macmillan.

Geis, Anna, Harald Müller and Niklas Schörnig, eds (2013). *The Militant Face of Democracy: Liberal Forces for Good*. Cambridge: Cambridge University Press.

Geldenhuys, Deon (2004). *Deviant Conduct in World Politics*. Basingstoke: Palgrave Macmillan.

Ghelfi, Gerald John (1968). 'European Opinions of American Republicanism during the "Critical Period", 1781–1789'. PhD dissertation, Claremont Graduate School and University Center.

Giddens, Anthony (1985). *The Nation-state and Violence: Volume Two of a Contemporary Critique of Historical Materialism*. Cambridge: Polity.

Giddings, Franklin Henry (1900). *Democracy and Empire*. New York: Macmillan.

Goble, Paul (2014). '"Patriots" of Putin's Party Want to Dispense with Democracy'. *The Interpreter*, 2 November.

Godkin, Edwin Lawrence (1898). *Unforeseen Tendencies of Democracy*. London: Archibald Constable.

Godwin, William (1793). *An Enquiry Concerning Political Justice, and Its Influence on General Virtue and Happiness*, vol. 2. London: G. G. J. & J. Robinson.

Gong, Gerrit W. (1984). *The Standard of 'Civilization' in International Society*. Oxford: Clarendon Press.

Graebner, Norman, ed. (1963). *The Cold War: Ideological Conflict or Power Struggle?* Boston: D. C. Heath.

Grant, Alfred (2000). *The American Civil War and the British Press*. Jefferson, NC: McFarland.

Graudbard, Stephen (1973). 'Democracy'. In Philip P. Wiener (ed.), *The Dictionary of the History of Ideas: Studies of Selected Pivotal Ideas*, vol. 1. New York: Charles Scribner's Sons.

Guins, George (1950). 'Constitutions of the Soviet Satellites'. *Annals of the American Academy of Political and Social Science* 271(1): 64–7.

Guizot, François (1849). *Democracy in France*, 3rd ed. London: John Murray.

Haack, Kirsten (2011). *The United Nations Democracy Agenda: A Conceptual History*. Manchester: Manchester University Press.

Haas, Richard N. (2014). 'The Unraveling: How to Respond to a Disordered World'. *Foreign Affairs*, November–December.

Hagan, Kenneth J. and Ian J. Bickerton (2007). *Unintended Consequences: The United States at War*. London: Reaktion.

Hall, John Stewart, ed. (1951). *A Documentary Survey of the French Revolution*. New York: Macmillan.

Hall, Rodney Bruce (1999). *National Collective Identity: Social Constructs and International Systems*. New York: Columbia University Press.

Halliday, Fred (1999). *Revolution and World Politics: The Rise and Fall of the Sixth Great Power*. Basingstoke: Macmillan.

Hampson, Norman (1988). 'La Patrie'. In *The French Revolution and the Creation of Modern Political Culture, Volume 2: The Political Culture of the French Revolution*, ed. Colin Lucas. Oxford: Pergamon Press.

Hansard (1914). House of Commons Debate, 3 August, vol. 65, col. 1867. Available at http://net.lib.byu.edu/estu/wwi/gifs/commonsdebate3aug1914.pdf (accessed 20 February 2015).

Harrison, Mark (2003). 'Counting Soviet Deaths in the Great Patriotic War: Comment'. *Europe–Asia Studies* 55(6): 939–44.

Hart, Albert Bushnell *et al.* (1915). 'The War and Democracy'. In Albert Bushnell Hart *et al., Problems of Readjustment after the War*. New York: D. Appleton.

Hassan, Oz and Andrew Hammond (2011). 'The Rise and Fall of American's [*sic*] Freedom Agenda in Afghanistan: Counter-terrorism, Nation-building and Democracy'. *International Journal of Human Rights* 15(4): 532–51.

Havel, Václav (1995). 'Democracy's Forgotten Dimension'. *Journal of Democracy* 6(2): 3–10.

Hayes, Jarrod (2012). 'The Democratic Peace and the New Evolution of an Old Idea'. *European Journal of International Relations* 18(4): 767–91.

Hearnshaw, F. J. C. (1920). *Democracy and the British Empire*. London: Constable.

Heater, Derek (1994). *National Self-determination: Woodrow Wilson and His Legacy*. Basingstoke: Macmillan.

Hegre, Håvard (2014). 'Democracy and Armed Conflict'. *Journal of Peace Research* 51(2): 159–72.

Hendrickson, David C. (2003). *Peace Pact: The Lost World of the American Founding*. Lawrence: University Press of Kansas.

Hertslet, Edward, ed. (1875). 'Troppau Protocol'. In *The Map of Europe by Treaty*. London: Butterworths.

Hinsley, F. H. (1966). *Sovereignty*. London: C. A. Watts.

Hinsley, F. H. (1973). *Nationalism and the International System*. London: Hodder & Stoughton.

Hinsley, F. H. (1982). 'The Rise and Fall of the Modern International System'. *Review of International Studies* 8(1): 1–8.

Hitler, Adolf ([1925] 1939). *Mein Kampf*. New York: Reynal & Hitchcock.

Hobbes, Thomas (1975). *Thucydides*, ed. Richard Schlatter. New Brunswick, NJ: Rutgers University Press.

Hobsbawm, Eric (1962). *The Age of Revolution: Europe 1789–1848*. London: Weidenfeld & Nicolson.

Hobson, Christopher (2005). 'A Forward Strategy of Freedom in the Middle East: US Democracy Promotion and the "War on Terror"'. *Australian Journal of International Affairs* 59(1): 39–53.

Hobson, Christopher (2008a). 'Democracy as Civilisation'. *Global Society* 22(1): 75–95.

Hobson, Christopher (2008b). 'Revolution, Representation and the Foundations of Modern Democracy'. *European Journal of Political Theory* 7(4): 449–71.

Hobson, Christopher (2009). 'Beyond the End of History: The Need for a "Radical Historicisation" of Democracy in International Relations'. *Millennium* 37(3): 631–57.

Hobson, Christopher (2011). 'Towards a Critical Theory of Democratic Peace'. *Review of International Studies* 37(4): 1903–22.

Hobson, Christopher and Milja Kurki, eds (2011). *The Conceptual Politics of Democracy Promotion*. Abingdon: Routledge.

Hobson, Christopher, Tony Smith, John M. Owen, Anna Geis, Christopher Hobson and Piki Ish-Shalom (2011). 'Between the Theory and Practice of Democratic Peace'. *International Relations* 25(2): 147–84.

Hobson, John (1934). *Democracy and a Changing Civilisation*. London: John Lane.

Hogan, James (1938). *Modern Democracy*. Dublin: Cork University Press.

Holbraad, Carsten (1970). *The Concert of Europe: A Study in German and British International Theory 1815–1914*. London: Longman.

Hont, Istvan (1994). 'The Permanent Crisis of a Divided Mankind: "Contemporary Crisis of the Nation State" in Historical Perspective'. *Political Studies* 42(S1): 166–231.

Hont, Istvan (2005). *Jealousy of Trade: International Competition and the Nation State in Historical Perspective*. Cambridge, MA: Belknap Press.

Huntington, Samuel P. (1984). 'Will More Countries Become Democratic?' *Political Science Quarterly* 99(2): 193–218.

Huntington, Samuel P. (1993). *The Third Wave: Democratization in the Late Twentieth Century*. Norman: University of Oklahoma Press.

Huntington, Samuel P. (1997). 'After Twenty Years: The Future of the Third Wave'. *Journal of Democracy* 8(4): 3–12.

Hurd, Ian (1999). 'Legitimacy and Authority in International Politics'. *International Organization* 53(2): 379–408.

Ignatieff, Michael (2014). 'Are the Authoritarians Winning?' *New York Review of Books*, 10 July.

Ikenberry, G. John (2000). 'America's Liberal Grand Strategy: Democracy and National Security in the Post-war Era'. In Michael Cox, G. John Ikenberry and Takashi

Inoguchi (eds), *American Democracy Promotion: Impulses, Strategies, and Impacts*. Oxford: Oxford University Press.

Ikenberry, G. John (2001). *After Victory: Institutions, Strategic Restraint, and the Rebuilding of Order after Major Wars*. Princeton, NJ: Princeton University Press.

Ikenberry, G. John (2011). *Liberal Leviathan: The Origins, Crisis, and Transformation of the American World Order*. Princeton, NJ: Princeton University Press.

Inter-Allied Council (1941). 'Inter-Allied Council Statement on the Principles of the Atlantic Charter', 24 September. Avalon Project website, http://avalon.law.yale.edu/wwii/interall.asp (accessed 23 February 2015).

Isaac, Jeffrey C. (1998). *Democracy in Dark Times*. Ithaca, NY: Cornell University Press.

Ish-Shalom, Piki (2006). 'Theory as a Hermeneutical Mechanism: The Democratic-peace Thesis and the Politics of Democratization'. *European Journal of International Relations* 12(4): 565–98.

Ish-Shalom, Piki (2007). '"The Civilization of Clashes": Misapplying the Democratic Peace in the Middle East'. *Political Science Quarterly* 122(4): 533–54.

Ish-Shalom, Piki (2008a). 'The Rhetorical Capital of Theories: The Democratic Peace and the Road to the Roadmap'. *International Political Science Review* 29(3): 281–301.

Ish-Shalom, Piki (2008b). 'Theorization, Harm, and the Democratic Imperative: Lessons from the Politicization of the Democratic-peace Thesis'. *International Studies Review* 10(4): 680–92.

Ish-Shalom, Piki (2009). 'Theorizing Politics, Politicizing Theory, and the Responsibility that Runs Between'. *Perspectives on Politics* 7(2): 303–16.

Ish-Shalom, Piki (2013). *Democratic Peace: A Political Biography*. Ann Arbor: University of Michigan Press.

Jackson, Patrick Thaddeus (2008). 'Hunting for Fossils in International Relations'. *International Studies Perspectives* 9(1): 99–105.

Jackson, Peter (2006). 'Post-war Politics and the Historiography of French Strategy and Diplomacy before the Second World War'. *History Compass* 4(5): 870–905.

Jackson, Robert (1993). 'The Weight of Ideas in Decolonization'. In Judith Goldstein and Robert O. Keohane (eds), *Ideas and Foreign Policy: Beliefs, Institutions, and Political Change*. Ithaca, NY: Cornell University Press.

Jackson, Robert (2005). *Classical and Modern Thought on International Relations: From Anarchy to Cosmopolis*. New York: Palgrave Macmillan.

Jackson, Robert (2007). *Sovereignty: Evolution of an Idea*. Cambridge: Polity.

Jahn, Beate (2013). *Liberal Internationalism: Theory, History, Practice*. Basingstoke: Palgrave Macmillan.

Jennings, Ivor (1956). *The Approach to Self-government*. Cambridge: Cambridge University Press.

Kagan, Robert (2015). 'The Weight of Geopolitics'. *Journal of Democracy* 26(1): 21–31.

Kalyvas, Andreas (2005). 'Popular Sovereignty, Democracy, and the Constituent Power'. *Constellations* 12(2): 223–44.

Kamenka, Eugene (1976). 'Political Nationalism: The Evolution of the Idea'. In Eugene Kamenka (ed.), *Nationalism: The Nature and Evolution of an Idea*. London: Edward Arnold.

Kant, Immanuel (1970). 'Perpetual Peace: A Philosophical Sketch'. In *Political Writings*, ed. H. S. Reiss. Cambridge: Cambridge University Press.

Keane, John (2009). *The Life and Death of Democracy*. New York: W. W. Norton.

Keene, Edward (2002). *Beyond the Anarchical Society: Grotius, Colonialism and Order in World Politics*. Cambridge: Cambridge University Press.

Keitner, Chimène I. (2007). *The Paradoxes of Nationalism: The French Revolution and Its Meaning for Contemporary Nation Building*. Albany: State University of New York Press.

Kelsen, Hans (1955). 'Foundations of Democracy'. *Ethics* 66(1): 1–101.

Kenyon, Cecelia (1962). 'Republicanism and Radicalism in the American Revolution: An Old-fashioned Interpretation'. *William and Mary Quarterly* 19(2): 154–82.

Kerber, Linda K. (1985). 'The Republican Ideology of the Revolutionary Generation'. *American Quarterly* 37(4): 474–95.

Kissinger, Henry ([1957] 1973). *A World Restored*. London: Victor Gollancz.

Knock, Thomas J. (1998). 'Wilsonian Concepts and International Realities at the End of the War'. In Manfred Boemeke, Gerald Feldman and Elisabeth Glaser (eds), *The Treaty of Versailles: A Reassessment after 75 Years*. Cambridge: Cambridge University Press.

Kohn, Hans (1942). *World Order in Historical Perspective*. Cambridge, MA: Harvard University Press.

Koselleck, Reinhart (1985). *Futures Past: On the Semantics of Historical Time*, tr. Keith Tribe. Cambridge, MA: MIT Press.

Koselleck, Reinhart (1996). 'A Response to Comments on *Geschichtliche Grundbegriffe*'. In *The Meaning of Historical Terms and Concepts: New Studies on* Begriffsgeschichte, ed. Hartmut Lehmann and Melvin Richter. Washington, DC: German Historical Institute.

Krastev, Ivan (2010). 'Deepening Dissatisfaction'. *Journal of Democracy* 21(1): 113–19.

Kratochwil, Friedrich (2006). 'History, Action and Identity: Revisiting the "Second" Great Debate and Assessing Its Importance for Social Theory'. *European Journal of International Relations* 12(1): 5–29.

Kurlantzick, Joshua (2013). *Democracy in Retreat: The Revolt of the Middle Class and the Worldwide Decline of Representative Government*. New Haven, CT: Yale University Press.

Lake, David A. (2013). 'Theory Is Dead, Long Live Theory: The End of the Great Debates and the Rise of Eclecticism in International Relations'. *European Journal of International Relations* 19(3): 567–87.

Lamartine, Alphonse de (1849). *History of the French Revolution of 1848*, vol. 2, tr. Francis A. Durivage and William S. Chase. Boston: Phillips, Sampson.

Lamartine, Alphonse de (1850). *The Past, Present, and Future of the Republic*. New York: Harper & Brothers.

Langhorne, Richard (1986). 'Reflections on the Significance of the Congress of Vienna'. *Review of International Studies* 12(4): 313–24.

Lansing, Robert (1919). 'The Power of Democracy'. Address before the regents of the University of the State of New York, New York, 17 October.

Lebow, Richard Ned (2003). *The Tragic Vision of Politics: Ethics, Interests and Orders.* Cambridge: Cambridge University Press.

Lecky, William Edward Hartpole (1899). *Democracy and Liberty*, vol. 1. London: Longmans, Green.

Lefebvre, Georges ([1962] 2001). *The French Revolution: From Its Origins to 1793*, tr. Elizabeth Moss Evanson. London: Routledge.

Lenin, Vladimir (1917a). 'Decree on Peace'. Presented at the Second All-Russia Congress of Soviets of Workers' and Soldiers' Deputies, 8 November (NS). Available at http://www.marxists.org/archive/lenin/works/1917/oct/25-26/26b.htm (accessed 20 February 2015).

Lenin, Vladimir (1917b). 'The Tasks of the Proletariat in the Present Revolution', tr. Bernard Isaacs. *Pravda*, 7 April (OS). Available at http://www.marxists.org/archive/lenin/works/1917/apr/04.htm (accessed 2 March 2015).

Lenin, Vladimir (1919a). 'Democracy and Dictatorship'. *Pravda*, 3 January. Lenin Internet Archive, http://www.marxists.org/archive/lenin/works/1918/dec/23.htm (accessed 2 March 2015).

Lenin, Vladimir (1919b). 'Thesis and Report on Bourgeois Democracy and the Dictatorship of the Proletariat', First Congress of the Communist International, 4 March. Available at http://www.marxists.org/archive/lenin/works/1919/mar/comintern. htm (accessed 20 February 2015).

Lenin, Vladimir ([1917] 1993). *The State and Revolution.* Available at http://www.marxists. org/archive/lenin/works/1917/staterev/index.htm (accessed 20 February 2015).

Levin, Michael (1992). *The Spectre of Democracy: The Rise of Modern Democracy as Seen by Its Critics.* New York: New York University Press.

Levitsky, Steven and Lucan Way (2015). 'The Myth of Democratic Recession'. *Journal of Democracy* 26(1): 45–58.

Levy, Jack S. (1988). 'Domestic Politics and War'. *Journal of Interdisciplinary History* 18(4): 653–73.

Levy, Jack S. (2011). 'Theories and Causes of War'. In Christopher J. Coyne and Rachel L. Mathers (eds), *The Handbook on the Political Economy of War.* Cheltenham: Edward Elgar.

Lincoln, Abraham (1863). The Gettysburg Address. Abraham Lincoln Online, http:// www.abrahamlincolnonline.org/lincoln/speeches/gettysburg.htm (accessed 2 March 2015).

Lindsay, A. D. ([1935] 1951). *The Essentials of Democracy*, 2nd ed. Oxford: Oxford University Press.

Link, Arthur S. (1979). *Woodrow Wilson: Revolution, War, and Peace.* Arlington Heights, IL: AHM.

Linz, Juan (1997). 'Some Thoughts on the Victory and Future of Democracy'. In Axel Hadenius (ed.), *Democracy's Victory and Crisis.* Cambridge: Cambridge University Press.

Lipson, Leslie (1964). *The Democratic Civilization.* New York: Oxford University Press.

Lloyd George, David (1918). 'Prime Minister Lloyd George on the British War Aims', 5 January. World War I Document Archive website, http://wwi.lib.byu.edu/index.php/

Prime_Minister_Lloyd_George_on_the_British_War_Aims (accessed 20 February 2015).

Lokken, Roy (1959). 'The Concept of Democracy in Colonial Political Thought'. *William and Mary Quarterly* 16(4): 568–80.

Lucas, Sir Charles (1916). 'Empire and Democracy'. In M. E. Sadler *et al.* (eds), *The Empire and the Future*. London: Macmillan.

Luckey, G. W. A. (1920). *Education, Democracy and the League of Nations*. Boston: Richard G. Badger.

Lynch, Allen (2002). 'Woodrow Wilson and the Principle of "National Self-determination": A Reconsideration'. *Review of International Studies* 28(12): 419–36.

McClelland, J. S. (1989). *The Crowd and the Mob: From Plato to Canetti*. London: Unwin Hyman.

McFaul, Michael (2004). 'Democracy Promotion as a World Value'. *Washington Quarterly* 28(1): 147–63.

McFaul, Michael (2010). *Advancing Democracy Abroad: Why We Should and How We Can*. Lanham, MD: Rowman & Littlefield.

MacLeod, Emma Vincent (1999). *A War of Ideas: British Attitudes to the Wars against Revolutionary France 1792–1802*. Aldershot: Ashgate.

McManners, John (1966). *Lectures on European History 1789–1914: Men, Machines and Freedom*. Oxford: Basil Blackwell.

MacMurray, John (1943). *Constructive Democracy*. London: Faber & Faber.

Macpherson, C. B. (1966). *The Real World of Democracy*. Oxford: Clarendon Press.

Madison, James (1787). 'Madison Debates', 20 July. Avalon Project website, http://avalon.law.yale.edu/18th_century/debates_720.asp (accessed 19 March 2015).

Madison, James (1795). 'Political Observations, 20 April 1795'. Founders Online, http://founders.archives.gov/documents/Madison/01-15-02-0423 (accessed 2 March 2015).

Madison, James (2001). '55th Federalist Paper'. In Alexander Hamilton, John Jay and James Madison, *The Federalist*, ed. George Carey and James McClellan. Indianapolis: Liberty Fund.

Maine, Henry Sumner (1886). *Popular Government: Four Essays*. London: John Murray.

Maistre, Joseph de (1996). *Against Rousseau: 'On the State of Nature' and 'On the Sovereignty of the People'*, tr. and ed. Richard A. Lebrun. Montreal: McGill-Queen's University Press.

Manela, Erez (2007). *The Wilsonian Moment: Self-determination and the International Origins of Anticolonial Nationalism*. New York: Oxford University Press.

Manent, Pierre (2014). 'The Crisis of Liberalism'. *Journal of Democracy* 25(1): 131–41.

Manin, Bernard (1996). *The Principles of Representative Government*. Cambridge: Cambridge University Press.

Mann, Michael (2004). *Fascists*. Cambridge: Cambridge University Press.

Mann, Michael (2005). *The Dark Side of Democracy: Explaining Ethnic Cleansing*. New York: Cambridge University Press.

Mann, Michael (2012a). *The Sources of Social Power, Volume 3: Global Empires and Revolution 1890–1945*. New York: Cambridge University Press.

Mann, Michael (2012b). *The Sources of Social Power, Volume 4: Globalizations 1945–2011*. New York: Cambridge University Press.

Manning, C. A. W. (1962). *The Nature of International Society*. London: G. Bell.

Marx, Karl ([1852] 1995). *The Eighteenth Brumaire of Louis Bonaparte*. Marx/Engels Internet Archive, http://www.marxists.org/archive/marx/works/1852/18th-brumaire (accessed 16 February 2015).

Marx, Karl and Frederick Engels (1848). *The Manifesto of the Communist Party*. Available at http://www.newyouth.com/archives/classics/marxengels/communist-manifesto.html (accessed 2 March 2015).

Maus, Ingeborg (2006). 'From Nation-state to Global State, or the Decline of Democracy'. *Constellations* 13(4): 465–84.

Mayall, James (1990). *Nationalism and International Society*. Cambridge: Cambridge University Press.

Mayall, James (2000a). 'Democracy and International Society'. *International Affairs* 76(1): 61–75.

Mayall, James (2000b). *World Politics: Progress and Its Limits*. Cambridge: Polity.

Mayer, Arno J. (1959). *Political Origins of the New Diplomacy 1917–1918*. New Haven, CT: Yale University Press.

Mazower, Mark (1998). *Dark Continent: Europe's Twentieth Century*. London: Penguin.

Mazzini, Giuseppe (2001). *Thoughts upon Democracy in Europe (1846–1847)*. Florence: Centro Editoriale Toscano.

Meaney, Thomas and Yascha Mounk (2014). 'What Was Democracy?' *The Nation*, 2 June.

Merriam, Charles (1939). *The New Democracy and the New Despotism*. New York: Whittlesey House.

Metternich, Richard, ed. (1880). *Memoirs of Prince Metternich 1773–1815*, vol. 2, tr. Mrs Alexander Napier. London: Richard Bentley.

Mill, James (1820). 'Government'. In *Encyclopædia Britannica*, 6th ed. Available at http://studymore.org.uk/xmilgov.htm (accessed 19 February 2015).

Mill, John Stuart (1991). *On Liberty and Other Essays*, ed. John Gray. Oxford: Oxford University Press.

Miller, David Hunter (1928a). *The Drafting of the Covenant*, vol. 1. New York: G. P. Putnam's Sons.

Miller, David Hunter (1928b). *The Drafting of the Covenant*, vol. 2. New York: G. P. Putnam's Sons.

Møller, Jørgen and Svend-Erik Skaaning (2013). 'The Third Wave: Inside the Numbers'. *Journal of Democracy*, October: 97–109.

Morantz, Regina Ann Morkell (1971). '"Democracy" and "Republic" in American Ideology (1787–1840)'. PhD dissertation, Columbia University.

Morgan, Edmund (1988). *Inventing the People: The Rise of Popular Sovereignty in England and America*. New York: W. W. Norton.

Morgenthau, Hans J. (1947). *Scientific Man vs. Power Politics*. London: Latimer House.

Morris, Richard B. (1965). *The Peacemakers: The Great Powers and American Independence*. New York: Harper & Row.

 


Mousseau, Michael (2013). 'The Democratic Peace Unraveled: It's the Economy'. *International Studies Quarterly* 57(1): 186–97.

Muir, Ramsay (1939). *Future for Democracy*. London: Nicholson & Watson.

Müller, Jan-Werner (2013). *Contesting Democracy: Political Ideas in Twentieth-century Europe*. New Haven, CT: Yale University Press.

Naess, Arne, Jens A. Christophersen and Kjell Kvalo (1956). *Democracy, Ideology and Objectivity: Studies in the Semantics and Cognitive Analysis of Ideological Controversy*. Oslo: Oslo University Press.

Nardin, Terry (1983). *Law, Morality, and the Relations of States*. Princeton, NJ: Princeton University Press.

Näsström, Sofia (2007). 'The Legitimacy of the People'. *Political Theory* 35(5): 624–58.

National Assembly of France (1789). 'Declaration of the Rights of Man and of the Citizen'. Avalon Project website, http://avalon.law.yale.edu/18th_century/rightsof.asp (accessed 17 February 2015).

National Assembly of France (1951). 'Declaration of Peace to the World'. In John Stewart Hall (ed.), *A Documentary Survey of the French Revolution*. New York: Macmillan.

Navari, Cornelia (2007). 'States and State Systems: Democratic, Westphalian or Both?' *Review of International Studies* 33(4): 577–95.

Newman, Edward and Roland Rich, eds (2004). *The UN Role in Promoting Democracy: Between Ideals and Reality*. Tokyo and New York: United Nations University Press.

Nicolson, Harold (1933). *Peacemaking 1919*. London: Constable.

Nicolson, Harold (1946). *The Congress of Vienna: A Study in Allied Unity 1812–1822*. London: Constable.

Niebuhr, Reinhold ([1946] 2011). *The Children of Light and the Children of Darkness: A Vindication of Democracy and a Critique of Its Traditional Defense*. Chicago: University of Chicago Press.

Nietzsche, Friedrich ([1967] 1989). *On the Genealogy of Morals and Ecce Homo*, tr. Walter Kaufmann and R. J. Hollingdale. New York: Vintage.

Ober, Josiah (1998). *Political Dissent in Democratic Athens: Intellectual Critics of Popular Rule*. Princeton, NJ: Princeton University Press.

O'Donnell, Guillermo A. (2007). 'The Perpetual Crises of Democracy'. *Journal of Democracy* 18(1): 5–11.

Onuf, Nicholas Greenwood (1991). 'Sovereignty: Outline of a Conceptual History'. *Alternatives* 16(4): 425–46.

Onuf, Peter (1998). 'A Declaration of Independence for Diplomatic Historians'. *Diplomatic History* 22(1): 71–83.

Onuf, Peter and Nicholas Onuf (1993). *Federal Union, Modern World: The Law of Nations in an Age of Revolutions 1776–1814*. Madison, WI: Madison House.

Oppenheim, Lars (1919). *The League of Nations and Its Problems: Three Lectures*. London: Longmans, Green.

Orbán, Viktor (2014). 'Speech at Băile Tuşnad (Tusnádfürdő)'. *Budapest Beacon*, 26 July.

Oren, Ido (1995). 'The Subjectivity of the "Democratic" Peace: Changing US Perceptions of Imperial Germany'. *International Security* 20(2): 147–84.

Oren, Ido (2002). *Our Enemies and US: America's Rivalries and the Making of Political Science*. Ithaca, NY: Cornell University Press.

OSCE (1990a). 'Charter of Paris for a New Europe'. Available at http://www.osce.org/mc/39516?download=true (accessed 2 March 2015).

OSCE (1990b). 'Document of the Copenhagen Meeting of the Conference on the Human Dimension of the CSCE', 29 June. OSCE website, http://www.osce.org/odihr/elections/14304 (accessed 2 March 2015).

Osiander, Andreas (1994). *The States System of Europe 1640–1990: Peacemaking and the Conditions of International Stability*. Oxford: Clarendon Press.

Osiander, Andreas (2001). 'Sovereignty, International Relations, and the Westphalian Myth'. *International Organization* 55(2): 251–87.

Owen, John (2011). 'Liberal Tradition, Not Social Science'. *International Relations* 25(2): 158–63.

Ozouf, Mona (1989). 'Danton'. In François Furet and Mona Ozouf (eds), *A Critical Dictionary of the French Revolution*, tr. Arthur Goldhammer. Cambridge, MA: Belknap Press.

Paine, Thomas (1988). *The Thomas Paine Reader*, ed. Michael Foot and Isaac Kramnick. Harmondsworth: Penguin.

Pallain, M. G., ed. (1881). *The Correspondence of Prince Talleyrand and King Louis XVIII during the Congress of Vienna*. London: Richard Bentley.

Palmer, R. R. (1959). *The Age of the Democratic Revolution, Volume 1: The Challenge*. Princeton, NJ: Princeton University Press.

Palmer, R. R. (1964). *The Age of the Democratic Revolution, Volume 2: The Struggle*. Princeton, NJ: Princeton University Press.

Palonen, Kari (2001). 'The History of Concepts as a Style of Political Theorizing: Quentin Skinner's and Reinhart Koselleck's Subversion of Normative Political Theory'. *European Journal of Political Theory* 1(1): 91–106.

Palonen, Kari (2003). *Quentin Skinner: History, Politics, Rhetoric*. Cambridge: Polity.

Paris, Roland (2002). 'International Peacebuilding and the "Mission Civilisatrice"'. *Review of International Studies* 28(4): 637–56.

Parmar, Inderjeet (2013). 'The "Knowledge Politics" of Democratic Peace Theory'. *International Politics* 50(2): 231–56.

Passmore, Kevin (2002). *Fascism: A Very Short Introduction*. Oxford: Oxford University Press.

Phelps, Edith, ed. (1919). *Selected Articles on a League of Nations*, 4th ed. New York: H. W. Wilson.

Philpott, Daniel (2001). *Revolutions in Sovereignty: How Ideas Shaped Modern International Relations*. Princeton, NJ: Princeton University Press.

Pitkin, Hannah (1967). *The Concept of Representation*. Berkeley: University of California Press.

Pitt, William (1940). *The War Speeches of William Pitt*, ed. R. Coupland. Oxford: Clarendon Press.

Pitts, Jennifer (2005). *A Turn to Empire: The Rise of Imperial Liberalism in Britain and France*. Princeton, NJ: Princeton University Press.

Plato (1901). *The Republic of Plato*. New York: Collier.

Pocock, J. G. A. (1975). *The Machiavellian Moment: Florentine Political Thought and the Atlantic Republican Tradition*. Princeton, NJ: Princeton University Press.

Pocock, J. G. A. (1995). 'Political Thought in the English-speaking Atlantic: The Imperial Crisis'. In J. G. A. Pocock (ed.), *The Varieties of British Political Thought 1500–1800*. Cambridge: Cambridge University Press.

Poggi, Gianfranco (1990). *The State: Its Nature, Development and Prospects*. Cambridge: Polity.

Polybius (1927). *The Histories of Polybius*, tr. W. P. Paton. Loeb Classical Library, vol. 3, books 5–8. New York: G. P. Putnam's Sons.

Pomerance, Michla (1976). 'The United States and Self-determination: Perspectives on the Wilsonian Conception'. *American Journal of International Law* 70(1).

Ponsonby, Arthur (1915). *Democracy and Diplomacy: A Plea for Popular Control of Foreign Policy*. London: Methuen.

Popper, Karl (1966). *The Open Society and Its Enemies, Volume 1: The Spell of Plato*, 5th ed. London: Routledge & Kegan Paul.

Prazmowska, Anita J. (1995). *Britain and Poland 1939–1943: The Betrayed Ally*. Cambridge: Cambridge University Press.

Price, Richard and Christian Reus-Smit (1998). 'Dangerous Liaisons? Critical International Theory and Constructivism'. *European Journal of International Relations* 4(3): 259–94.

Putin, Vladimir (2014). 'Meeting of the Valdai International Discussion Club', 24 October. President of Russia website, http://eng.kremlin.ru/news/23137 (accessed 2 March 2015).

Rainbolt, John (1973). 'Americans' Initial View of Their Revolution's Significance for Other Peoples 1776–1788'. *The Historian* 35(3): 418–33.

Rappard, William (1938). *The Crisis of Democracy*. Chicago: University of Chicago Press.

Rasmussen, Mikkel Vedby (2003). *The West, Civil Society and the Construction of Peace*. Basingstoke: Palgrave Macmillan.

Rawls, John (2001). *The Law of Peoples: With 'The Idea of Public Reason Revisited'*. Cambridge, MA: Harvard University Press.

Ray, James Lee (2013). 'War on Democratic Peace'. *International Studies Quarterly* 57(1): 198–200.

Reid, John Phillip (1989). *The Concept of Representation in the Age of the American Revolution*. Chicago: University of Chicago Press.

Reus-Smit, Christian (1999). *The Moral Purpose of the State: Culture, Social Identity, and Institutional Rationality in International Relations*. Princeton, NJ: Princeton University Press.

Reus-Smit, Christian (2005a). 'Constructivism'. In Scott Burchill *et al.* (eds), *Theories of International Relations*, 3rd ed. Basingstoke: Palgrave Macmillan.

Reus-Smit, Christian (2005b). 'Liberal Hierarchy and the Licence to Use Force'. *Review of International Studies* 31(S1): 71–92.

Reves, Emery (1943). *A Democratic Manifesto*. London: Jonathan Cape.

Rhodes, P. J. (2003). *Ancient Democracy and Modern Ideology*. London: Duckworth.

Richter, Melvin (1995). *The History of Political and Social Concepts: A Critical Introduction*. New York: Oxford University Press.

Richter, Melvin (2000). 'Conceptualizing the Contestable: Begriffsgeschichte and Political Concepts'. In Gunter Scholtz (ed.), *Die Interdisziplinarität der Begriffsgeschichte*. Hamburg: Meiner.

Richter, Melvin (2003). 'Towards a Lexicon of European Political and Legal Concepts: A Comparison of Begriffsgeschichte and the "Cambridge School"'. *Critical Review of International Social and Political Philosophy* 6(2): 91–120.

Ringen, Stein (2013). *Nation of Devils: Democratic Leadership and the Problem of Obedience*. New Haven, CT: Yale University Press.

Risse-Kappen, Thomas (1995). 'Democratic Peace – Warlike Democracies? A Social Constructivist Interpretation of the Liberal Argument'. *European Journal of International Relations* 1(4): 491–517.

Roberts, Jennifer Tolbert (1994). *Athens on Trial: The Antidemocratic Tradition in Western Thought*. Princeton, NJ: Princeton University Press.

Roberts, Richard (1920). *The Unfinished Programme of Democracy*. New York: B. W. Huebsch.

Robespierre, Maximilien (1794). 'On the Enemies of the Nation', 26 May, tr. Mitch Abidor. Available at http://www.marxists.org/history/france/revolution/robespierre/1794/enemies.htm (accessed 2 March 2015).

Robespierre, Maximilien (2007). *Virtue and Terror*, ed. Jean Ducange, tr. John Howe. London: Verso.

Robinson, Eric (2001). 'Reading and Misreading the Ancient Evidence for Democratic Peace'. *Journal of Peace Research* 38(5): 593–608.

Roosevelt, Franklin D. (1940). 'Arsenal of Democracy'. Fireside Chat, Washington, DC, 29 December. Available at http://xroads.virginia.edu/~1930s2/time/1940/fdrsenal.html (accessed 2 March 2015).

Roosevelt, Franklin D. (1941a). '1941 State of the Union Address', 6 January. Available at http://www.fdrlibrary.marist.edu/pdfs/fftext.pdf (accessed 2 March 2015).

Roosevelt, Franklin D. (1941b). 'Declarations of a State of War with Japan, Germany, and Italy, Part 4', 8 December. Avalon Project website, http://avalon.law.yale.edu/wwii/dec04.asp (accessed 23 February 2015)

Roosevelt, Franklin D. (1941c). 'Message to Congress on the Atlantic Charter', 21 August. Avalon Project website, http://avalon.law.yale.edu/wwii/atcmess.asp (accessed 2 March 2015).

Roosevelt, Franklin D. and Winston S. Churchill (1941). 'The Atlantic Charter', 14 August. Avalon Project website, http://avalon.law.yale.edu/wwii/atlantic.asp (accessed 23 February 2015).

Roper, Jon (1989). *Democracy and Its Critics: Anglo-American Democratic Thought in the Nineteenth Century*. London: Unwin Hyman.

Rosanvallon, Pierre (2002). 'Political Rationalism and Democracy in France in the 18th and 19th Centuries'. *Philosophy and Social Criticism* 28(6): 687–701.

Rosanvallon, Pierre (2006). *Democracy Past and Future*, tr. Samuel Moyn. New York: Columbia University Press.

Rosato, Sebastian (2003). 'The Flawed Logic of Democratic Peace Theory'. *American Political Science Review* 97(4): 585–602.

Rothwell, V. H. (1971). *British War Aims and Peace Diplomacy 1914–1918*. Oxford: Clarendon Press.

Rousseau, Jean-Jacques (1923). *The Social Contract and Discourses*, tr. G. D. H. Cole. London: J. M. Dent.

Rude, George (1972). *Debate on Europe 1815–1850*. New York: Harper & Row.

Ruggie, John Gerard (1982). 'International Regimes, Transactions, and Change: Embedded Liberalism in the Postwar Economic Order'. *International Organization* 36(2): 379–415.

Rummel, R. J. (1979). *Understanding Conflict and War, Volume 4: War, Power, Peace*. London: Sage.

Rummel, R. J. (1981). *Understanding Conflict and War, Volume 5: The Just Peace*. London: Sage.

Runciman, David (2013). *The Confidence Trap: A History of Democracy in Crisis from World War I to the Present*. Princeton, NJ: Princeton University Press.

Russett, Bruce (1993). *Grasping the Democratic Peace: Principles for a Post-Cold War World*. Princeton, NJ: Princeton University Press.

Russett, Bruce and William Antholis (1992). 'Do Democracies Fight Each Other? Evidence from the Peloponnesian War'. *Journal of Peace Research* 29(4): 415–34.

Salter, Mark (2002). *Barbarians and Civilization in International Relations*. London: Pluto Press.

Schmitt, Carl ([1923] 1985). *The Crisis of Parliamentary Democracy*, tr. Ellen Kennedy. Cambridge, MA: MIT Press.

Schmitt, Carl (2008). *Constitutional Theory*, tr. and ed. Jeffrey Seitzer. Durham, NC: Duke University Press.

Schmitter, Philippe C. (2015). 'Crisis and Transition, but Not Decline'. *Journal of Democracy* 26(1): 32–44.

Schroeder, Paul W. (1994). *The Transformation of European Politics 1763–1848*. Oxford: Clarendon Press.

Schumpeter, Joseph (1943). *Capitalism, Socialism, and Democracy*. London: George Allen & Unwin.

Schwarzenberger, Georg (1936). *The League of Nations and World Order*. London: Constable.

Scott, James Brown, ed. (1918). *President Wilson's Foreign Policy: Messages, Addresses, Papers*. New York: Oxford University Press.

Sen, Amartya (1999). 'Democracy as a Universal Value'. *Journal of Democracy* 10(3).

Sharp, Alan (1991). *The Versailles Settlement: Peacemaking in Paris 1919*. Basingstoke: Macmillan.

Shaw, Martin (2001). 'Democracy and Peace in the Global Revolution'. In Tarak Barkawi and Mark Laffey (eds), *Democracy, Liberalism, and War*. Boulder, CO: Lynne Rienner.

Shinoda, Hideaki (2000). *Re-examining Sovereignty: From Classical Theory to the Global Age*. Basingstoke: Palgrave Macmillan.

Shoemaker, Robert W. (1966). '"Democracy" and "Republic" as Understood in Late Eighteenth-century America'. *American Speech* 41(2): 83–95.

Sieyès, Emmanuel (2003). *Political Writings*, ed. Michael Sonenscher. Indianapolis: Hackett.

Simpson, Gerry (2004). *Great Powers and Outlaw States: Unequal Sovereigns in the International Legal Order*. Cambridge: Cambridge University Press.

Skinner, Quentin (1969). 'Meaning and Understanding in the History of Ideas'. *History and Theory* 8(1): 3–53.

Skinner, Quentin (1973). 'The Empirical Theorists of Democracy and Their Critics: A Plague on Both Their Houses'. *Political Theory* 1(3): 287–306.

Skinner, Quentin (1978). *The Foundations of Modern Political Thought, Volume 1: The Renaissance*. Cambridge: Cambridge University Press.

Skinner, Quentin (2002). *Visions of Politics, Volume 1: Regarding Method*. Cambridge: Cambridge University Press.

Smith, Hazel, ed. (2000). *Democracy and International Relations: Critical Theories/ Problematic Practices*. Basingstoke: Macmillan.

Smith, Tony (1994). *America's Mission: The United States and the Worldwide Struggle for Democracy in the Twentieth Century*. Princeton, NJ: Princeton University Press.

Smith, Tony (2007). *A Pact with the Devil: Washington's Bid for World Supremacy and the Betrayal of the American Promise*. New York: Routledge.

Smuts, J. C. (1917). *War-time Speeches*. London: Hodder & Stoughton.

Sorel, Albert (1969). *Europe and the French Revolution: The Political Traditions of the Old Régime*, tr. Alfred Cobban and J. W. Hunt. London: Collins.

Sperber, Jonathan (1994). *The European Revolutions 1848–1851*. Cambridge: Cambridge University Press.

Stalin, Joseph (1941). 'Radio Broadcast', 3 July. Available at https://www.marxists.org/reference/archive/stalin/works/1941/07/03.htm (accessed 2 March 2015).

Stalin, Joseph (1947). 'Greetings Message to Moscow', 8 September. Available at https://www.marxists.org/reference/archive/stalin/works/1947/09/08.htm (accessed 23 February 2015).

Stalin, Joseph (1953). *The Foundations of Leninism*. Moscow: Foreign Language Publishing House.

Steele, Brent J. (2007). 'Liberal-idealism: A Constructivist Critique'. *International Studies Review* 9(1): 23–52.

Steele, Brent J. (2010). 'Of "Witch's Brews" and Scholarly Communities: The Dangers and Promise of Academic Parrhesia'. *Cambridge Review of International Affairs* 23(1): 49–68.

Steiner, Zara (2007). *The Lights that Failed: European International History 1919–1933*. Oxford: Oxford University Press.

Steiner, Zara (2011). *The Triumph of the Dark: European International History 1933– 1939*. Oxford: Oxford University Press.

Stourzh, Gerald (1970). *Alexander Hamilton and the Idea of Republican Government*. Stanford, CA: Stanford University Press.

Stow, Simon (2007). 'Pericles at Gettysburg and Ground Zero: Tragedy, Patriotism, and Public Mourning'. *American Political Science Review* 101(2): 195–208.

Suzuki, Shogo (2009). *Civilization and Empire: China and Japan's Encounter with International Society*. Abingdon: Routledge.

Tanji, Miyume and Stephanie Lawson (1997). '"Democratic Peace" and "Asian Democracy": A Universalist–Particularist Tension'. *Alternatives* 22(1): 135–55.

Tarchi, Marco (2002). 'The Role of Fascist Movements'. In Dirk Berg-Schlosser and Jeremy Mitchell (eds), *Authoritarianism and Democracy in Europe 1919–39: Comparative Analyses*. Basingstoke: Palgrave Macmillan.

Thompson, Mark R. (2002). 'Building Nations and Crafting Democracies: Competing Legitimacies in Interwar Eastern Europe'. In Dirk Berg-Schlosser and Jeremy Mitchell (eds), *Authoritarianism and Democracy in Europe 1919–39: Comparative Analyses*. Basingstoke: Palgrave Macmillan.

Thomson, Janice E. (1994). *Mercenaries, Pirates, and Sovereigns: State-building and Extraterritorial Violence in Early Modern Europe*. Princeton, NJ: Princeton University Press.

Three Heads of Government of the USSR, USA and UK (1945). 'Potsdam Conference', 1 August. Avalon Project website, http://avalon.law.yale.edu/20th_century/decade17.asp (accessed 23 February 2015).

Thucydides (1954). *History of the Peloponnesian War*, rev. ed., tr. Rex Warner. Harmondsworth: Penguin.

Timasheff, N. S. (1950). 'The Soviet Concept of Democracy'. *Review of Politics* 12(4): 506–18.

Tocqueville, Alexis de (1958). *Journeys to England and Ireland*, tr. George Lawrence and K. P. Mayer. London: Faber & Faber.

Tocqueville, Alexis de (2003). *Democracy in America*, tr. Gerald E. Bevan. London: Penguin.

Todorov, Tzvetan (1993). *On Human Diversity: Nationalism, Racism, and Exoticism in French Thought*, tr. Catherine Porter. Cambridge, MA: Harvard University Press.

Trotsky, Leon (1918). 'The International: Will the Allies Throw Away the Last Chance?' *The Call*, 10 January. Available at http://www.marxists.org/archive/trotsky/1918/01/international-appeal.htm (accessed 20 February 2015).

Ulfelder, Jay (2015). 'A Forecast of Global Democratization Trends through 2025', Dart-throwing Chimp blog, 11 January, https://dartthrowingchimp.wordpress.com/2015/01/11/a-forecast-of-global-democratization-trends-through-2025 (accessed 13 February 2015).

UNESCO (1951). *Democracy in a World of Tensions*. Chicago: University of Chicago Press.

United Nations (1943). 'Casablanca Conference 1943', 12 February. Avalon Project website, http://avalon.law.yale.edu/wwii/casablan.asp.

United Nations (1945). Charter of the United Nations. United Nations website, http://www.un.org/en/documents/charter/index.shtml (accessed 23 February 2015).

United Nations (1960). Declaration on the Granting of Independence to Colonial Countries and Peoples. United Nations website, http://www.un.org/en/decolonization/declaration.shtml (accessed 23 February 2015).

United Nations (2005). *2005 World Summit Outcome*, 24 October. Available at http://www.un.org/womenwatch/ods/A-RES-60-1-E.pdf (accessed 2 March 2015).

Urbinati, Nadia (2006). *Representative Democracy: Principles and Genealogy*. Chicago: University of Chicago Press.

Van Belle, Douglas A. (2006). 'Dinosaurs and the Democratic Peace: Paleontological Lessons for Avoiding the Extinction of Theory in Political Science'. *International Studies Perspectives* 7(3): 287–306.

Venturi, Franco (1991). *The End of the Old Regime in Europe 1776–1789, Volume 1: The Great States of the West*, tr. R. Burr Litchfield. Princeton, NJ: Princeton University Press.

Walker, R. B. J. (1993). *Inside/Outside: International Relations as Political Theory*. Cambridge: Cambridge University Press.

Walt, Stephen M. (1996). *Revolution and War*. Ithaca, NY: Cornell University Press.

Waltz, Kenneth (1979). *Theory of International Politics*. Reading, MA: Addison-Wesley.

Walzer, Michael, ed. (1974). *Regicide and Revolution: Speeches at the Trial of Louis XVI*, tr. Marian Rothstein. Cambridge: Cambridge University Press.

Weisser, Henry (1971). 'Chartist Internationalism 1845–1848'. *Historical Journal* 14(1): 49–66.

Welch, David A. (2003). 'Why International Relations Theorists Should Stop Reading Thucydides'. *Review of International Studies* 29(3): 301–19.

Wells, H. G. (1918). *In the Fourth Year: Anticipations of a World Peace*. New York: Macmillan.

Wendt, Alexander (1996). 'Identity and Structural Change in International Polities'. In Yosef Lapid and Friedrich Kratochwil (eds), *The Return of Culture and Identity in IR Theory*. Boulder, CO: Lynne Rienner.

Whelan, Anthony (1994). 'Wilsonian Self-determination and the Versailles Settlement'. *International and Comparative Law Quarterly* 43(1): 99–115.

Whelan, Frederick (1983). 'Democratic Theory and the Boundary Problem'. In J. P. Pennock and J. W. Chapman (eds), *Liberal Democracy*. New York: New York University Press.

Wight, Martin (1966). 'Western Values in International Relations'. In Herbert Butterfield and Martin Wight (eds), *Diplomatic Investigations: Essays in the Theory of International Politics*. London: George Allen & Unwin.

Wight, Martin (1972). 'International Legitimacy'. *International Relations* 4(1).

Wight, Martin (1977). *Systems of States*. Leicester: Leicester University Press.

Wight, Martin (1978). *Power Politics*, rev. ed. Leicester: Leicester University Press.

Williams, Michael C. (2001). 'The Discipline of the Democratic Peace: Kant, Liberalism and the Social Construction of Security Communities'. *European Journal of International Relations* 7(4): 525–53.

Wolin, Sheldon (2004). *Politics and Vision*, rev. ed. Princeton, NJ: Princeton University Press.

Wolverton, Joe (2005). 'The Founding Fathers and the Classics'. *New American*, September.

Wood, Gordon S. (1969). *The Creation of the American Republic 1776–1787*. New York: W. W. Norton.

Yack, Bernard (2001). 'Popular Sovereignty and Nationalism'. *Political Theory* 29(4): 517–36.

Zakaria, Fareed (2007). *The Future of Freedom: Illiberal Democracy at Home and Abroad*, rev. ed. New York: W. W. Norton.

Zakaria, Fareed (2013). 'Can America Be Fixed? The New Crisis of Democracy'. *Foreign Affairs*, January–February.

Zimmern, Alfred (1929). *The Prospects of Democracy*. London: Chatto & Windus.

EU representative:
Easy Access System Europe
Mustamäe tee 50, 10621 Tallinn, Estonia
Gpsr.requests@easproject.com

www.ingramcontent.com/pod-product-compliance
Lightning Source LLC
Chambersburg PA
CBHW070753240726

48654CB00007B/70